BIC

A Concise (

GW01549889

20

BIOLOGY

A Concise Guide for First Examinations

B. L. Thomas, B.A., M.I.Biol.
Solihull School, West Midlands

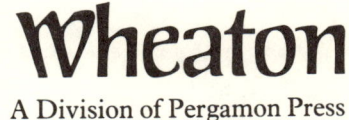

Wheaton

A Division of Pergamon Press

A. Wheaton & Company Limited
A Division of Pergamon Press

Hennock Road, Exeter EX2 8RP

Pergamon Press Ltd
Headington Hill Hall, Oxford OX3 0BW

Pergamon Press Inc.
Maxwell House, Fairview Park, Elmsford, New York 10523

Pergamon of Canada Ltd
Suite 104, 150 Consumers Road, Willowdale, Ontario M2 J 1P9, Canada

Pergamon Press (Australia) Pty Ltd
P.O. Box 544, Potts Point, N.S.W. 2011

Pergamon Press GmbH
6242 Kronberg/Taunus, Pferdstrasse 1, Frankfurt-am-Main,
Federal Republic of Germany

First published 1979

To my parents

The illustration on the cover is reproduced by permission of
Heather Angel.

Typeset by Oxprint Ltd, Oxford

Printed in Great Britain by A. Wheaton & Co. Ltd, Exeter
ISBN 0 08 022879 8

Contents

Introduction

This book is designed to be used:

1. For revision at the end of a course prior to 'O' level or 'CSE' examinations.

2. For consolidation and revision at intervals throughout a course leading to first examinations.

3. As a source of questions for homework.

Whichever alternative is adopted, it is suggested that the student should read through one chapter at a time which will help to highlight the main points. The student should then read up the relevant notes relating to that chapter, which are provided either by the teacher or extracted from a suitable textbook. Finally, the student writes out the answers to the questions without the aid of notes, and only referring to the answer section at the end of this book when all the questions in a particular chapter have been attempted.

Throughout this book there are words which are printed in bold type. These are important biological words of which the reader should know the meanings. It would be useful for the student to write down a description of these words at intervals throughout the course.

It is not intended that this book should replace the standard textbooks used at this level, but to complement them. The core of material in modern syllabuses, including Nuffield Biology, is covered.

The book will have served its purpose if it helps the student to learn and revise the subject in a systematic and thorough manner.

I should like to thank the following for their help in the preparation of this book:

Mr C. Gould for so patiently advising me on the manuscript.

Mrs I. E. G. Biggs for typing the manuscript.

Messrs R. W. Beach, K. H. Sach, R. J. Spence and D. H. Tomlin for their suggestions and criticisms.

The British Museum for Fig. 36.1.

Dr J. Hannay, Department of Botany, Imperial College of Science and Technology, for Fig. 11.2.

Dr G. H. Jones, Department of Genetics, University of Birmingham, for Fig. 22.1.

Mr R. J. Spence for Figs 6.2, 6.3 and 17.3.

The Wellcome Museum of Medical Science for Figs 7.1 and 36.1.

The pupils of Solihull School, 1971–77.

B. L. T.

Part One Organisation of Cells and Organisms

1 Classifying Living Things

Biology is the study of living things. There are so many different organisms that it is impossible for anyone to be able to recognise all of them. A system is needed to place organisms into groups to make their identification easier.

The usual way to do this is to use a **key**. A key consists of a series of questions about the organism to be identified. By answering these questions (e.g. shape, size, colour) you can identify the organism. Here is a simple key for identifying some common seaweeds:

(i)(a) Plant not bearing visible fruiting bodies
        . . . . *see* (ii)

  (b) Plant bearing fruiting bodies . . . . *see* (iii)

(ii)(a) Long flat ribbon-like frond (up to 4 metres in length) . . . . *Laminaria saccharina*

  (b) Broad flat frond (up to 0.5 metres in length) . . . . *Ulva lactuca*

(iii)(a) Air bladders absent . . . . *see* (iv)

  (b) Air bladders present . . . . *see* (v)

(iv)(a) Serrated edge to frond . . . . *Fucus serratus*

  (b) Smooth edge to frond . . . . *Fucus spiralis*

(v)(a) Air bladders present in pairs, midrib present . . . . *Fucus vesiculosus*

  (b) Single air bladders, no midrib present
        . . . . *Ascophyllum nodosum*

1.1 Look at the drawing of the plant in Fig. 1.1 and try to identify it using the key above.

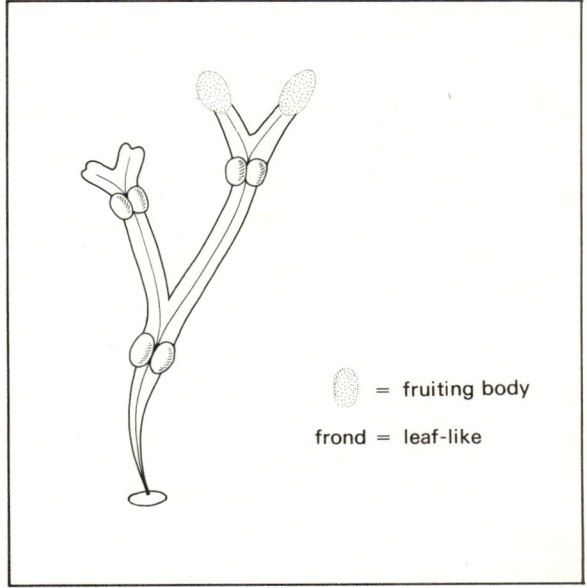

= fruiting body

frond = leaf-like

Fig. 1.1

In using such a key you have been forced to examine the characteristics of that organism. Its identification needs careful observation and judgement.

1.2 Try to make your own key for the animals drawn in Fig. 1.2. (It will help you if you first make a list of the main features of each animal.)

To avoid confusion every type of organism must have its own name which is different from every other name. In the eighteenth century Linnaeus, a Swedish scientist, developed a system of naming organisms which is still used today. He began by sorting organisms into very large groups called kingdoms (animals and plants). These large groups were then subdivided into smaller groups. As the large groups were subdivided the sub-groups contained fewer and fewer organisms but the organisms within the sub-groups became more alike.

1

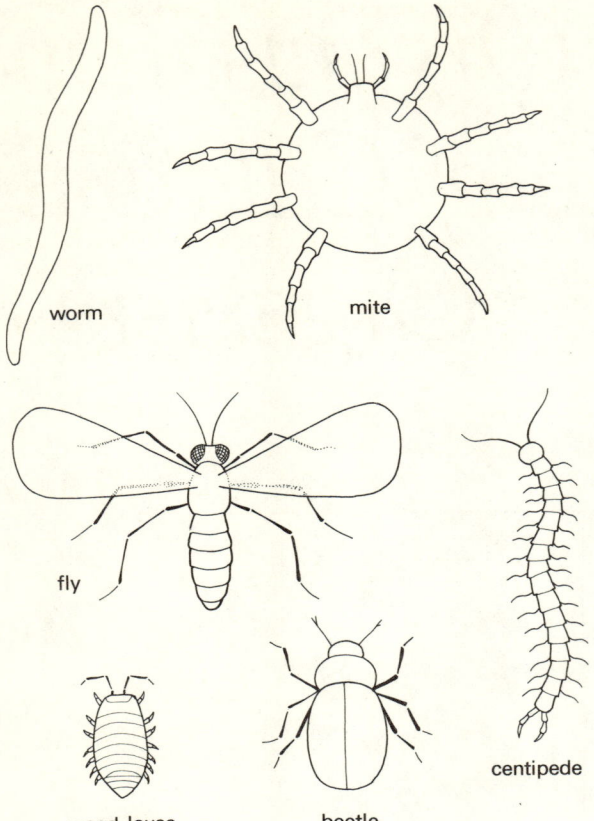

Fig. 1.2

An example of how an organism is classified is illustrated in Table 1. The organism in this case is the earthworm.

Table 1. Classification of the Earthworm

Kingdom: Animal
Phylum: Annelida
Class: Chaetopoda
Order: Oligochaeta
Family: Lumbricidae
Genus: *Lumbricus*
Species: *L. terrestris*

1.3 The words listed below are all used in the full classification of man:
Vertebrata: Hominidae: *sapiens*; animal; *Homo*; Mammalia; Primate; Use these words to draw up a classification table for man like the one given for the earthworm.

Every known organism has been given a special scientific name. Two Latin words are used. The first name (the first letter of which is always capitalised) is the name of the **genus** to which it belongs (the generic name). The second name (the first letter of which is always written with a small letter) is the name of the **species** (the specific name). Both the generic and the specific name must be underlined when written, or put in italic type if printed.

1.4 A laboratory strain of fruit-fly is classified with the name *Drosophila melanogaster*. Which part of the name refers to
(a) the genus
(b) the species?

2 Animal and Plant Cells

Living things are made up of units called **cells**. We can examine cells by using a **microscope**.

2.1 What is the function of a microscope? Draw a simple diagram to illustrate your answer.

Specimens of cells may be obtained in a variety of ways. For example, thin slices of tissue can be cut from plants and animals. Alternatively, cells may be obtained by mounting a small piece of tissue on a microscope slide and then squashing it with a cover slip.

Cheek cells may be obtained by scraping your finger-nail over the inside of your cheek. The cells are then mounted on a microscope slide with a drop of saliva, covered with a cover slip, and examined under the microscope.

2.2 (a) What is the purpose of the saliva?
(b) Make a list of the uses of a cover slip.
(c) How can details within the cells be made clearer?

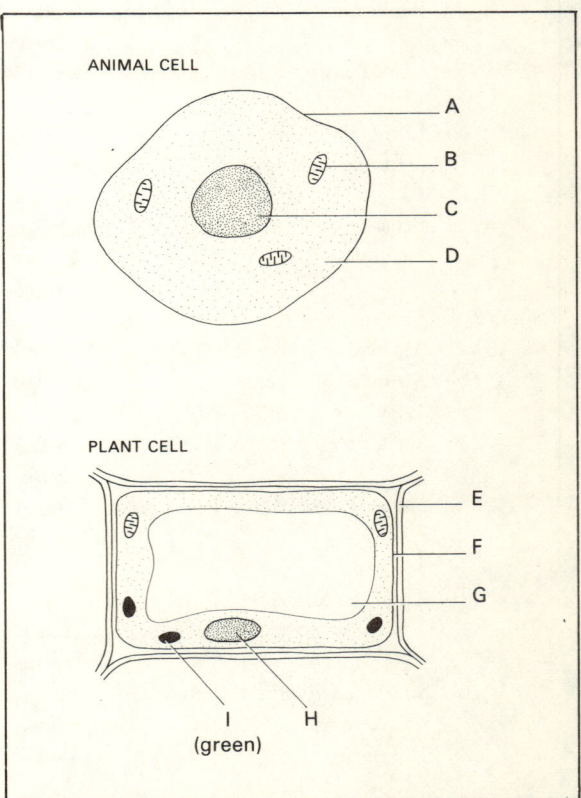

Fig. 2.1

2.3 (a) Look at Fig. 2.1 which shows a plant and an animal cell, and write down the names and functions of the structures labelled A–I.

(b) Make a list of the similarities and of the differences between plant and animal cells.

3 Simple Organisms (Unicells)

Most organisms are made up of many cells. However, there are some organisms that exist as a single cell which can carry out all the vital processes of life.

3.1 List seven vital processes of life.

Unicells have no need for a special breathing organ. They rely on diffusion to obtain oxygen through the cell membrane.

3.2 Explain what is meant by diffusion.

Waste products also move from the inside of the cell to the outside by diffusion.

3.3 What waste products are produced by unicells?

As with other organisms, unicells respond to stimuli.

3.4 What type of stimuli do unicells respond to?

Light is one important stimulus which affects the lives of some unicells.

3.5 What type of unicell needs light in order to live?

Different types of unicells obtain their food in one of two ways. If they are plant-like they use the sun to make their own food from carbon dioxide and water. If they are animal-like they consume other animals or plants by the cell surrounding the food particle.

3.6 Draw a series of simple diagrams to show how *Amoeba* feeds.

Unicells move in a variety of ways.

3.7 Name one unicell which moves by
(a) flowing cytoplasm
(b) cilia
(c) flagella.

However, not all unicells can move. Some live attached to some object by a "stalk". Others are simply carried by water currents.

Most unicells reproduce by **binary fission** (a form of asexual reproduction where the organism divides into two).

3.8 The stages in the asexual reproduction of *Amoeba* are labelled A–E in Fig. 3.1. Write down the letters which show the correct order of the stages.

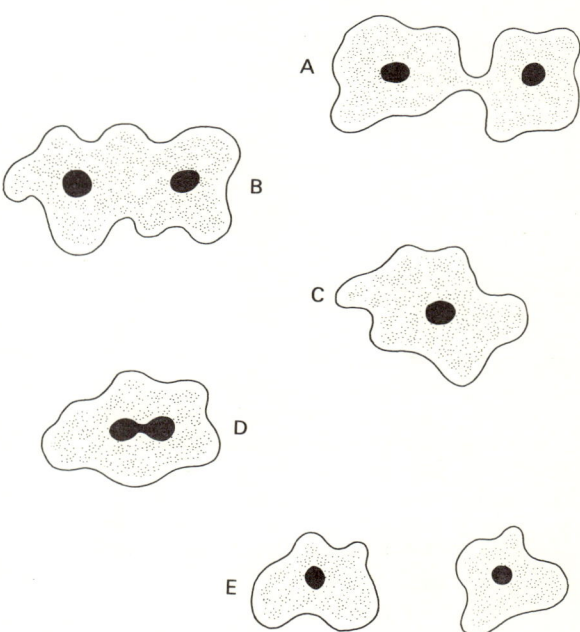

Fig. 3.1

In some unicells both asexual reproduction and sexual reproduction occur. Growth means simply an increase in size. The unicell usually undergoes asexual reproduction once it has reached its optimum size.

Part Two   Maintenance of Life

4 Gas Exchange in Animals

Let us consider what differences there are between the air we **breathe** in and the air we breathe out.

4.1 (a) What happens when you place a lighted candle into (i) a gas jar of atmospheric air (ii) a gas jar of exhaled air?
(b) What do you conclude from this?

This experiment, however, does not show you what gases are present in these two air samples.

4.2 (a) Describe a simple experiment to compare the amount of **carbon dioxide** in atmospheric air with that in exhaled air.
(b) What results would you expect?

We can find out more about gas exchange by calculating the percentage volume of carbon dioxide and **oxygen** in exhaled and inhaled air. Two reagents, **potassium hydroxide** and **potassium pyrogallate,** can be used.

4.3 (a) Draw a simple diagram of the apparatus you would use.
(b) How are the reagents, potassium hydroxide and potassium pyrogallate, used in this experiment?
(c) The order in which the reagents are used is important. Why?
(d) Calculate the percentage volume of gases in a given air sample from the following experimental results:

Original volume of gas sample = 100 mm³
Volume after addition of potassium hydroxide = 96 mm³
Volume after addition of potassium pyrogallate = 80 mm³

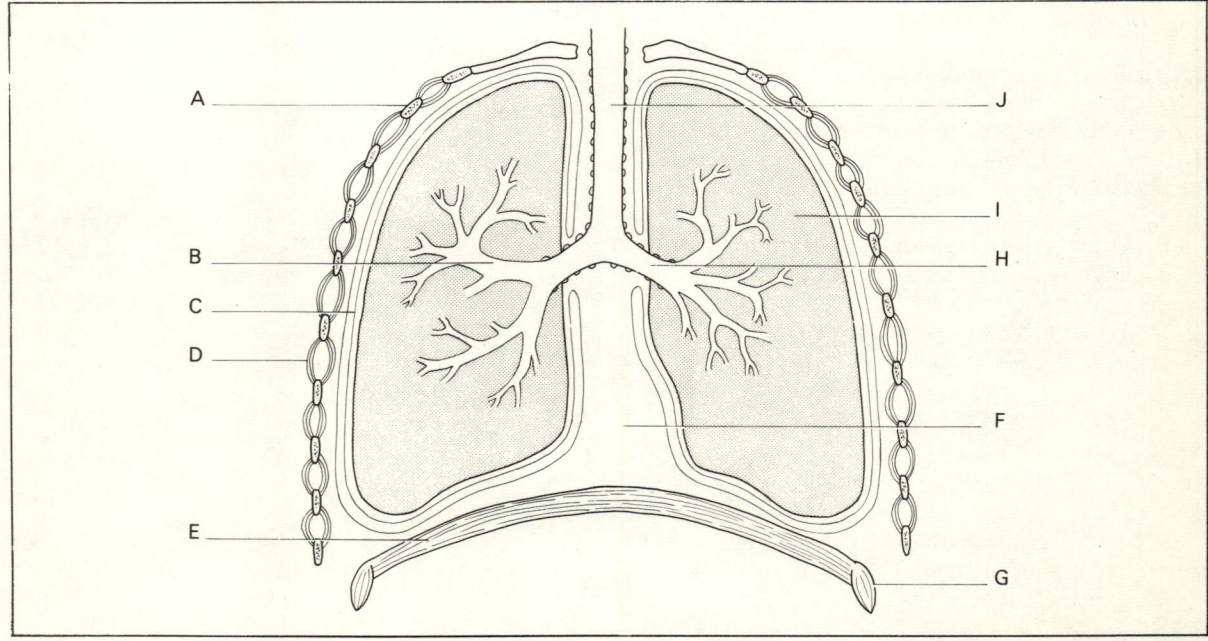

Fig. 4.1

(e) What do you think the remaining volume of gas contains?

(f) Do you think the source of the gas sample in the experiment is exhaled or inhaled air?

4.4 Devise an experiment to find out whether wood-lice or other small animals give off carbon dioxide. Do not forget to include suitable controls.

Carbon dioxide is not the only gas breathed out. **Water** vapour is also produced.

4.5 How could you prove that we breathe out water vapour?

Your **rate of breathing** depends on what you are doing at the time.

4.6 Compare your rate and depth of breathing when resting with that
(a) after vigorous exercise
(b) when standing on the top of a high mountain.
Explain in each case the differences that you describe.

How does the air reach the **lungs** where gas exchange takes place?

4.7 (a) List the structures making up the pathway through which air entering the mouth passes to the lungs.
(b) Name the structures which are labelled A–J in Fig. 4.1.

When you breathe in (**inhale**) the volume of the lungs is increased. One thing you may notice is that the **ribs** move upwards and outwards.
Between the ribs, there are muscles called the **intercostal muscles.**

4.8 What is the function of the intercostal muscles?

When the **rib cage** moves up and out this increases the volume of the chest cavity.
Breathing is also achieved with the aid of the **diaphragm.** The diaphragm is a dome-shaped sheet of tissue at the base of the **thorax,** and is illustrated in Fig. 4.1.

4.9 What happens to (i) the diaphragm (ii) the chest volume when the muscles on the edge of the diaphragm contract?

The principle of breathing can be demonstrated by reference to the model illustrated in Fig. 4.2.

4.10 (a) What happens to (i) the volume (ii) the pressure when you pull down the sheet?

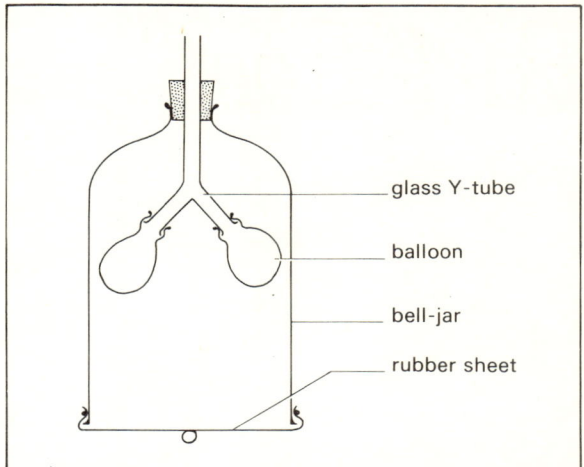

Fig. 4.2

(b) How does this cause air to move into the lungs?
(c) Now explain how the movement of the ribs and diaphragm causes air to move into the lungs.

So far, we have considered how we inhale.

4.11 (a) What happens to (i) the ribs (ii) the diaphragm when we exhale?
(b) What effect does this have on the volume of the chest?
(c) Why does this cause us to breathe out?

The chest wall and lungs are separated by two thin layers of cells. These form two airtight sacs (the **pleural sacs**) around the lungs.

4.12 What would happen to the lung if the pleural sacs were punctured from the outside?

Our lungs can hold quite a large volume of air.

4.13 (a) Describe an experiment to measure the volume of air that your lungs can hold.
(b) Does the apparatus measure all the air in your lungs? Explain your answer.
(c) What is the name given to the volume of air which moves in and out in normal breathing?

The lung is made up of very finely divided tubes, at the end of which are found a large number of air sacs called **alveoli.** The alveoli are well supplied with blood **capillaries.**

4.14 (a) Why are the capillaries found close to the alveoli?
(b) How is the oxygen transferred from the air inside the alveoli to the blood in the capillaries?

Different ways of obtaining oxygen can be seen in

5

different animals. Fish, for example, have to obtain their oxygen directly from the water.

4.15 (a) What features would you expect to find in the gas-exchange organ of a fish?
(b) What is the name of the gas-exchange organ in fish?

Another active animal is the insect. It solves the problem of obtaining oxygen in a completely different way. If you make a microscopic examination of the tissue of an insect you will find many tubes called **tracheae** in it.

4.16 Describe briefly how oxygen gets to the tissues in an insect.

5 Respiration

Why do organisms take in oxygen and give out carbon dioxide? Food is used (oxidised) in the body to give **energy** and carbon dioxide. Oxygen is needed for this process. Water is also produced in addition to carbon dioxide.

5.1 Describe a simple chemical test for water.

How much energy is there in food? A simple way to find out is to measure the heat given off when food is burnt. Consider the experiment illustrated in Fig. 5.1.

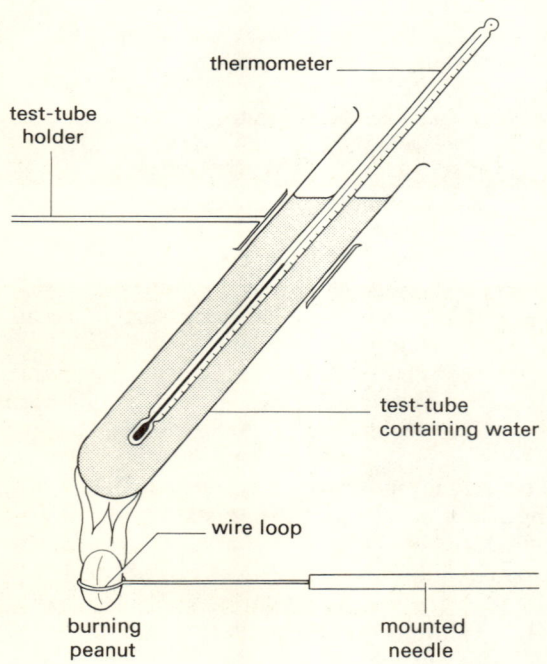

Fig. 5.1

5.2 (a) What measurements would you make in this experiment?

(b) How would you calculate the energy given out by the peanut?
(c) What errors would occur in this experiment and how would you reduce them?
(d) Calculate the energy given out by 1 gram of peanut when 0.1 g of peanut is burnt. The amount of water in the test-tube is 40 cm³. The temperature of water is raised from 19 °C to 50 °C.

We need energy to carry out work, e.g. using muscles to run.

5.3 Where is this energy produced?

Energy in the body is obtained from food by a number of small chemical changes rather than one large change. This energy is stored in a chemical called **adenosine triphosphate** (ATP). This is made as follows:

Adenosine diphosphate (ADP) + phosphate
+ energy = ATP

Energy is needed for muscles to contract. This energy is obtained from ATP as follows:

ATP = ADP + phosphate + energy

The ADP can then be reconverted to ATP using more energy from food. Release of energy from food in the body is called **respiration.**

5.4 What do we call the type of respiration that uses oxygen?

5.5 Write out the basic chemical equation for the oxidation of glucose by oxygen to carbon dioxide and water.

5.6 In which structures inside the cell is ATP produced?

Respiration can also occur without oxygen.

5.7 What do we call the type of respiration that occurs without oxygen?

If muscles continue to contract for a period of time an **oxygen debt** builds up. This means that energy produced by **aerobic respiration** is not sufficient to meet the demands of continued exertion.

5.8 What substance builds up in the muscle when **anaerobic respiration** takes place?

An experiment can be set up to show that yeast can live on glucose in the absence of air (see Fig. 5.2).

5.9 (a) What products are produced by the yeast when using this type of respiration?
(b) What is the purpose of placing paraffin above the yeast and glucose solution?

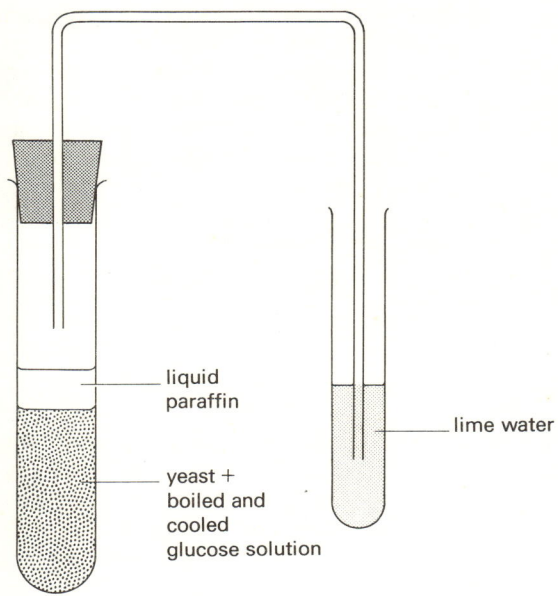

liquid
paraffin

yeast +
boiled and
cooled
glucose solution

lime water

Fig. 5.2

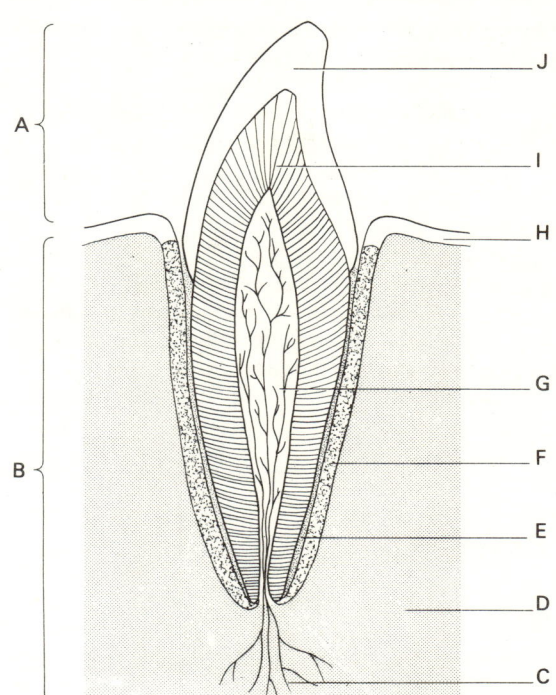

Fig. 6.1

(c) What change would you expect to occur in the lime water?

5.10 (a) Write out the basic chemical equation for the anaerobic respiration of glucose by yeast.
  (b) What use is made by man of this type of respiration by yeast?

6 Feeding Mechanisms in Animals

In many animals food must be broken down into smaller pieces before it can be swallowed. The biting devices of mammals are called **teeth.** There are four types of teeth.

6.1 (a) Name the four types of teeth in mammals.
  (b) Describe the functions of these four types of teeth.

The basic structure of all teeth is the same.

6.2 Fig. 6.1 is a diagram of an **incisor** tooth. Write the names of the parts labelled A–J.

The shape and number of teeth is called the **dentition.** The dentition of an animal varies according to its **diet.**

6.3 (a) Look at the photograph of a cat's skull in Fig. 6.2. Describe briefly how the teeth are suitable for eating meat.

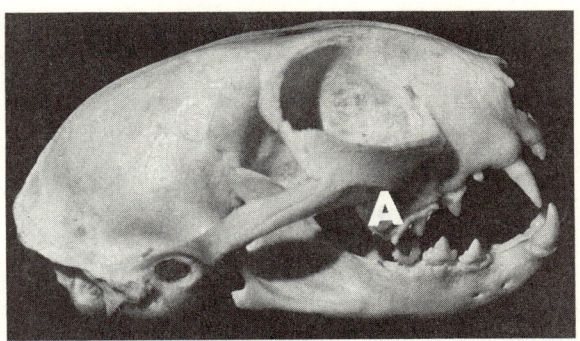

Fig. 6.2

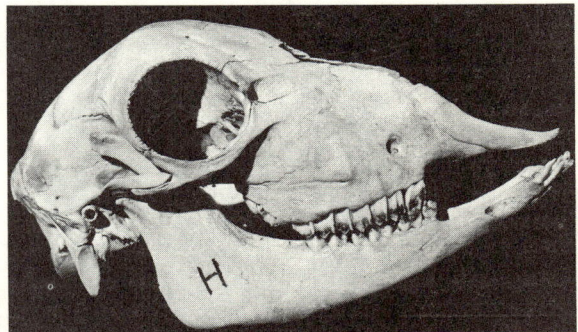

Fig. 6.3

(b) What is the name of the huge teeth labelled A in the photograph?
(c) In what way must the jaw move in order for the teeth to cut the meat efficiently?

6.4 (a) Look at the photograph of a sheep's skull in Fig. 6.3. Describe briefly how the teeth are suitable for eating grass.
(b) How must the jaw move to enable the teeth to grind the grass into small pieces?

The **locust** eats large quantities of vegetation by means of its **mouthparts.**

6.5 (a) Write down the letter in Fig. 6.4 which corresponds to the following mouthparts of a locust: (i) **mandibles** (ii) **maxilla** (iii) **labium** (iv) **labrum.**
(b) Briefly describe the functions of each of these mouthparts.

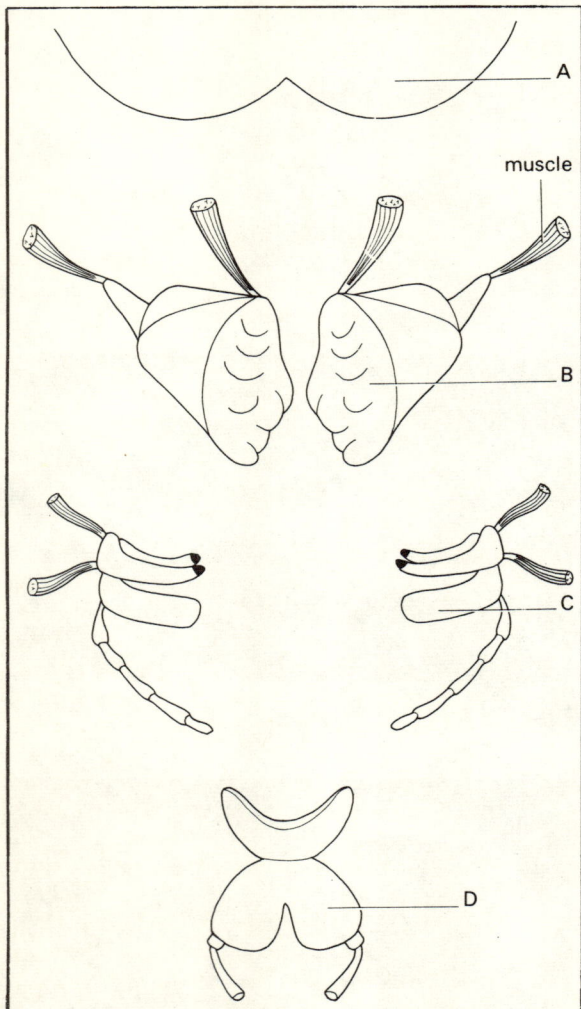

Fig. 6.4

The **house-fly** cannot feed on solid food.

6.6 Look at Fig. 6.5 which shows the mouthparts of the house-fly. Explain how the insect feeds.

The variety of ways in which animals catch their food is enormous.

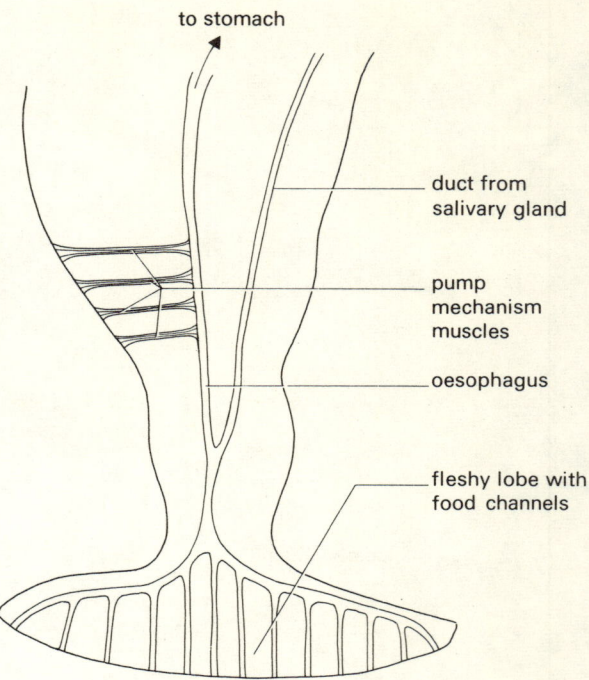

Fig. 6.5

6.7 Describe briefly how the following animals obtain their food:
(a) *Amoeba*
(b) *Hydra*
(c) mosquito
(d) butterfly

7 Food

All organisms require **food** of some sort.

7.1 Why does man need food?

Food is classified by scientists into different groups according to its chemical structure. The main groups of food substances are **carbohydrates, fats** and **proteins.**

CARBOHYDRATES
Starches and sugars are both carbohydrates.

7.2 What elements are present in carbohydrates?

7.3 Draw a simple diagram of the chemical structure of starch.

7.4 (a) Describe a simple chemical test for the presence of starch in a food.
(b) What would be a positive result?

Most sugars are able to reduce an alkaline solution of

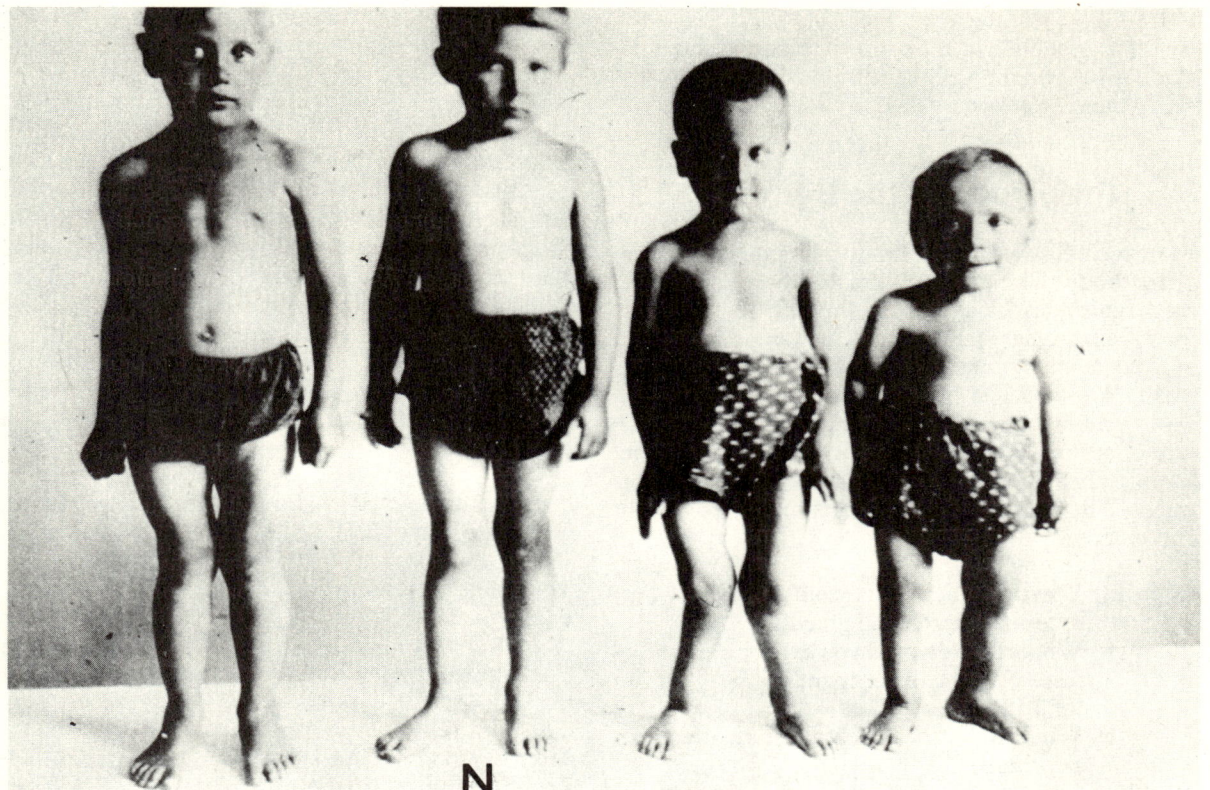

Fig. 7.1 *Rickets in children aged 5 years; child N is almost normal.*

copper sulphate to copper oxide. These sugars are called **reducing sugars.**

7.5 (a) Describe a simple chemical test for the presence of reducing sugars in a food.
(b) What would be a positive result when (i) a small amount of reducing sugar is present (ii) a medium amount of reducing sugar is present (iii) a large amount of reducing sugar is present?

The test does not work with ordinary **sucrose** sugar but can be used if the sucrose is first broken down to reducing sugar.

7.6 How can you change sucrose into a reducing sugar?

FATS
7.7 What elements do fats contain?

7.8 Describe a simple test for the presence of fat in a food.

PROTEINS
7.9 (a) What chemical elements do proteins contain?
(b) From what smaller molecules are proteins built up?
(c) Why do the many proteins differ from each other?

7.10 (a) Describe a simple chemical test for the presence of protein in a food.
(b) What would be a positive result?

VITAMINS
There are also other important substances called **vitamins** present in food. Although we get no energy from vitamins they are necessary for the normal functioning of the body. Only tiny amounts of these vitamins are necessary. If they are absent from the diet we suffer from deficiency diseases.

7.11 (a) The children in the photograph suffer from **rickets.** Which vitamin is lacking in the children's diet?
(b) What kinds of foods are required to prevent this?
(c) Give another example of a vitamin. Which foods are a rich source of this vitamin? What happens to man if there is a deficiency of it?

MINERAL SALTS
Mineral salts are also needed for the healthy functioning of the body.

7.12 (a) What is the use of (i) **iron** (ii) **phosphorus** (iii) **calcium** in the body?
(b) What food source is rich in (i) iron (ii) phosphorus (iii) calcium?

WATER

Water is essential in the diet. The human body is made up of about 65 per cent water. It must replace that which it loses every day.

8 Getting Food to the Body

After food is swallowed it has to pass into the tissues of the body. The **gut** wall acts as a barrier and the food molecules have to pass through it. Consider food containing starch and glucose. The starch molecules are large whilst the glucose molecules are small. A model gut can be set up (as in Fig. 8.1), using a **membrane** called **Visking tubing** and a mixture of starch and glucose solution placed inside the tubing. The tubing is then placed in a beaker of water. The water in the beaker is tested for starch and glucose.

8.1 (a) What chemical tests would you carry out to test for starch and glucose?
   (b) What results would you expect from these tests after the experiment has been set up for 30 minutes?
   (c) What do you conclude from this experiment?

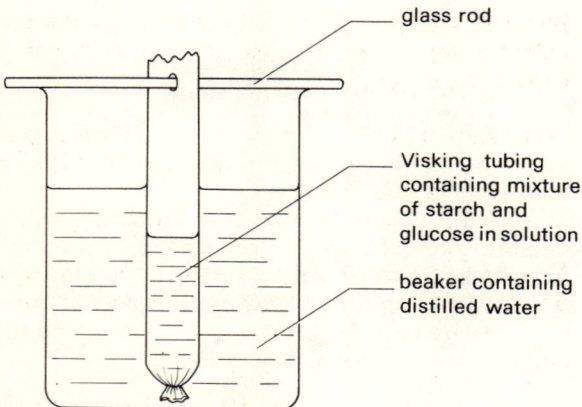

Fig. 8.1

The Visking tubing is **permeable** to glucose but **impermeable** to starch.

8.2 What type of membrane do we call Visking tubing?

It seems that the gut wall acts as a similar kind of barrier. How can starch be broken down so that it can pass through the gut wall?

8.3 (a) What is mixed with food in the mouth?
   (b) What happens if this liquid is mixed with starch solution?

You should now be able to understand what happens to starch in the **alimentary canal.**

8.4 Use the information from Questions 8.1 and 8.3 to explain how starch in our food is able to enter the tissues of the body.

There must be something in saliva which can break down starch into glucose. In other words we have found that a chemical reaction has taken place and has been helped by a substance in saliva. In chemistry, substances which help reactions to take place are called **catalysts.** Biological catalysts are called **enzymes.** Enzymes can only work efficiently in the body under special conditions.

8.5 List as many as you can of the special conditions that enzymes need to function efficiently.

Enzymes are named according to the food substance (substrate) they work on. The name of an enzyme always ends in **-ase**, e.g. protease is the enzyme which acts on protein.

8.6 **Salivary amylase** is an enzyme which is found in saliva. On which food substances does it act?

After the food has been swallowed it passes through a tube running through the body from the mouth, where the food enters, to the anus, where the waste material comes out as **faeces.** This tube is called the alimentary canal.

8.7 Name the structures labelled A–L in Fig. 8.2.

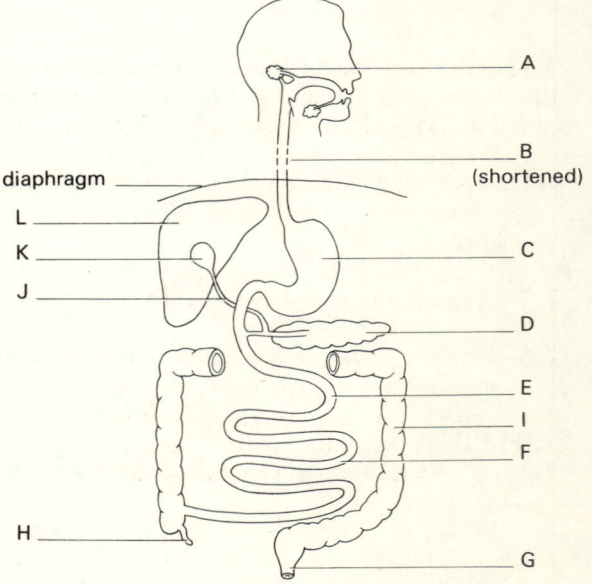

Fig. 8.2

How does food travel down the alimentary canal? Close examination of a cross-section of the canal reveals two sets of muscles, longitudinal and circular (Fig. 8.3).

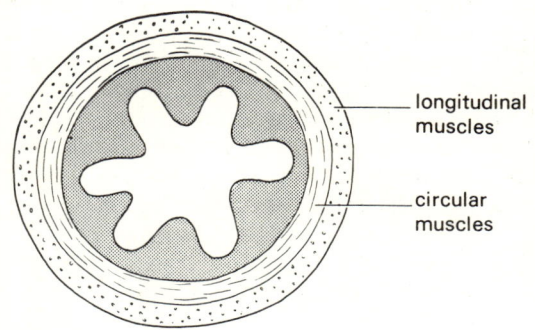

Fig. 8.3

8.8 (a) What is the name given to the process of muscle contraction which makes the food travel down the gut?
 (b) Explain how the muscles in the gut wall produce this contraction.

The most important digestive processes occur in the **stomach** and **small intestine.**

8.9 (a) What happens to the food in (i) the stomach (ii) the **duodenum?**
 (b) Name two digestive enzymes and the food substances on which they act.
 (c) What chemical substances are provided after digestion has taken place?

The digested food in the small intestine has to enter the body tissues.

8.10 How are the products of digestion absorbed into the body? Give details of the structures involved.

8.11 Some animals (**herbivores**) eat only plant material. Much of the plant material is made up of **cellulose** molecules. However, herbivores do not possess the enzymes capable of digesting cellulose, so how are they able to obtain nourishment from cellulose?

9 Transport in Animals

A small organism such as *Amoeba* can obtain food and oxygen simply by **diffusion**. There is a maximum size to which *Amoeba* can grow because as the cell's volume increases the surface of the cell decreases in proportion. This can be illustrated by a simple example:

Total surface area of cube with 1 cm sides = 6 cm²
Volume of cube with 1 cm sides = 1 cm³
The surface area/volume ratio is 6 : 1

9.1 (a) What would be the surface area/volume ratio of a cube with (i) 2 cm sides (ii) 3 cm sides?
 (b) What do you notice about the area/volume ratios as compared with that of the 1 cm cube?

As the volume of the organism increases the surface area does not increase in proportion. Therefore the organism cannot rely on diffusion alone for its supply of food and oxygen. Also, as the size of the organism increases so does the distance from the outside to the inside increase. This problem has been overcome by larger animals with **mass flow systems.** A mass flow system is a means of distributing food and oxygen around the body, often with the aid of tubes and pumps. The **blood system** is an example of a mass flow system.

9.2 Name three mass flow systems in the human body other than the blood system.

9.3 (a) List the main components of blood.
 (b) What are the functions of each component?
 (c) Draw a simple diagram of each type of blood cell to show the main features.
 (d) Where are the red blood cells made?

Blood is transported around the body by the **circulatory (or blood) system.** This is a system of vessels and a pump.

9.4 Refer to Fig. 9.1 and write down the names of
 (a) the major organs the system supplies (labelled 1–6)
 (b) the major blood vessels (labelled A–G).

You can compare the circulatory system with **parallel** and **series** circuits in an electricity circuit.

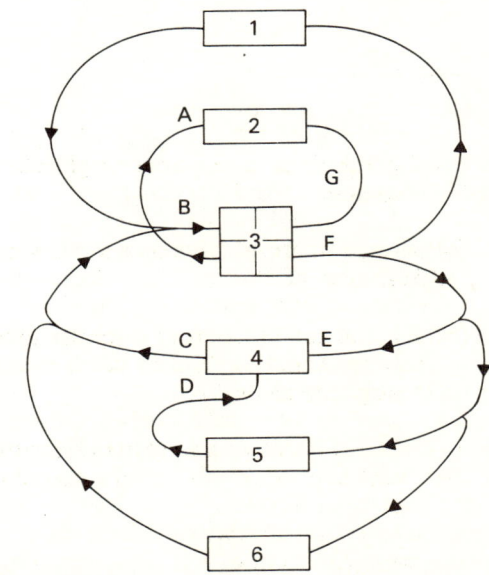

Fig. 9.1

9.5 **(a)** Which parts of the blood system illustrated in Fig. 9.1 are (i) parallel circuits (ii) series circuits?
   (b) What are the advantages of (i) parallel circuits (ii) series circuits?

Another vital part of the circuit is the pump (the **heart**) which moves the blood around the body. Refer to the diagram of the heart (Fig. 9.2) and answer the following questions.

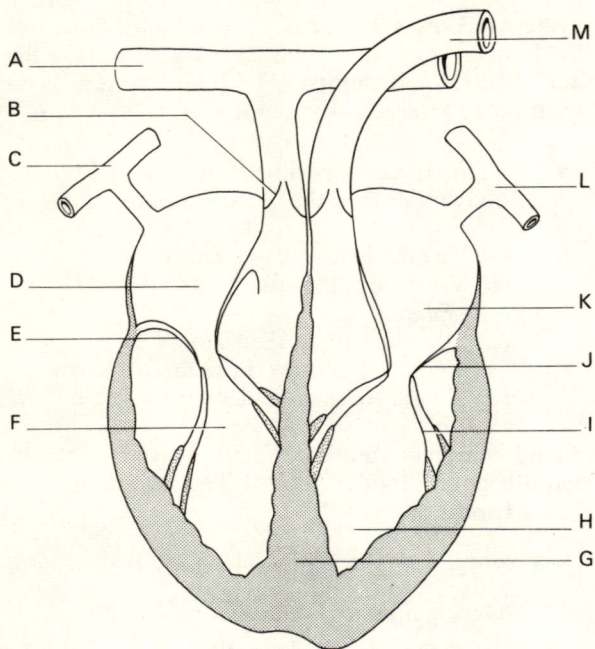

Fig. 9.2

9.6 **(a)** Write down the names of the parts labelled A–M.
   (b) Why is there a difference between the thickness of the muscular walls of the auricles and those of the ventricles?
   (c) Why is there a difference between the thickness of the muscular walls of the right and left ventricles?
   (d) What is the function of the cords which are attached to the valve edges and the ventricle walls?
   (e) Where do the vessels attached to the heart (labelled A, C, L and M) go to or come from?

In the circulatory system, there are three main types of **blood vessel**. One type of vessel transports blood away from the heart and is under great pressure.

9.7 **(a)** Name the type of vessel shown in Fig. 9.3.
   (b) How is this vessel adapted to carry blood away from the heart?

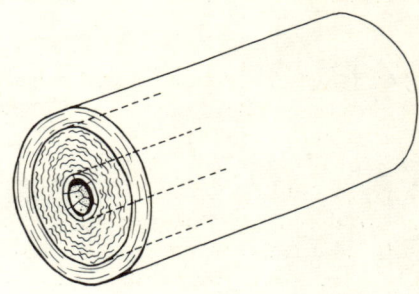

Fig. 9.3

Another type of blood vessel transports blood back to the heart.

9.8 **(a)** Name the type of vessel shown in Fig. 9.4.
   (b) How is this vessel adapted to carry blood back to the heart?

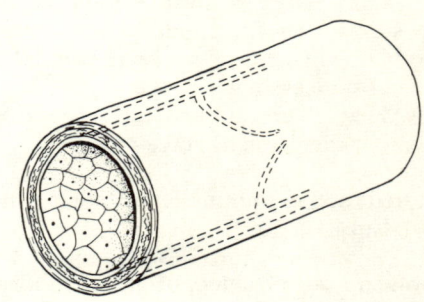

Fig. 9.4

A third type of vessel enables the exchange of gases, food and waste products between the blood and the tissues to take place.

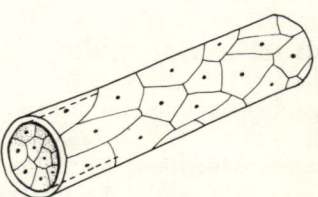

Fig. 9.5

9.9 **(a)** Name the type of vessel shown in Fig. 9.5.

(b) How is this vessel adapted to carry out this exchange of materials between the blood and tissues?

One of the functions of the blood is the transport of gases.

9.10 (a) What gases are transported by the blood?
(b) Describe how each of these gases is carried by the blood.

THE LYMPHATIC SYSTEM

Fluid leaks from the capillaries into the surrounding tissues. The clear fluid which emerges and bathes the cells is called **tissue fluid.** Tissue fluid contains the food and oxygen necessary to keep the cells alive. The fluid is then drained into an open-ended system of tubes called the **lymphatic system.**

9.11 (a) How is the **lymph** moved along the lymphatic vessels?
(b) Into which blood vessel do the lymphatic vessels drain?

9.12 What is the function of the **lymph nodes** which are situated along the lymphatic vessels?

10 Photosynthesis

Analysis of the atmosphere over a period of time shows that the concentration of gases remains constant. Yet we know that animals give out carbon dioxide whilst taking in oxygen for respiration. Why then are the atmospheric levels of these gases constant? Measurement of gases in areas of green vegetation shows that the level of carbon dioxide is lower during the hours of daylight.

10.1 Suggest what is happening to the carbon dioxide.

10.2 (a) Describe an experiment to find out if carbon dioxide is taken up by green plants in the light. Remember to include suitable controls.
(b) What results would you expect to find?

10.3 Remembering that green plants respire aerobically, summarise diagrammatically the CO_2 output and intake of a green plant in both light and dark conditions.

Carbon dioxide is not the only gas involved. Experiments carried out by Priestley in the nineteenth century showed that mice could live in a closed container such as a bell-jar as long as there was a green plant in there as well.

10.4 (a) How is the mouse able to keep alive?
(b) How would you carry out an experiment to collect and analyse the gas given off by pondweed?
(c) What is the name of the gas you should collect?

10.5 Now summarise the CO_2 and O_2 output and input of a green plant in (i) light (ii) dark conditions.

Why does a green plant need carbon dioxide? Plants, like animals, need food for energy. Carbohydrates can be made in the plant for this purpose. One way to show this is to carry out simple chemical tests on green leaves.

10.6 Describe how you would carry out an experiment to find out if carbohydrates are formed in green leaves in light. (Answer the questions below to help you.)
(a) How do you kill the leaf?
(b) Why must you remove the green colour of the leaves?
(c) How is the green colour removed?
(d) How do you test for starch in the leaf?

10.7 Devise simple experiments to show that (i) light (ii) carbon dioxide is necessary for starch production in green leaves.

Carbon dioxide, water and light are all necessary for green plants to form food. Oxygen is given off as a waste product.

The process can be summarised as follows:

$$2H_2O \xrightarrow{\text{light}} 4H + O_2$$
$$CO_2 + 4H \longrightarrow (CH_2O) + H_2O$$

simplified
glucose

Remember that the atoms in the glucose molecule are in the ratio 1(C) : 2(H) : 1(O).

$$\text{Therefore } 6(CH_2O) \longrightarrow C_6H_{12}O_6$$

glucose

10.8 Write down the chemical equation which represents the over-all process of starch production in leaves.

This process of carbohydrate production from carbon dioxide and water in green leaves and light is called **photosynthesis.**

Light is important in this process and so is the fact that plants are green. The green substance in plants is called chlorophyll.

You can extract the chlorophyll from plants and put it in a hollow glass slide. The slide can then be placed in front of a light beam which is passed into a prism. The light is then projected on to a screen.

10.9 (a) What colour(s) would you see on the screen?

(b) What do you conclude from this experiment?

10.10 Describe an experiment to show that chlorophyll is essential for photosynthesis.

Refer to Fig. 10.1 which illustrates a vertical section through a leaf.

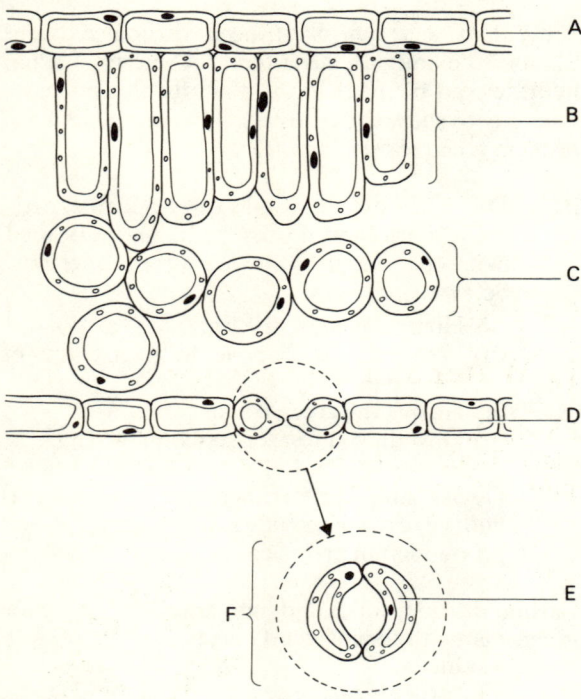

Fig. 10.1

10.11 (a) Which part of the leaf would receive the most light?

(b) Name the structures labelled A–F.

(c) State briefly the functions of these parts.

10.12 Make a step by step comparison of the processes of respiration and photosynthesis.

Photosynthesis is important in food production. Plants are able to make their own food. Animals, however, cannot do this, for they are ultimately dependent on plants for food.

10.13 Draw a simple flow diagram showing the direction of energy flow from sunlight through a food chain.

11 Transport in Plants

Food, water and minerals need to be transported within the plant. Therefore a mass flow system is necessary to transport these substances around the plant.

Let us first look at the way in which water and minerals are transported within the plant.

11.1 (a) If you were given a fresh leafy shoot and a solution of a red dye in water, how would you investigate the path of water and ions in the stem?

(b) Write down the letter in Fig. 11.1 which labels the tissue in which you would find the red dye.

(c) What is the name of this tissue?

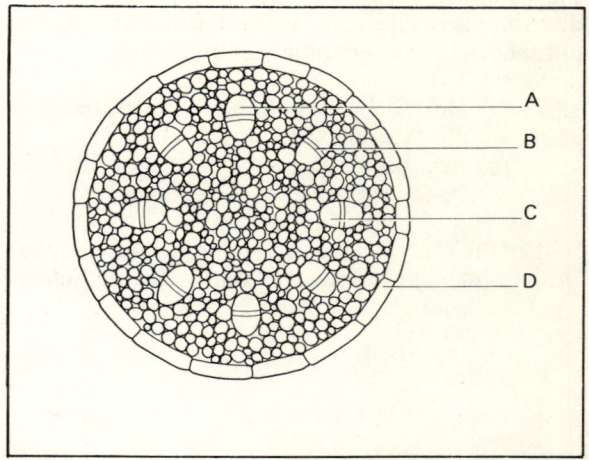

Fig. 11.1

Minerals are also transported in the same structures. Minerals are important in many processes.

11.2 Briefly describe why (i) **magnesium** (ii) **nitrate** (iii) **phosphate** ions are needed in a plant.

If any ions are missing then the growth of the plant may be affected in some way. This is called **mineral deficiency.**

11.3 What experiment would you carry out to see if a deficiency of an ion would make any difference to the growth of a plant?

Cells are capable of storing within them high concentrations of ions, many times those of concentrations outside the cell.

11.4 Experiments have shown that ions are taken into the root cells at a much faster rate than could occur by diffusion alone. When this happens, carbohydrates are used up and the oxygen consumption increases in the plant. Using this information, try to explain how ions are transported into the plant.

Let us now look at the way a plant transports food to its various parts. A way of demonstrating this is by **ringing** the plant. Ringing is achieved by removing a ring of outside tissue from the stem.

11.5 (a) What happens to the plant if you ring it?
　　　(b) What do you conclude from this?
　　　(c) What is the name of the plant tissue which transports food around the plant?

A modern way of demonstrating this food transport system is to use food which contains sucrose made up of **radioactive carbon atoms (C^{14})**. This labels the food so that its path may be traced throughout the plant. This radioactive sucrose may be placed on the leaves (as shown in Fig. 11.2) and allowed to distribute itself around the plant. Next, the plant is placed on a photographic film which is then developed.

11.6 Fig. 11.2 shows the appearance of the photographic plate after it has been developed. What do you conclude about the distribution of food around the plant?

11.7 Complete the naming of the labelled structures in Fig. 11.1 and briefly state the function of each of the plant tissues.

11.8 Using Fig. 11.3, describe how the section of a **woody** stem differs from that of a non-woody stem.

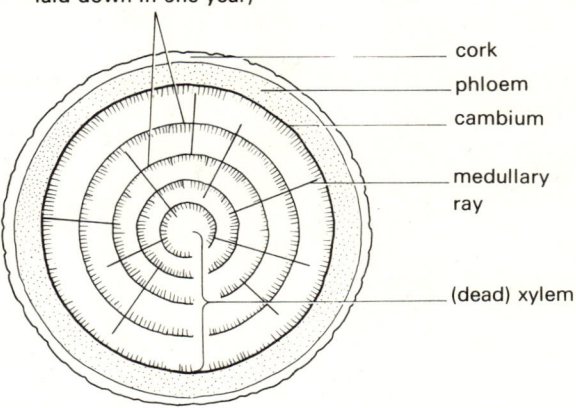

annual rings (1 ring of xylem laid down in one year)

cork
phloem
cambium
medullary ray
(dead) xylem

Fig. 11.3

12 Water and the Organism

Living organisms contain a high proportion of water. Both plants and animals need water to stay alive.

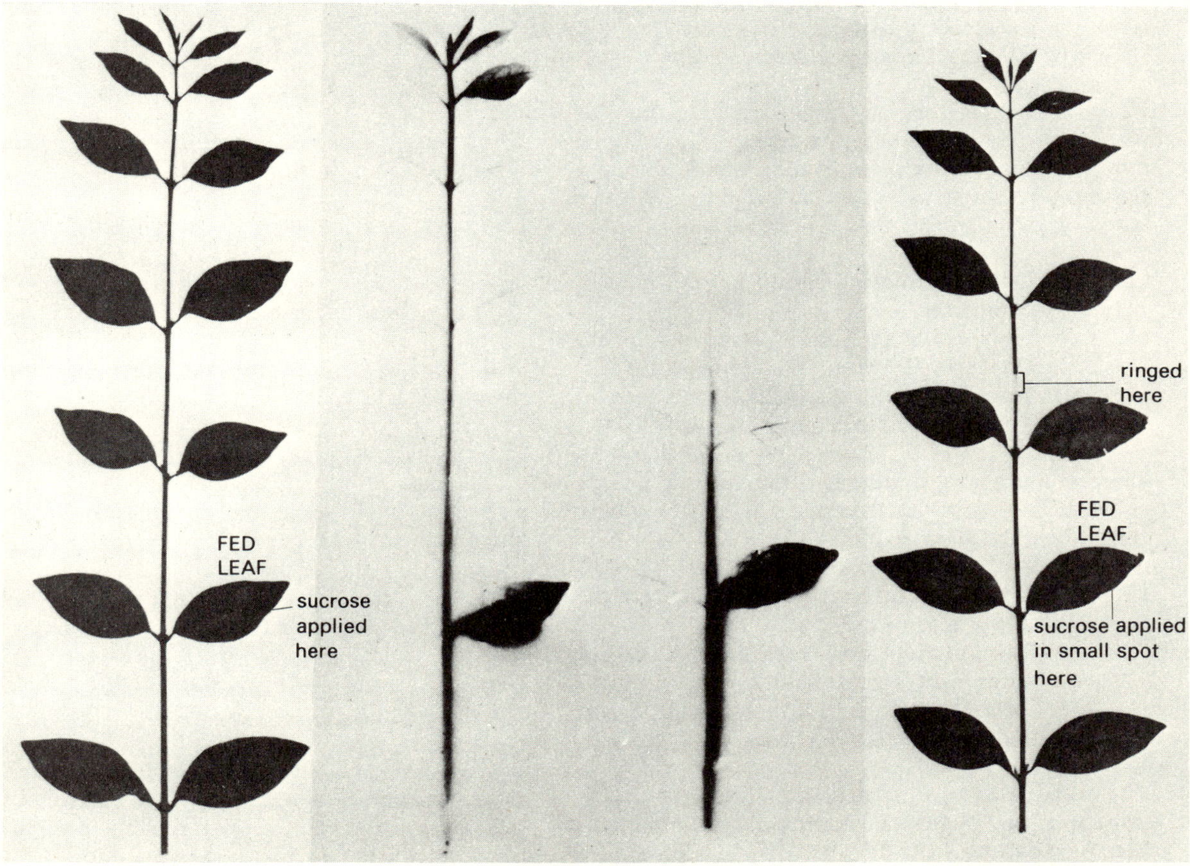

FED LEAF
sucrose applied here

ringed here

FED LEAF
sucrose applied in small spot here

Pressed and dried control twig

Autoradiograph of twigs made after allowing 24 hours for ^{14}C labelled sucrose to translocate.

Pressed and dried twig from which a ring of bark was removed

Fig. 11.2

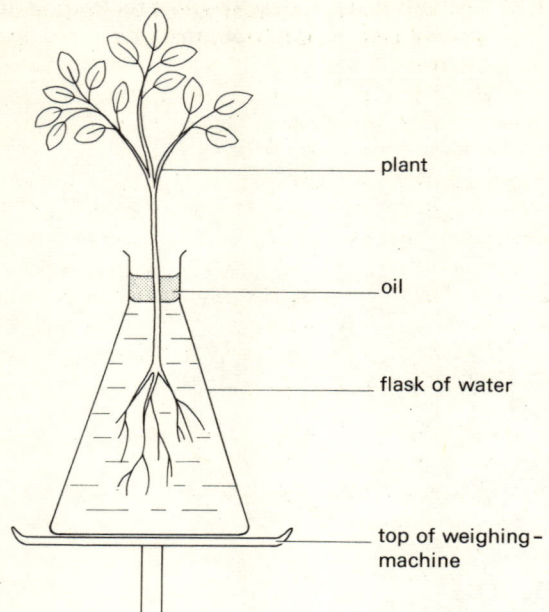

plant

oil

flask of water

top of weighing-machine

Fig. 12.1

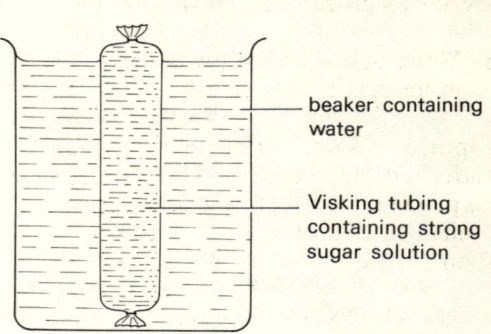

beaker containing water

Visking tubing containing strong sugar solution

EXPERIMENT 2

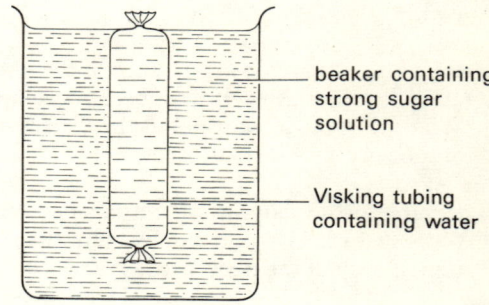

beaker containing strong sugar solution

Visking tubing containing water

Fig. 12.2

12.1 (a) Fig. 12.1 illustrates an experiment to find out whether or not water is lost from a plant. What do you expect to happen after a short period of time?

(b) What is the purpose of the oil film?

From this experiment we may conclude that the plant loses water to the atmosphere. You may be familiar with another piece of apparatus known as a **potometer** which measures the amount of water taken up by a plant.

12.2 (a) Draw a simple diagram of one type of potometer.

(b) How would you use a potometer to find out how (i) wind (ii) temperature (iii) humidity (iv) light affects the rate at which water is taken into the plant?

The leaf must have some way of controlling the rate of water loss to avoid drying up in hot or windy conditions.

12.3 (a) What structures in the leaf control the rate of water loss?

(b) How do these structures affect the rate of water loss from the plant?

(c) How else are these structures important to the plant?

The word used to describe water loss in plants is **transpiration.** Water is taken into the plant to maintain the balance.

Where does water enter the plant? Let us look more closely at how water gets into cells. We can do this by using a **model.** An experiment can be set up

using lengths of Visking tubing immersed in different solutions, as illustrated in Fig. 12.2.

12.4 (a) What happens in experiments 1 and 2 of Fig. 12.2?

(b) What conclusions can you draw from these experiments?

Water passes through the Visking tubing but the sugar does not.

12.5 What do we call this type of membrane?

The experiment described in Question **12.4** provides a clue to what happens inside the plant cell.

12.6 (a) Draw a diagram of what you would expect to see under the microscope if onion cells were immersed in (i) tap water and (ii) a strong sugar solution.

(b) Explain your answers.

12.7 (a) What is the name given to the condition of the cell when it is full of water and pressure is exerted on the cell membrane from the inside?

(b) What is the name given to the condition of the cell when it is short of water and the cell membrane is under low pressure?

The movement of water in and out of cells is achieved by a process called **osmosis.**

12.8 Write out a concise but accurate description of the process of osmosis.

The process is also important in animal cells. Consider red blood cells which are surrounded by **blood plasma.** Plasma has a concentration of solutes equivalent to that of a 0.85% salt solution (**saline** solution).

12.9 (a) What would happen if red blood cells were placed in (i) distilled water (ii) 0.85% saline solution (iii) 2% saline solution?
(b) Explain your answers.

Organisms which live in water have osmotic problems. Think, for example, of a one-celled organism such as *Amoeba* which lives in pond water.

12.10 (a) Which way is water going to flow across the cell membrane of *Amoeba*? Explain why.
(b) What is the name of the structure in *Amoeba* which regulates its water balance?

Larger organisms such as fish also have osmotic problems, but these depend on whether they live in sea-water or fresh water.

12.11 (a) Which way does water flow in a fresh-water fish such as a carp? Explain why.
(b) How does the carp regulate its water balance?

12.12 (a) Which way does water flow in a sea-water fish such as a cod? Explain why.
(b) How does the cod regulate its water balance?

Part Three Adjustment and Control

13 Steady State Mechanisms

Organisms constantly need to make adjustments to counteract changes in the environment.

13.1 What name do we give to the processes that maintain the steady state of an organism?

One example of such a process is keeping the body temperature constant even though the external temperature changes.

13.2 (a) List those factors which can affect the rate at which heat is lost from the body.
(b) How can you reduce the amount of heat being lost from your body?
(c) What does your body do to compensate for the heat loss?

13.3 (a) What happens to you when your temperature rises (e.g. on a hot summer's day)?
(b) Why would the response by your body be less useful in a hot humid jungle?

The detection of temperature changes is also important. In the body there are receptors in the **hypothalamus** (in the brain) which detect changes in the temperature of the blood.
    The regulation of body temperature illustrates the main principles in **homeostasis**:

   (i) A receptor detects a change in the environment.
   (ii) The information is fed into a control centre (often the brain).
   (iii) The control centre sends messages to effectors which counteract that change in the environment.

13.4 Draw a simple diagram to summarise the changes in (i)–(iii) above.

If homeostasis is to be maintained, a **feedback** system is necessary. Feedback involves the sending of continuous information to the control centre.

13.5 On the diagram you have drawn for Question **13.4** indicate where feedback occurs.

Another example of homeostasis is the control of breathing in mammals.

13.6 (a) What happens to oxygen intake and carbon dioxide output when you do vigorous exercise?
(b) What happens to your rate of breathing if you rest after vigorous exercise?

If you undertake vigorous exercise you need more oxygen and you also give out more carbon dioxide. The breathing rate might depend on the concentration of either carbon dioxide or oxygen.

13.7 If a person rebreathes his air in the apparatus illustrated in Fig. 13.1 the subject rapidly becomes unconscious without any increase in his rate of breathing. Which gas does this experiment suggest is normally responsible for stimulating an increase in the rate of breathing?

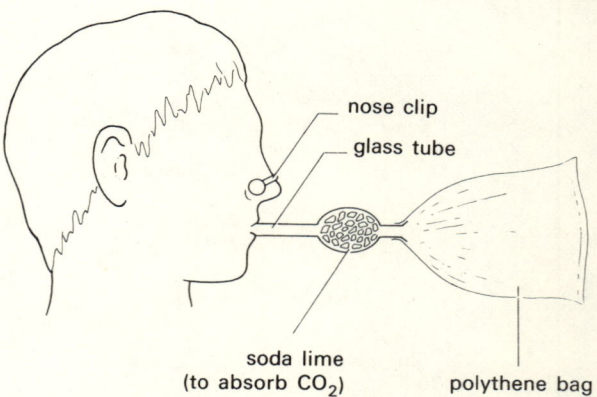

nose clip
glass tube
soda lime (to absorb CO_2)
polythene bag

Fig. 13.1

A third example of a homeostatic system occurs in the **liver**. Its prime function is to regulate the amount of food reaching the tissues. The liver and the pancreas (which produces a hormone) control the amount of sugar in the blood.

13.8 (a) What is the name of this hormone secreted by the pancreas?
(b) In what way does this hormone alter the level of blood sugar?
(c) What disease occurs if there is a lack of this hormone?

Some blood sugar is obtained from **glycogen** which is stored in the liver. Glycogen is converted to glucose when necessary.

13.9 The liver has a number of other important functions. List as many of these as you can.

14 Excretion and Osmoregulation

One of the most important homeostatic organs in the body is the **kidney,** which is illustrated in Fig. 14.1.

14.1 (a) Name the structures labelled A–G in Fig. 14.1.
(b) How is the flow of **urine** to the outside of the body controlled?
(c) What stimulus indicates that the bladder is full?

Referring to Fig. 14.2, it can be seen that the kidney is made up of thousands of structures each of which is called a **nephron.**

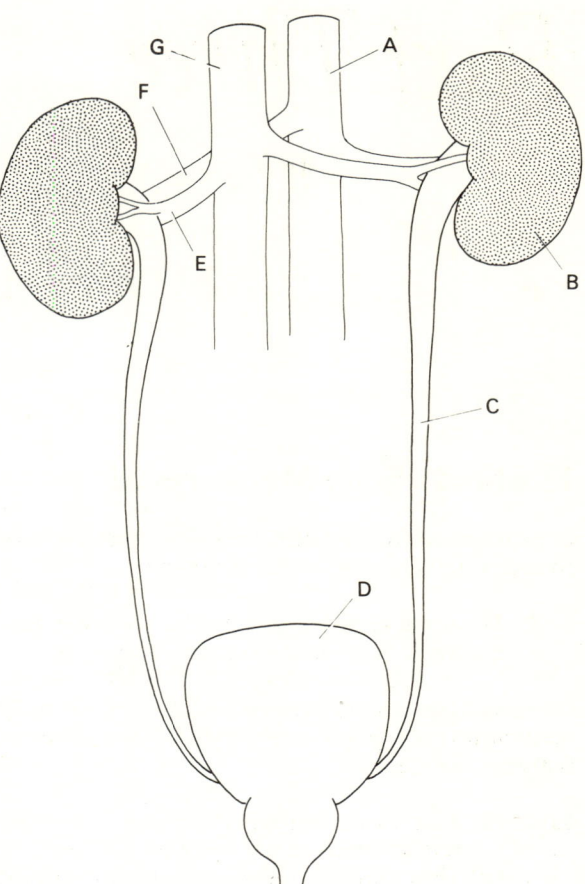

Fig. 14.1

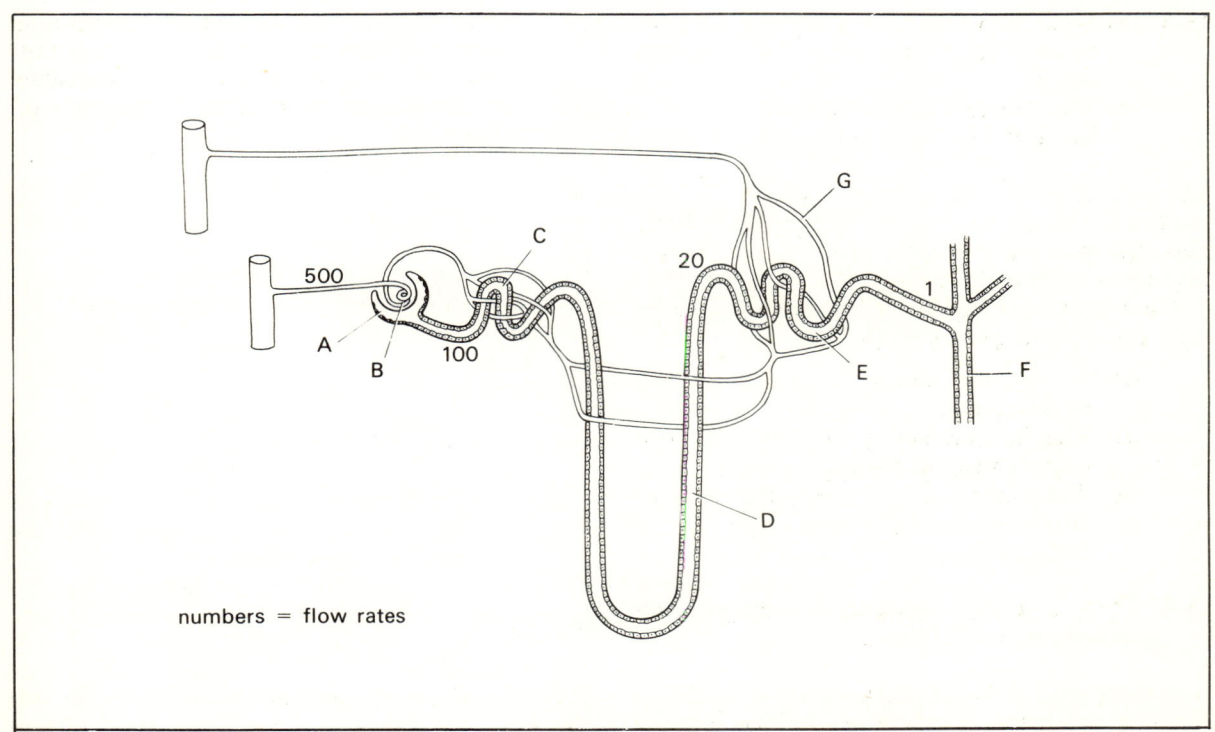

numbers = flow rates

Fig. 14.2

14.2 Name the components of the nephron in Fig. 14.2 (labelled by the letters A–G) and state which of them allow substances to pass from the capillary to the nephron.

The components of the nephron mentioned in Question **14.2** act as a filter, for they are permeable to some substances but not to others.

14.3 What will structures A and B allow to pass into the nephron?

The kidney removes **waste** molecules. Some molecules, however, need to be **reabsorbed** into the kidney.

14.4 (a) Which structures in Fig. 14.2 are responsible for the reabsorption of useful substances? Give both the names and the letters which refer to them.
(b) Which substances are likely to be reabsorbed?

Waste products will form as a result of the chemical processes in the body. Animals use proteins for making new tissue but an excess of protein cannot be stored. When protein is broken down **ammonia** (NH_3) is formed, but this is very toxic. The liver converts the ammonia into a less toxic soluble compound called **urea** ($CO(NH_2)_2$). The kidney removes this urea. The main components of urine are:

Water	94%
Urea	2%
Ammonia	0.05%
Na^+	0.6 %
K^+	0.16%
Cl^-	0.5 %

14.5 (a) Which compound makes up the largest percentage of urine?
(b) What is the importance of this compound in the urine?
(c) Look at the flow rates of fluids through the nephron in Fig. 14.2 and explain why the rate is becoming less as fluid flows through it.

14.6 What would happen to the amount of urine produced if
(a) you drank a large amount of water
(b) you drank a strong salt solution?
Explain your answers.

Freshwater fish also need to excrete nitrogenous waste. They excrete ammonia instead of urea. Ammonia is toxic and soluble.

14.7 Why is it safe for a fish to produce ammonia as waste, whereas it is dangerous for a land mammal like man?

15 Defence against Disease

Most of the time man enjoys good health. But he can be invaded by organisms which cause **disease**. These organisms are generally known as **pathogens** and most of them are microscopic – called **microorganisms.**

One important group of organisms are called **bacteria,** some of which cause disease.

15.1 (a) Draw simple diagrams of the following types of bacteria: (i) **micrococci** (ii) **diplococci** (iii) **staphylococci** (iv) **streptococci** (v) **spirilla** (vi) **bacilli.**
(b) Write down the names of three diseases which are caused by bacteria.

Another group of micro-organisms which cause disease are called **viruses.** They cannot grow or reproduce unless they invade cells of another organism.

15.2 Write down the names of three diseases which are caused by viruses.

Disease can be spread among people in many ways.

15.3 In what ways can disease be spread from person to person?

Much has been done to stop the spread of disease. For example, people have learnt about **health** and **hygiene.**

15.4 Make a list of the ways in which the spread of disease may be reduced by good hygiene. Explain your answers.

However, a healthy body puts up its own defence against disease.

15.5 In what ways can the body help to prevent the entry of micro-organisms?

Another way in which the body can combat disease is by acquiring **immunity.** If a person recovers from a disease he or she is unlikely to suffer from that particular disease again. That person is said to have become immune, which means that the body produces substances which can deal with the organisms.

15.6 (a) White blood cells produce substances which attack micro-organisms. What are these substances called?
(b) What are the harmful substances called which stimulate production of the substances in (a)?

The **immune system** which protects us from disease becomes a disadvantage when a person is given an **organ transplant.**

15.7 (a) What is an organ transplant?
(b) When is it necessary to be given a transplant?

The transplant is regarded by the body as a foreign substance and will be rejected unless the system which gives us immunity is suppressed by radiation or chemicals.

Man can combat disease artificially by a process called **artifical immunity.** This involves stimulating the body to produce **antibodies** to a particular micro-organism. This is done by injecting **vaccines** into the body to produce immunity against the disease in question.

15.8 (a) What is a vaccine?
(b) Edward Jenner discovered a way of protecting people from **smallpox.** How were people protected?

Sometimes it is necessary to use another animal to produce the antibodies to a micro-organism. These are then injected into humans to treat them for the disease.

15.9 (a) Describe briefly how this may be done.
(b) Name a disease which can be treated in this way.

Man can also combat disease by using chemicals which kill the pathogens. One well-known example is **penicillin.**

15.10 (a) Name the scientist who discovered penicillin.
(b) Where is penicillin obtained from?
(c) Describe how penicillin cures disease.
(d) Which type of micro-organism does it attack?

Part Four Response and Co-ordination

16 Nervous Communication in the Body

Organisms will only function properly if the organs of the body work at the correct speed and in the proper sequence. **Receptors** and **effectors** are connected via the **brain** or **spinal cord** by whitish strands called **nerves**. Nerve cells are called neurons and there are three different kinds which are grouped according to their function.

16.1 (a) One type of neuron takes messages from the receptor. What is this neuron called?
(b) The second type of neuron takes messages to the effector. What is this neuron called?
(c) The third type of neuron can be found in the spinal cord. It connects other neurons together. What is this neuron called?

The simplest nerve action is a **reflex** one. In most reflex actions the message is sent to the spinal cord and then directed to the effector without having to pass through the brain first.

16.2 Give one example of a reflex action.

The simplest pathway that a **nerve impulse** (an electrical signal which passes down the nerve fibre) can pass along is called a **reflex arc**.

16.3 Copy Fig. 16.1 into your books and draw in the main neurons. Label them and indicate the direction of the impulse.

16.4 (a) Look at Fig. 16.2 and write down the names of the parts labelled A–F.
(b) What is the function of the part labelled D?
(c) What is a synapse?

The control centre of the nervous system in man is the brain. It is very complex and still little understood.

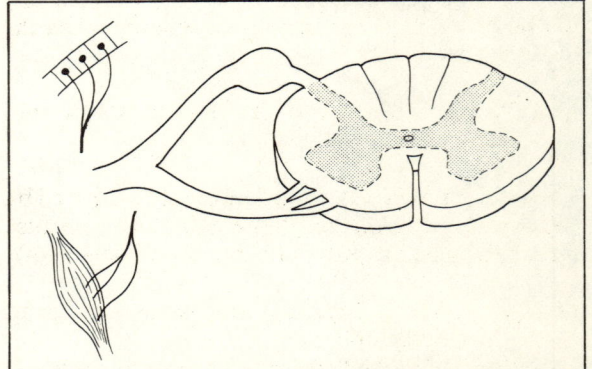

Fig. 16.1

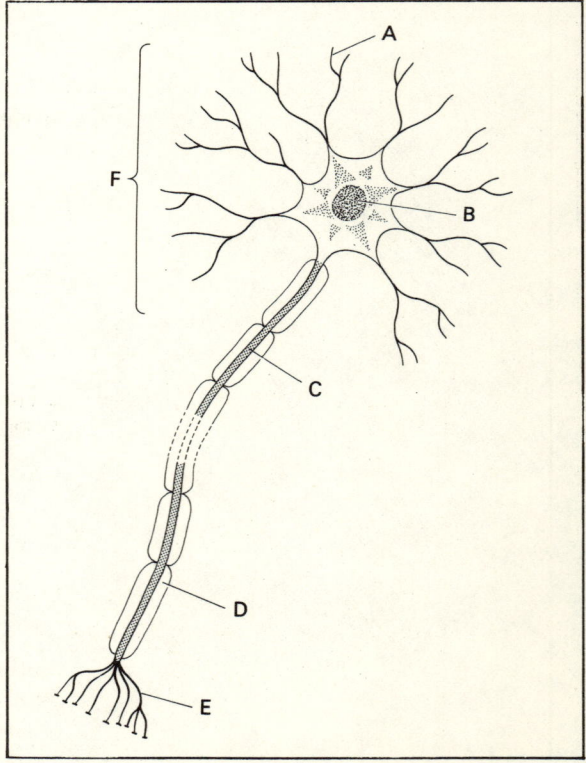

Fig. 16.2

16.5 Describe briefly the main functions of the following areas of the brain:
(a) the **cerebral hemispheres**
(b) the **cerebellum**
(c) the **medulla**

17 Chemical Communication in Animals and Plants

Changes occur in organisms which are not controlled by the nervous system. For example, if the testes are removed from a young cockerel it will grow into a fat bird with plumage similar to that of a hen. Normally the young cockerel would have grown into a bird with the features of a mature cock. This experiment suggests that the changes occur by means of certain chemical substances secreted into the body, because the nerves are severed when the testes are removed.

17.1 What is the name of these chemical substances or messengers?

These secretions (called **hormones**) are produced by **endocrine** or **ductless glands** (so called because these substances pass directly into the bloodstream).

17.2 (a) Look at Fig. 17.1 and name each gland labelled A–F.
(b) Name the hormones secreted by each gland.

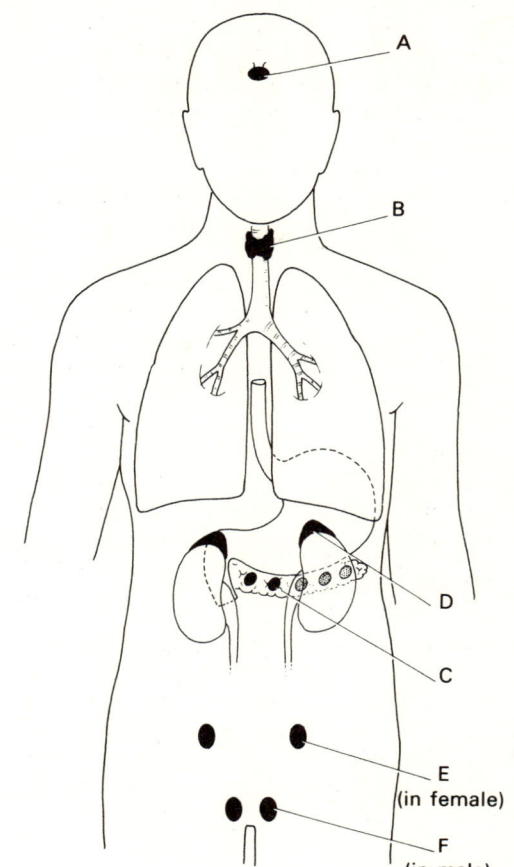

Fig. 17.1

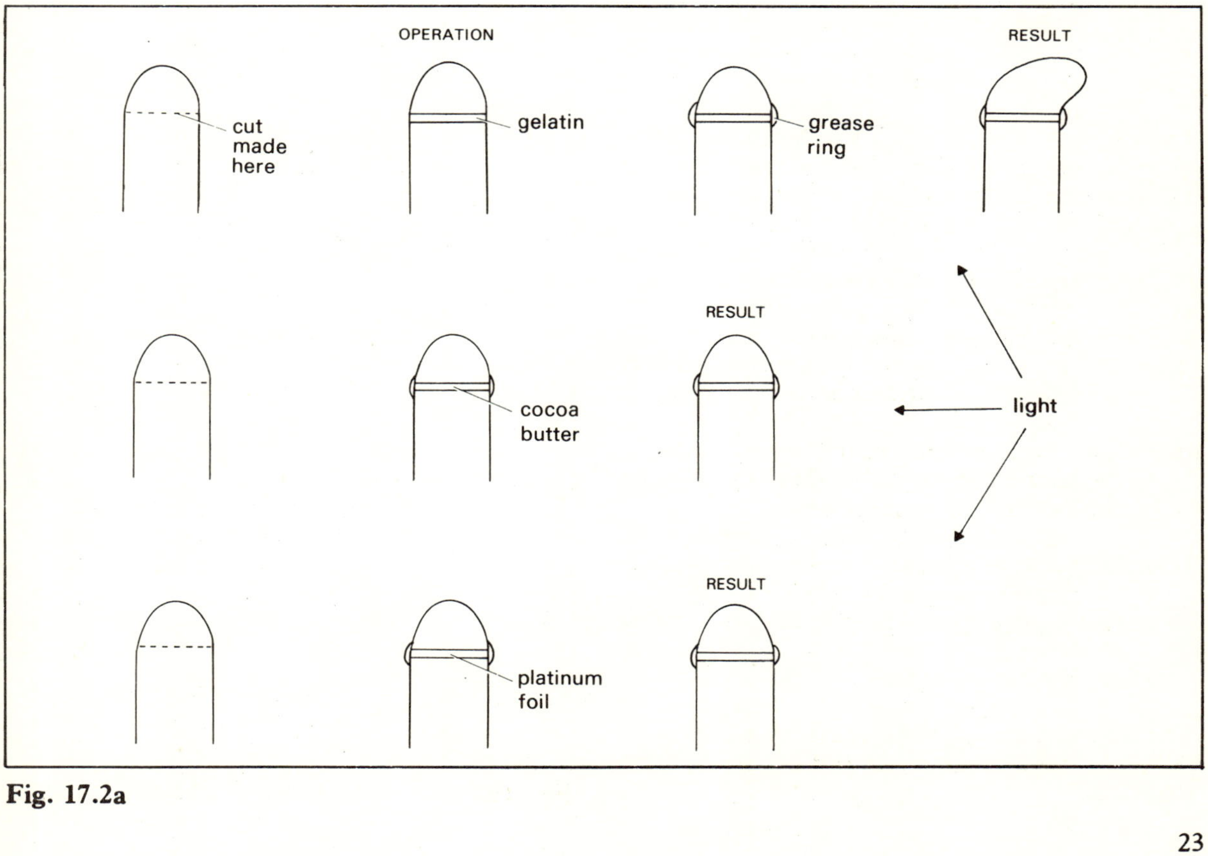

Fig. 17.2a

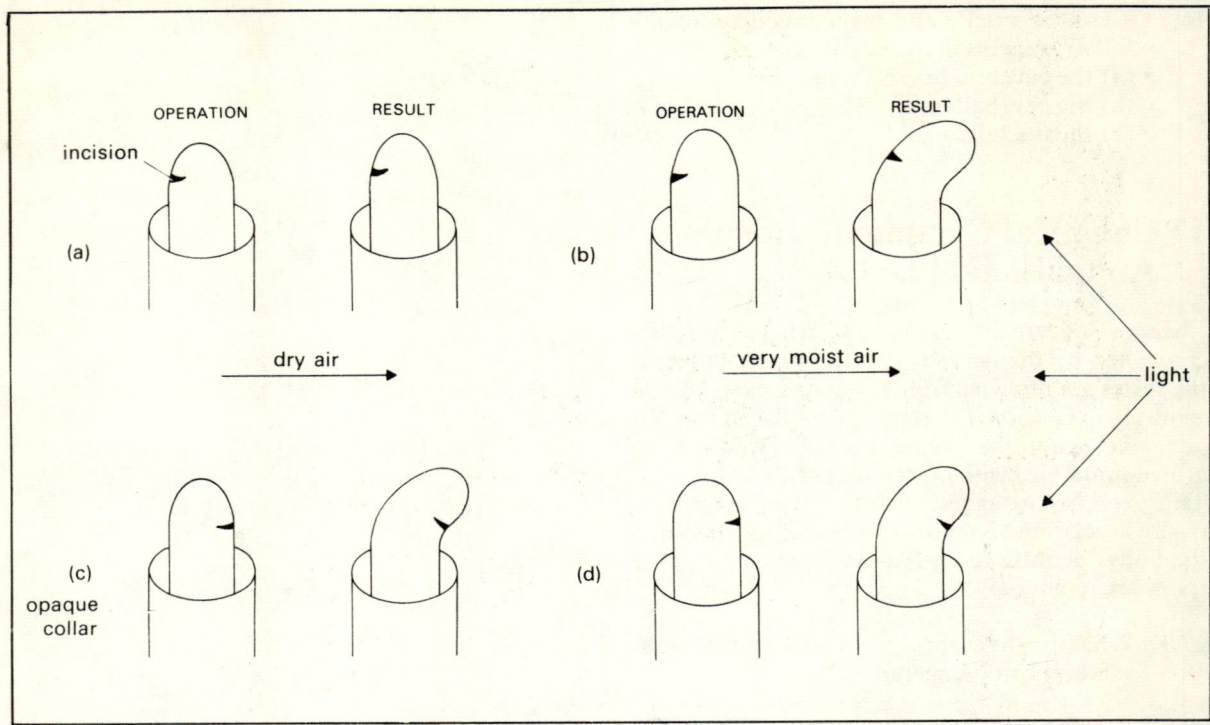

Fig. 17.2b

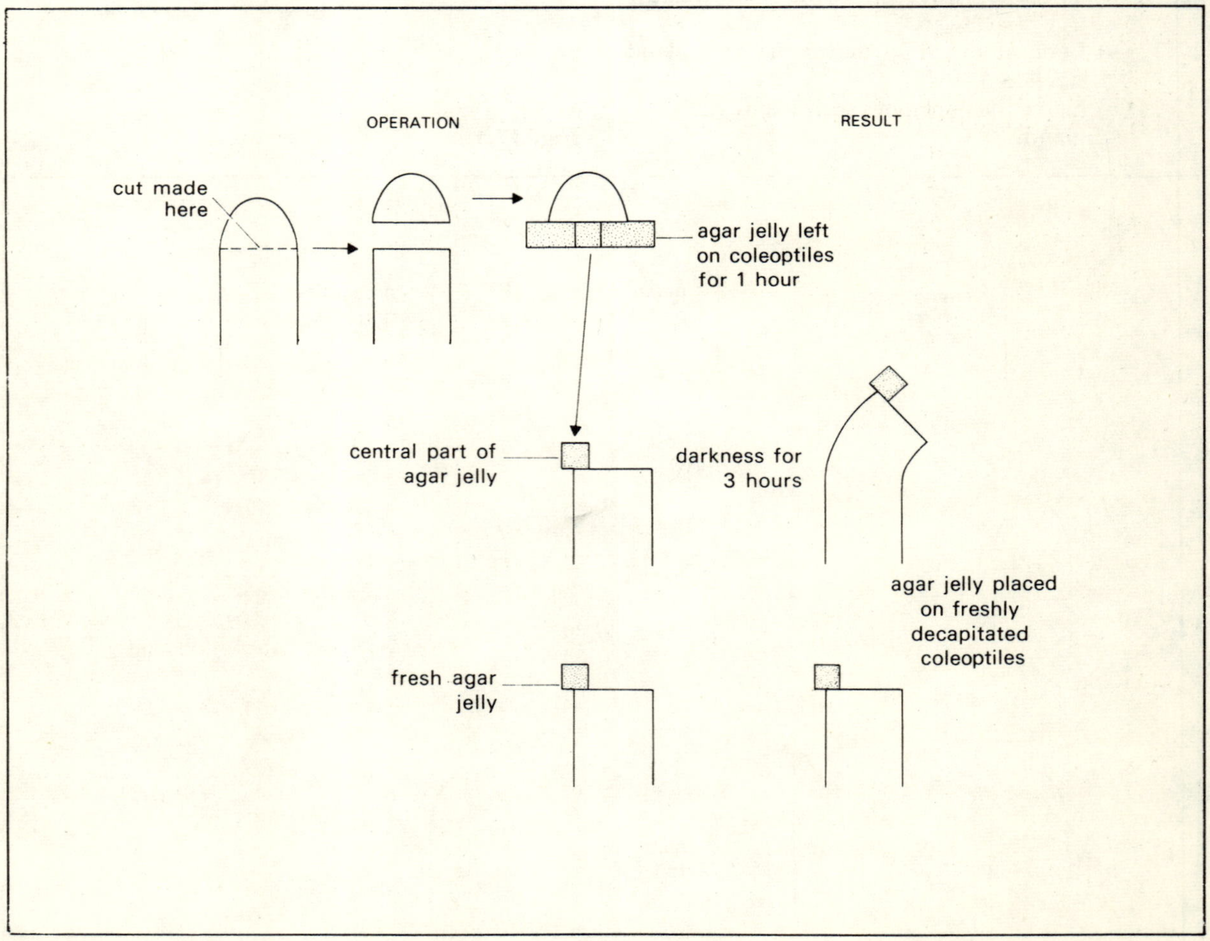

OPERATION · RESULT · OPERATION · RESULT

incision

(a)

dry air →

(b)

very moist air →

← light

(c)
opaque
collar

(d)

OPERATION · RESULT

cut made
here →

→ agar jelly left
on coleoptiles
for 1 hour

central part of
agar jelly

darkness for
3 hours

agar jelly placed
on freshly
decapitated
coleoptiles

fresh agar
jelly

Fig. 17.2c

(c) What would happen if there was an over-secretion of **thyroxine** in the body?

(d) Under what conditions is **adrenalin** secreted in the body? What effects does adrenalin have?

(e) List the effects on the human body when (i) **oestrogen** is secreted in the female (ii) **testosterone** is secreted in the male.

Plants have no nervous system. They rely entirely on the secretion of chemical substances called plant **growth substances** (sometimes called hormones).

17.3 Look at the experiments performed on young oat shoots which are illustrated in Figs. 17.2 (a), (b) and (c). What do you conclude from these experiments?

Hormones control the response of a plant to light. They also control the direction of a plant's growth in relation to gravity.

17.4 (a) Briefly describe an experiment to show that plants respond to gravity.

(b) Describe the results you would expect to see.

(c) What is the name of the apparatus illustrated in Fig. 17.3?

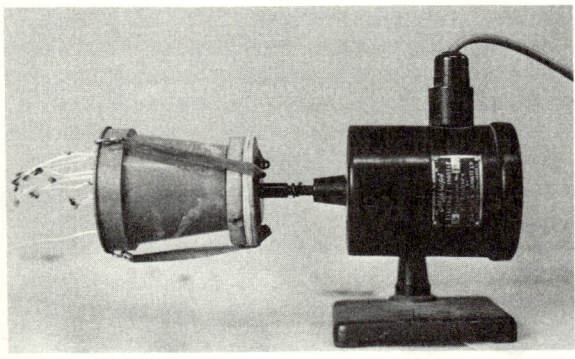

Fig. 17.3

18 Receptors in Animals

A living organism constantly responds to its environment. The organism must have the ability to pick up **stimuli** from the environment, process the information, and then respond by carrying out appropriate responses. We are continuously bombarded by many types of stimuli. In man, stimuli are picked up by organs called **receptors**.

18.1 (a) List the stimuli a human may pick up.

(b) List the main receptors in man and indicate which stimuli they are sensitive to.

CHEMICAL STIMULI

Organisms are sensitive to many forms of **chemical stimuli.**

18.2 (a) Where are the principal chemical receptors in humans found?

(b) What four main types of chemical substances are identified by the **tongue?**

VISUAL STIMULI

Many organisms are sensitive to light but a few, such as mammals, are capable of forming picture images of the outside world. This is called **vision.**

The mammalian **eye** is well adapted to pick up **light waves.**

18.3 List as many properties of light as you can.

18.4 List as many simple observations about eyes as you can (how many, how do they move, defects and so on).

Refer to Fig. 18.1 of the eye.

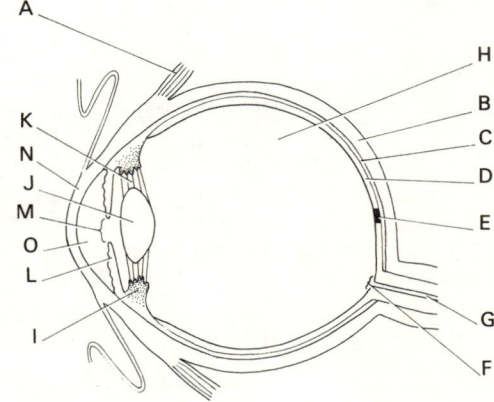

Fig. 18.1

18.5 Name the structures on the diagram labelled A–O. Write down the name of the structure which

(a) protects the front part of the eye

(b) allows light into the interior of the eyeball

(c) controls the amount of light entering the eye

(d) focuses the light rays

(e) acts as a light receptor (There are two types of cells on the light receptors. Name them and briefly describe their function.)

(f) prevents reflection inside the eyeball

(g) carries impulses to the brain

(h) protects the eyeball.

18.6 (a) Explain how the focusing device adjusts the image arriving from different distances.

(b) What keeps the eyeball in shape?

AUDIBLE STIMULI

The **ear** is the organ of hearing. It "picks up" **sound**

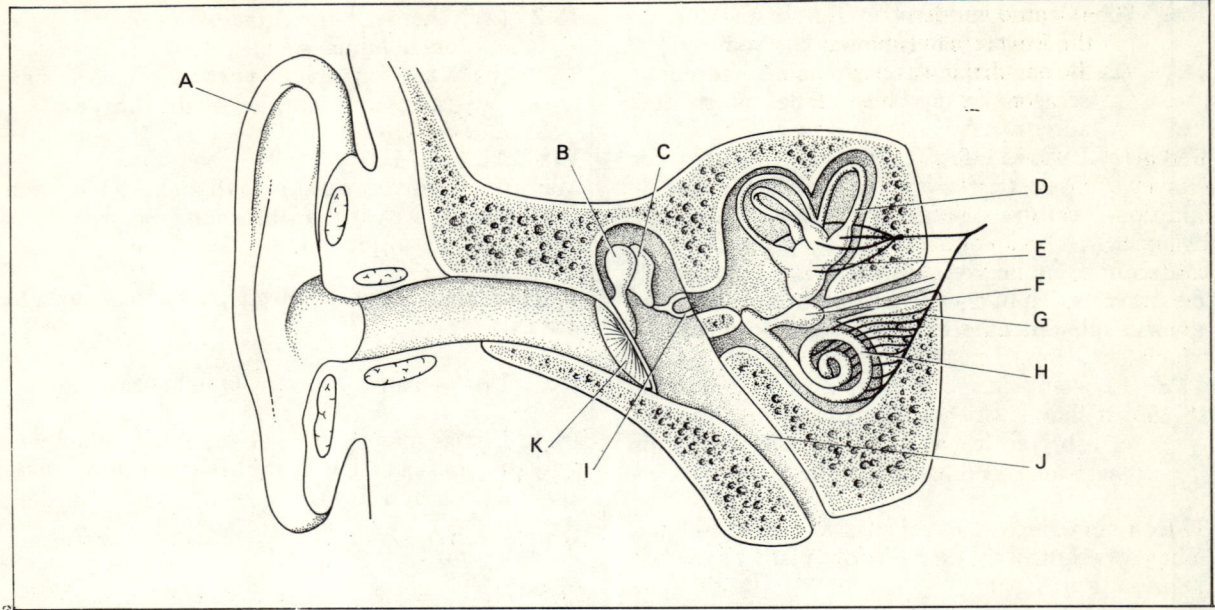

Fig. 18.2

waves. Sound is a series of vibrations which requires a medium, such as air or water, through which to pass. Ears in mammals are specially adapted to receive various **audible stimuli.**

18.7 What simple observations can you make about human ears (how many, ability to detect extremes of volume and pitch, lack of hearing, and so on)?

Fig. 18.2 is a diagram of the ear.

18.8 Name the structures in Fig. 18.2 labelled A–K. Write down the name of the structure which
(a) collects sound waves
(b) vibrates in sympathy with sound waves
(c) transmits vibrations through the middle ear and amplifies them
(d) equalises the pressure from the outer and middle ears
(e) picks up sound waves (receptors)
(f) transmits nerve impulses to the brain.

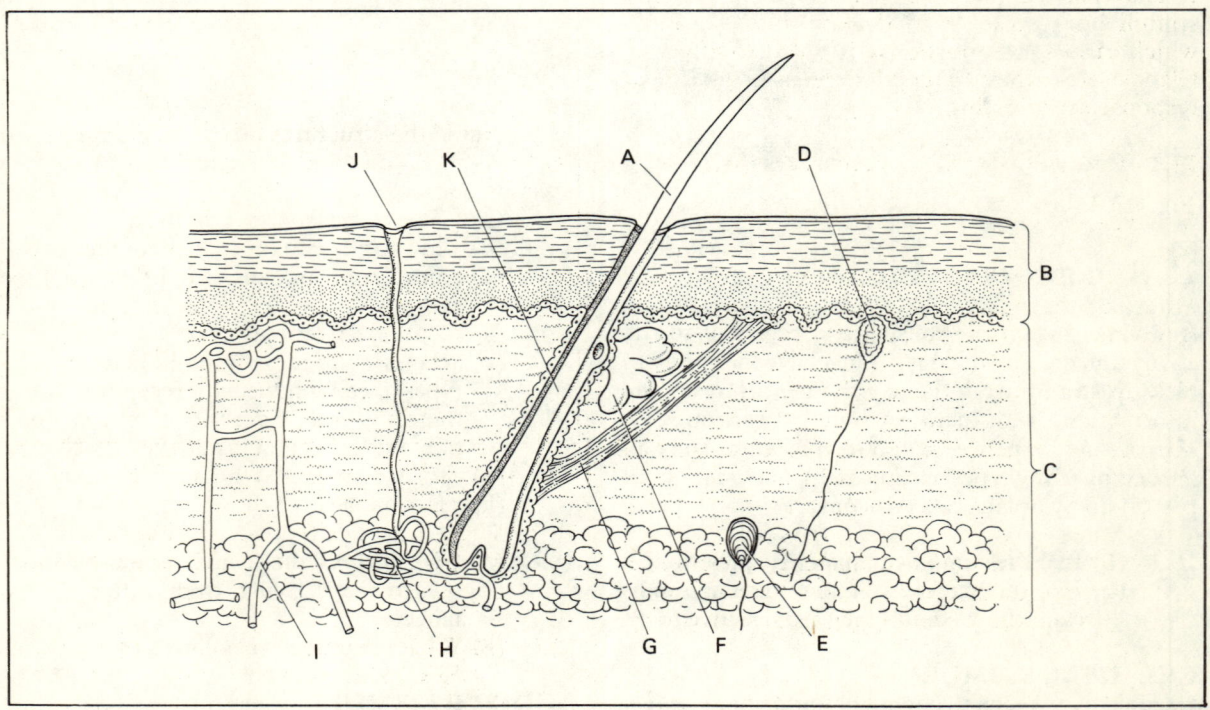

Fig. 18.3

18.9 What would happen if
  (a) the **Eustachian tube** was blocked
  (b) the **ear-drum** was perforated?
  Give reasons for your answers.

BALANCE AND GRAVITY

Our eyes tell us which way up we are. However an additional organ is needed to help us keep our balance. The organ of **balance** is found in the inner ear (see Fig. 18.2). It consists of two sacs (one above the other), on top of which are three **semicircular canals**. There is fluid in these canals at the base of which are hairs attached to nerve receptors.

18.10 (a) What happens to the hairs if you move?
  (b) Why are there three semicircular canals arranged in their particular positions?

THE SKIN

The **skin** performs many functions.

18.11 List the functions of the skin.

18.12 (a) Refer to Fig. 18.3 and write down the names of the structures labelled A–K.
  (b) What **sense organs** are found in the skin?

19 Structures Which Do Things (Effectors)

It is important for animals not only to pick up stimuli but also to respond to them. A structure which carries out a **response** is called an **effector**. Glands are effectors and **secrete** chemicals in response to a stimulus.

19.1 Give an example of a gland and its secretion.

Muscles and **bones** work as effectors. The muscle-bone system can be compared to a machine. A machine converts one form of energy into another. Muscles exert a **force**. When a force moves an object from one place to another, **work** has taken place.

19.2 How does a muscle work?

Muscles are attached to bones by a series of fine strands at each end of the muscle.

19.3 (a) What are these fine strands called?
  (b) What change would occur in the forces exerted by a muscle on a limb when the positions of attachment are changed (see Fig. 19.1)?

19.4 Why is it advantageous for a digging animal, such as the mole, to have short limbs?

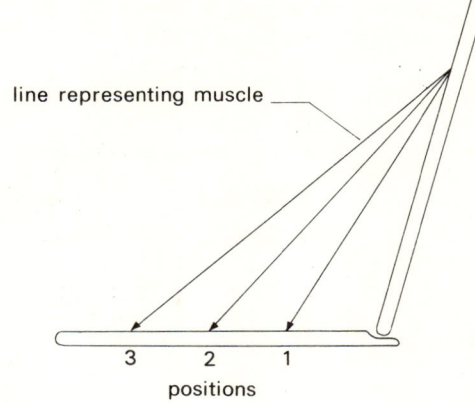

Fig. 19.1

Muscles can only exert a force when contracting.

19.5 How can two-way movements of limbs be achieved?

The muscles which cause the limbs to bend are called **flexors** and those which straighten the limb are called **extensors**.

19.6 Write down the names of the muscles in Fig. 19.2 which are flexors and those which are extensors.

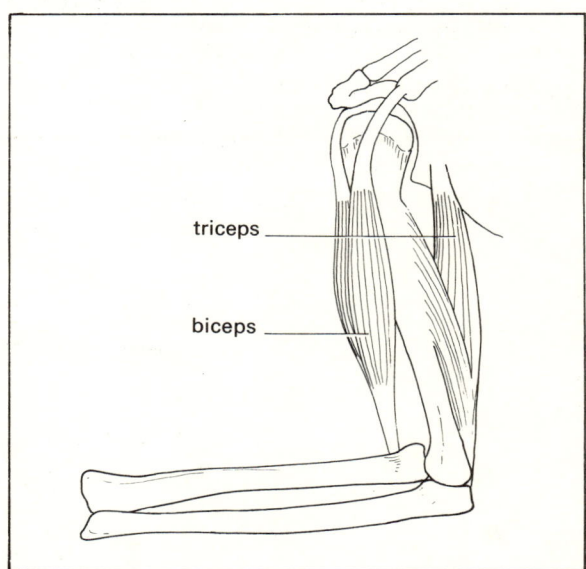

Fig. 19.2

19.7 What is the scientific term given to the situation where two muscles are in balanced opposition?

19.8 (a) What chemical substances do muscles need to function properly?
  (b) What waste products are produced from working muscles?

For movement to take place, a **limb** must be able to move relative to the rest of the body. In addition to muscles and bones there are **joints.**

19.9 (**a**) Refer to Fig. 19.3 of a joint and name those parts labelled A–E.
(**b**) What is the function of each part?

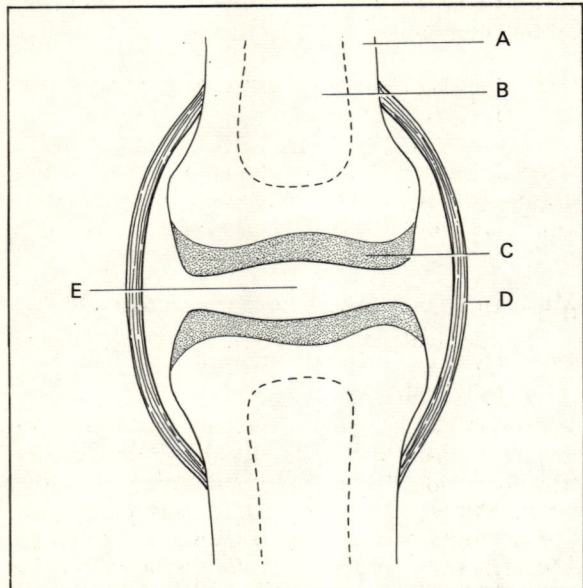

Fig. 19.3

The muscles are attached to an arrangement of bones called the **skeleton.** The bones move relative to one another by means of a system of **levers.** The **fulcrum** is the point around which the lever **pivots.** Levers are moved by **effort,** which in this case is the use of the muscles. Thirdly, levers need to support a **load.** Three types of lever are illustrated in Fig. 19.4.

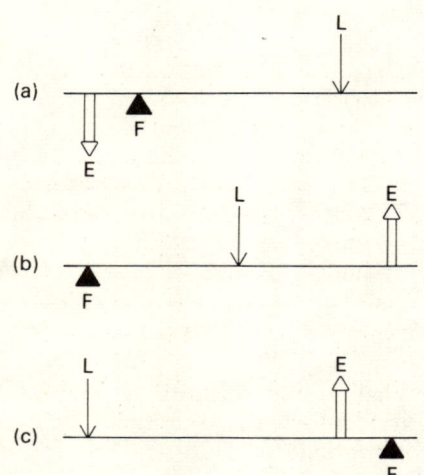

F = fulcrum or pivot
E = effort exerted by muscle
L = load exerted by limbs etc.

Fig. 19.4

19.10 Give one example of each of the levers illustrated in Fig. 19.4 that can be found in the human body.

20 Movement and Support

ANIMAL MOVEMENT AND SUPPORT

20.1 Make a list of the reasons why an animal may need to move from one place to another.

Animals move in different ways on land. Two main types of movement are **walking** and **running.**

20.2 List the main differences between running and walking.

Some animals are adapted for running at very fast speeds.

20.3 Name two animals which can move very fast over land.

In order to move fast, an animal needs large muscles. Unfortunately, the larger muscles are the slower they contract. Small animals do not have problems since their muscles are correspondingly small, but difficulties do arise in larger animals. These problems can be resolved by reducing the need for muscles. In the lower limbs of the horse, for example, there are special **springing ligaments** which stretch when the hoof touches the ground but spring the limb straight when the hoof leaves the ground (see Fig. 20.1).

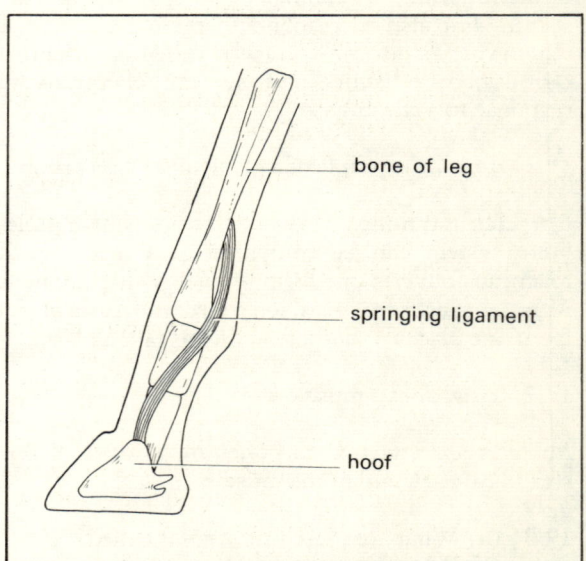

Fig. 20.1

A third method of movement on land is **jumping.**

20.4 Name two animals which can jump, and describe briefly how they do this.

Jumping may be impossible for some animals because they are so large.

The amount of **support** an animal needs depends on its **size**. The larger the animal is, the greater are its problems. A whale is very large indeed but it is well adapted to its way of life.

20.5 How is it possible for a whale to support its enormous size and weight?

Another way of moving from one place to another is by **flying.**

20.6 Draw a simple diagram showing a cross-section of a **wing** and show the principal forces acting on it.

The wing, however, is not rigid and birds are able to move their wings in a complicated series of movements. Yet there is one force which can slow down forward motion.

20.7 (a) Which force slows down forward motion?
      (b) In what ways can a bird overcome this force?

There are animals which move in water. Many live in fresh water or the sea and are specially adapted to move in this medium.

20.8 (a) Draw a fish the shape of which helps it to overcome **drag.**
      (b) Which part(s) of the fish are mainly concerned with forward motion?
      (c) What other parts of the fish are concerned with movement?
      (d) What simple experiments could you carry out to find out which shape is most suited to movement in water?

Plants vary in size and shape. All plants have to stand up to various forces to avoid being uprooted.

20.9 (a) What forces would expose plants to great strain?
      (b) What features would you expect a plant to possess in order to stand up to these natural forces?

Water may help a plant to remain upright. One example of this is when a plant is supported by the water in which it lives (as in the case of pondweed). However, it can also be demonstrated by means of a simple experiment. Two flexible shoots of a non-woody plant were taken; one was placed with its cut end in a jar of water, the other was left without water on a bench for an hour.

20.10 What would be the condition of (i) the plant in water (ii) the plant without water after an hour?

21 Behaviour

Behaviour is difficult to define. One example of it is movement but behaviour is much more than this.

There must be a reason for any sort of animal or plant movement. Gulls remove eggshells from their nest after their brood have hatched. This is a **behaviour pattern,** and it occurs because it is important for the survival of the organism.

21.1 Suggest a reason for gulls removing eggshells from their nests.

Many simple experiments can explore the behaviour of animals but accurate conclusions are often difficult. This is because behaviour can be controlled by many stimuli, some known, some unknown.

21.2 What experiment could you carry out to investigate the response of house-flies to light?

Behaviour can be examined using careful observation over a long period of time. Many animals exhibit behaviour which is **stereotyped.** In other words, they react in a predictable way when a particular stimulus is applied. Despite being complicated, the same type of behaviour can be observed in different individuals of the same species. For example, a young female bird may build a nest without being taught to do so by the parent. Such behaviour is said to be **instinctive.**

21.3 Give another example of instinctive behaviour.

Animals may be born with behaviour patterns (**innate**) or animals may **learn** behaviour patterns from others. Chicks start to peck at objects as soon as they are born. The gradually learn to peck only at objects which look like food.

21.4 Babies make the following innate responses as soon as they are born:
      (i)   They make mouthing and suckling movements with their lips.
      (ii) The lips are compressed when touched.
      (iii) If the cheek of the baby is touched with a finger, the baby moves towards the finger.
      What is the survival value for these responses?

Certain types of behaviour can be made to occur by the presentation of an unrelated stimulus. Pavlov carried out experiments on one particular response in dogs. Aware that a dog salivates on being presented with food (the first stimulus), Pavlov introduced a second unrelated stimulus – a bell which was rung every time food was presented to the animal. After a time the dog responded by salivating to a ringing bell only.

21.5 What is the name given to this type of response?

Imprinting is another important behaviour pattern. It means that soon after birth or hatching an animal will become deeply attached to the first large moving object it meets. This response occurs, for example, in chicks.

21.6 (a) What is the first large moving object a chick is likely to encounter?
(b) What is the value of such a response?
(c) What would you expect the chick to do if a man was the first moving object it encountered after hatching?

Animals with larger brains tend to have more complicated behaviour patterns, as they have a larger number of nerve pathways from receptors to effectors. Animals with larger brains tend to be more **intelligent.** Intelligent behaviour can be said to occur in those animals which can overcome a problem by thinking it out. Suppose we set up an experiment where a U-shaped piece of wire-netting is placed with food outside the U, and animals are put inside the U (see Fig. 21.1).

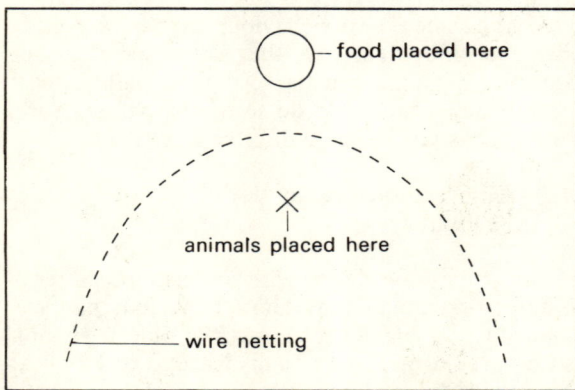

Fig. 21.1

21.7 How do you think (i) a hungry hen (ii) a hungry dog (iii) a hungry child would react to the situation?
Explain your answers.

The hunger will act as a further stimulus to solving their problem. In this case the animals are said to be **motivated.**

21.8 Name one example of human motivated behaviour.

A final example is **social behaviour.** Many responses are controlled by stimuli emitted by fellow animals. Such behaviour is often very complex.

21.9 Name one advantage of social behaviour in man.

Part Five

Reproduction, Development and Heredity

22 Cell Division

Most organisms are made up of more than one cell. A human is made up of many millions of cells. Since we begin life as a single cell (the fertilised egg), cells must be able to multiply. Cells increase by a process called **cell division.** This process can be examined quite easily. For example, the cells at the tip of a root can be examined.

22.1 Describe simply the experimental procedure necessary for the preparation and examination of cells at the root tip of a plant.

Under the microscope the stain used shows up structures called **chromosomes.**

22.2 (a) What is the function of chromosomes?
(b) Why must each chromosome make an exact copy of itself before the cell divides?

The stages of cell division you might see under the microscope can be classified as follows.

Stage 1: Individual chromosomes are grouped in the centre of the cell. Each chromosome is a double thread – each an exact copy of its "partner".
Stage 2: The chromosomes are arranged in a line across the centre of the cell.
Stage 3: Chromosome "copies" pull away from each other and go to opposite ends of the cell.
Stage 4: Two identical groups of chromosomes can be seen in the cell.
Stage 5: The cell divides to give two cells with identical chromosomes.

22.3 These five main stages of cell division are illustrated in Fig. 22.1. Each stage is labelled by a letter. Place these letters in the correct order of stages.

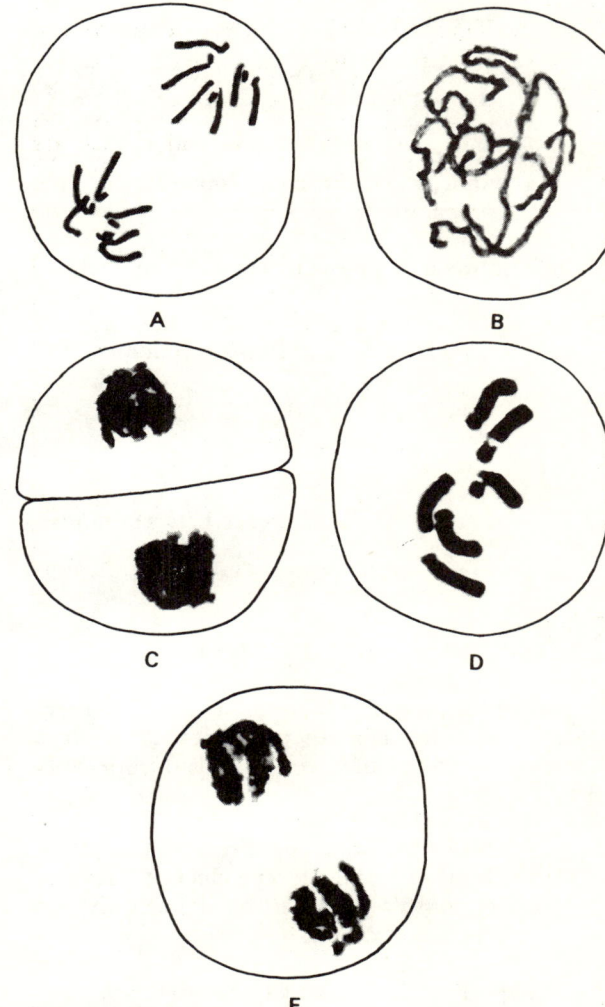

Fig. 22.1

This type of cell division produces growth and is called **mitosis.** The genetic information from one cell is passed on exactly to other cells. The number of chromosomes remains the same after each cell division has taken place.

22.4 Complete the following model of mitosis:

$$2n \longrightarrow ? \ (2n = \text{number of chromosomes in normal body cells})$$

There is a second form of cell division in which the cells after division are different from the original cell. This type of cell division is called **meiosis** (reduction division). It can be represented as follows:

$$2n \longrightarrow n \ (2n = \text{number of chromosomes in normal body cells})$$

22.5 What happens to the chromosomes in meiosis?

Where there are the normal number of chromosomes (i.e. $2n$), the condition of the cell is said to be **diploid**. When meiosis occurs **haploid** cells are formed (they contain n chromosomes). Meiosis can be observed in locust testes.

22.6 (a) Describe the experimental procedure for the preparation and examination of locust testes.
(b) What structures would you expect to see under the microscope if you examined the preparation?

Meiosis occurs in organs which make the **gametes**.

22.7 Why does the chromosome number need to be halved in gametes? Explain your answer.

22.8 What is the purpose of
(a) mitosis
(b) meiosis?

22.9 What is the main difference between mitosis and meiosis?

23 Asexual Reproduction

Organisms can only live for a certain length of time. If the species is to avoid dying out it must produce offspring by one of the two methods of **reproduction**.

23.1 (a) Name the two types of reproduction.
(b) In what type of reproduction are new organisms produced by the cell division process of mitosis?

23.2 Describe briefly what happens to the chromosomes in mitosis.

23.3 Explain why the offspring of asexual reproduction are identical to the parent.

One of the simplest types of asexual reproduction is found in unicellular organisms like *Amoeba*. They simply divide into two, a process known as **binary fission** (see Chapter 3).

Yeast reproduces by a process called **budding**.

23.4 Draw simple diagrams to illustrate the process of budding in yeast.

Parts of a plant such as the stem or the root may produce new plants. This type of reproduction is called **vegetative reproduction**.

23.5 List three different types of vegetative reproduction. Give examples to illustrate each.

24 Sexual Reproduction

In addition to asexual reproduction new organisms may also arise by the fusion of special cells called gametes. This is called **sexual reproduction**. One gamete comes from the male and the other from the female (i.e. two organisms are needed for the creation of a new organism).

24.1 (a) What are the male and female gametes in a mammal called?
(b) Where are the male and female gametes in a flowering plant situated?

Gametes are composed of a **nucleus** and **cytoplasm**. The male gamete is nearly all nucleus in which the genetic information is carried.

24.2 Write down the names of the structures labelled A–E in Fig. 24.1, which shows an egg and a sperm cell.

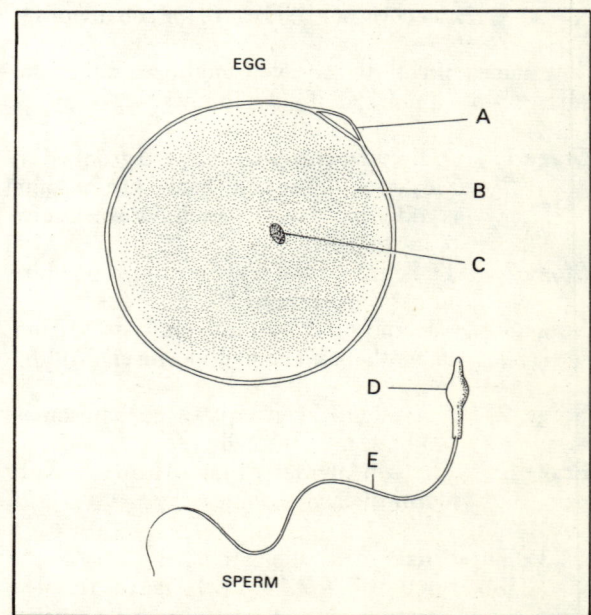

Fig. 24.1

The sperm and egg fuse to form a **fertilised egg.**

24.3 (**a**) How many chromosomes are there in a human gamete? (All other human cells contain 46 chromosomes.)
(**b**) What would be the chromosome number in the fertilised egg?
(**c**) What is the name given to the fertilised egg?

For fertilisation to take place the gametes must be brought together. Some sort of behaviour pattern in animals is needed to bring the male and female together before the egg can be fertilised. Some animals achieve fertilisation by the female laying the eggs and the male placing sperm on them afterwards.

24.4 Give one example of an organism which carries out this type of fertilisation (called **external fertilisation**).

In some animals, such as man, sperm are placed directly into the body of the female and the eggs are fertilised inside her.

24.5 What is the name given to this type of fertilisation?

24.6 Look at Fig. 24.2 which shows the human male reproductive organs and write down the names of those structures labelled A–J.

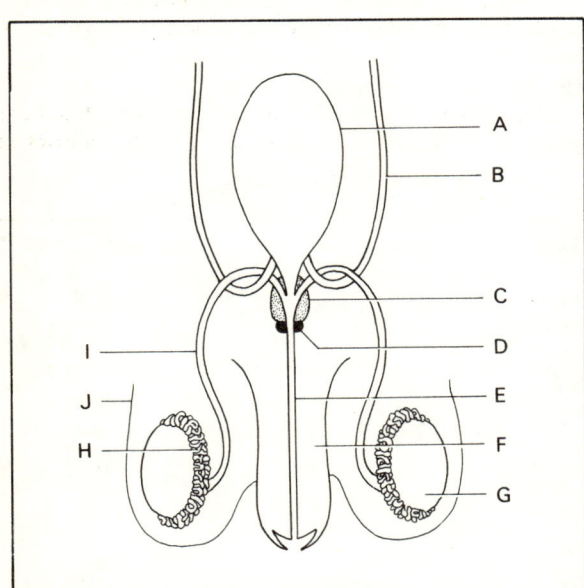

Fig. 24.2

24.7 Look at Fig. 24.3 which shows the human female reproductive organs and write down the names of those structures labelled A–I.

The woman's reproductive system passes through a regular sequence of events called the **menstrual cycle.**

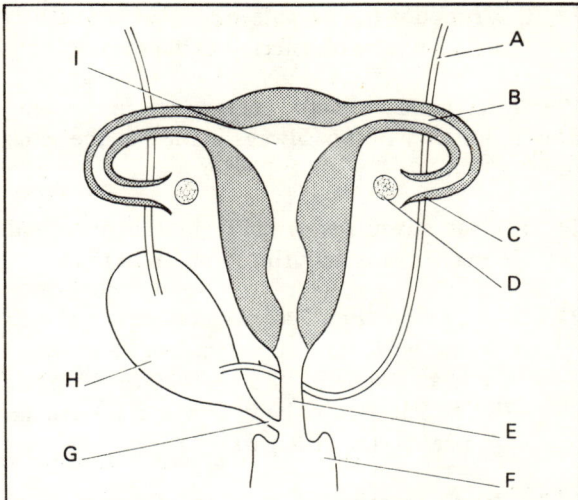

Fig. 24.3

24.8 Briefly describe the basic features of the menstrual cycle. (Use the following guidelines for your answer: How often is an egg released from an **ovary**? How long is the fertile period? What hormones are involved? What happens to the **uterus**?)

Men have no such cycle and continuously produce sperm from the time of **puberty** until about the age of seventy.

There is deep concern about the rapid increase in the world population, but the number of babies born can be controlled.

24.9 List the main methods of **birth control** which are available. Briefly describe how effective each method is.

The principle of sexual reproduction is the same in plants. However, the way in which the **pollen** travels to the ovary is rather more haphazard.

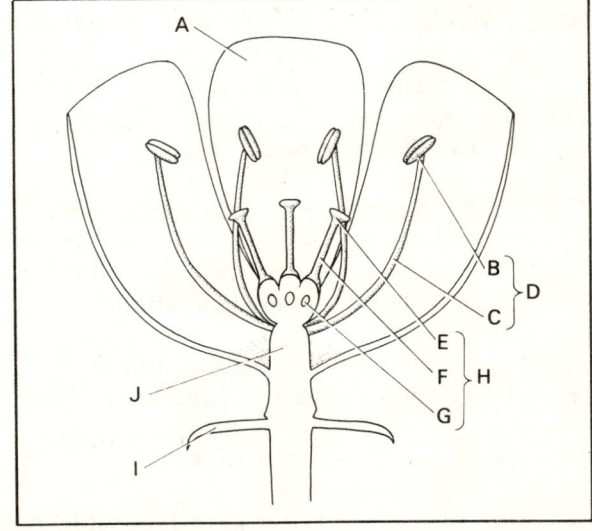

Fig. 24.4

24.10 Write down two different ways in which pollen may be transferred to the stigma.

Very often male and female organs are on the same flower but they do not always mature at the same time.

24.11 What advantage is there in the male and female organs maturing at different times?

24.12 (a) Look at Fig. 24.4 which shows a flower and write down the names of those structures labelled A–J.
(b) Which part of the flower is (i) the female part (ii) the male part?

24.13 Briefly describe the sequence of events which takes place after the pollen reaches the **stigma**.

25 Mendelian Genetics

If you look at your parents and grandparents you will observe some features which are similar to the ones you possess. Just over a hundred years ago the Abbot of Brünn, Gregor Mendel, carried out many experiments on **inheritance** using the garden pea. He worked out simple laws to explain inheritance which still hold true today. More recent work has often used the fruit-fly, *Drosophila melanogaster*, for genetic studies.

25.1 Suggest three advantages which make *Drosophila* a suitable organism with which to study **genetics.**

When carrying out genetics experiments with *Drosophila* it is important that the females are virgin (the adults only remain so for up to eight hours). In order to examine flies (e.g. to choose some for breeding experiments), they must be anaesthetised.

25.2 Briefly outline the procedure for examining the features of *Drosophila*.

25.3 What is meant by a **pure line culture?**

Suppose that a pure line normal winged fly is crossed with a pure line **vestigial** winged fly.

25.4 (a) What does a vestigial winged fly look like (i.e. its **phenotype**)?
(b) What would be the phenotype of the fly in the first of F1 generation?

The vestigial gene must be present even though we cannot see it. In this case the normal wing type dominates (is **dominant** to) the vestigial wing type (which is **recessive**). The resulting cross is not pure line but contains genes of both the normal and vestigial types (i.e. a **hybrid**). The genetic make-up (**genotype**) of the F1 flies is different from that of the pure line culture. The pure line culture has a **homozygous** genotype whilst the flies of the F1 generation have a **heterozygous** genotype.

25.5 (a) What is the genotype of the normal winged fly of the pure line culture (use the + symbol to represent the normal wing gene)?
(b) What is the genotype of a fly from a cross between a normal winged type (symbol +) and a vestigial wing type (symbol vg)?
(c) What would be the genotypes and proportions of flies in the following cross?

hybrid		hybrid
	×	
normal wing		normal wing

(d) What would be the genotypes and proportions of flies in the following cross?

hybrid		pure line
	×	
normal wing		vestigial wing

The cross in Question 25.5(d) is called a recessive backcross. This cross can be used to find out the genotype of a normal winged fly.

25.6 Why might you need to find out the genotype of a normal winged fly?

The sex of an animal is also determined genetically.

25.7 Using the symbols X and Y to represent the sex chromosomes, draw a diagram to show how sex may be inherited, remembering that the number of boys and girls born are approximately 50/50 (clue: recessive backcross).

26 The Material of Inheritance

If a chemical analysis is made of the chromosomes much of it is found to be made up of a substance known as **deoxyribonucleic acid** (**DNA**). An experiment that demonstrates that DNA is responsible for passing on genetic information from one generation to the next is illustrated in Fig. 26.1. DNA can be extracted from a "normal" strain of bacterium and placed in a culture containing a

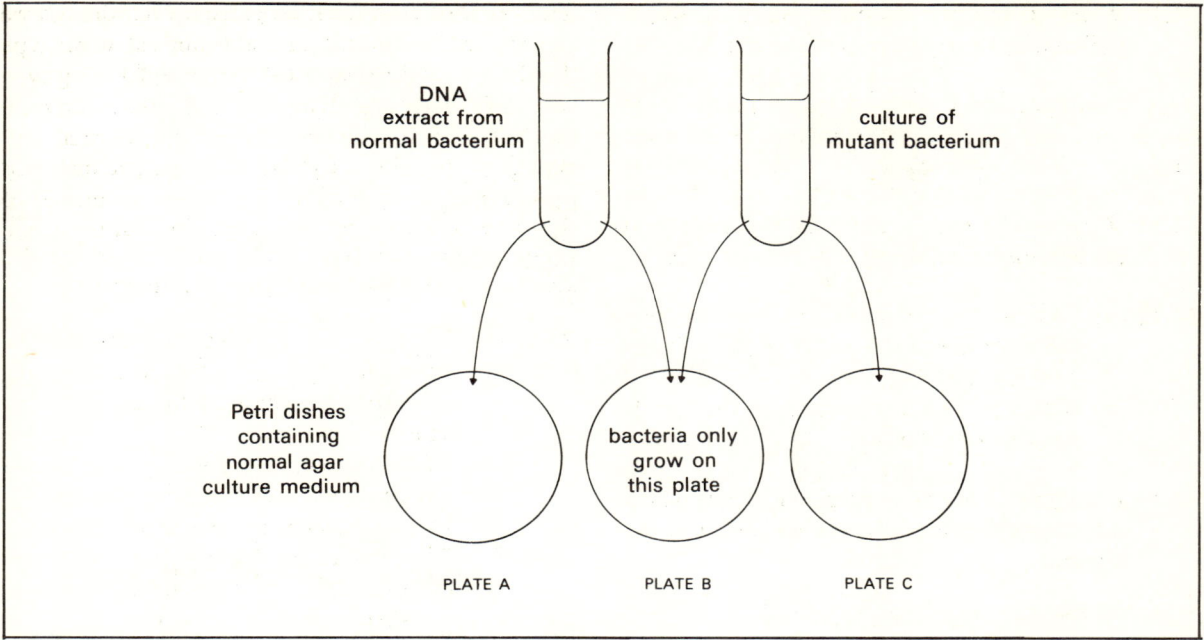

Fig. 26.1

mutant variety of the same species. (The mutant variety requires a special medium for growth.)

26.1 Look at Fig. 26.1 which summarises the experiment. What conclusions about the function of DNA can you draw from this experiment?

DNA carries a set of instructions for building new cells. These instructions are often called the "genetic code". This code is formed in the following way. DNA is made up of three main chemical parts: **sugar molecules (deoxyribose)**, phosphate molecules and four types of base – **adenine,** **thymine, guanine** and **cytosine.** The chemical parts are arranged together as in Fig. 26.2. It seems that these four bases in sequence form the code. This code is used to determine the sequence of amino-acids, which together form particular proteins. According to modern theory, three bases are needed to code for one amino-acid. DNA codes for enzymes (a particular type of protein) which are responsible for making chemical reactions go on within cells. These chemical reactions in turn build cells and then organisms.

DNA can also make an exact copy of itself.

26.2 What is the importance of this process?

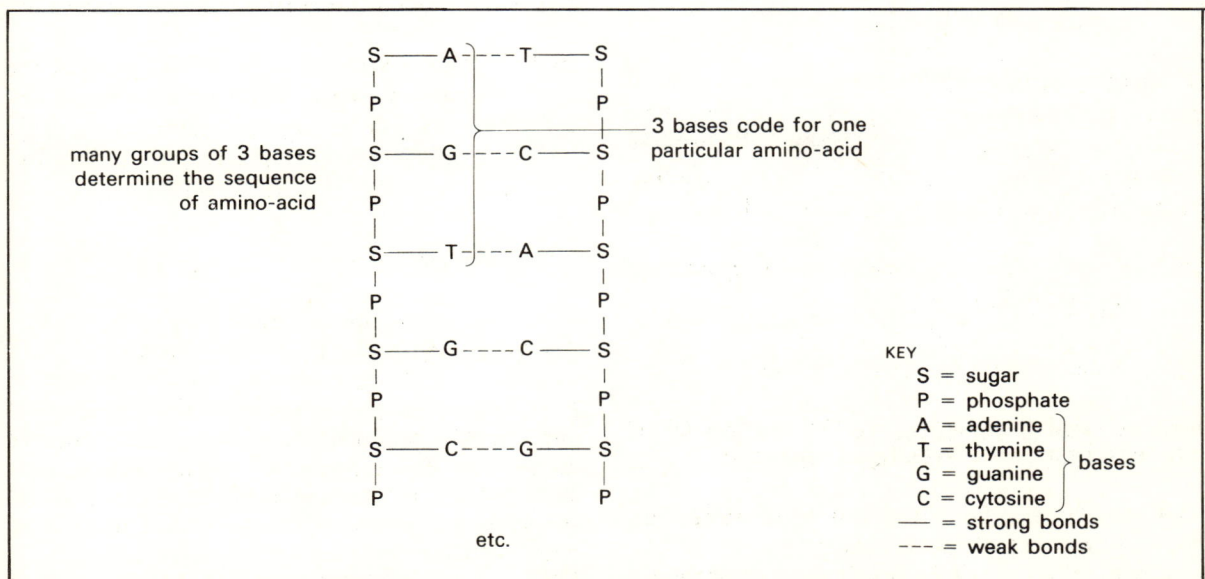

Fig. 26.2

27 Life Cycles

27.1 What do you understand by the term **"life cycle"?**

New generations are produced by means of sexual and asexual reproduction. Very often both meiosis and mitotis are involved in the life cycle of an organism. Man has a simple life cycle.

27.2 Draw a diagram of the life cycle of man.

Most animals such as mammals, birds and reptiles have similar life cycles.

Insect life cycles show a number of distinct stages. There are two main types of life cycle in insects. The first is illustrated by the locust. The offspring develop gradually into the adult by a series of stages called **nymphs.**

27.3 (a) Draw a simple diagram of the life cycle of the locust.
(b) Name two other insects which have similar life cycles.

The second group of insects have life cycles in which the adult is distinctly different from the **larval stage.**

27.4 What is the name given to the process whereby extensive breakdown and reorganisation of tissues takes place within the insect as it changes from the larval stage to the adult (**imago**)?

An example of an insect which has this stage in its life cycle is the butterfly.

27.5 (a) Draw a simple diagram showing the life cycle of a butterfly.
(b) Name two other insects which have similar life cycles.

The life cycles of plants follow similar patterns to those of animals. Yeast is a simple plant whose life cycle has a separate diploid and haploid phase; each phase is able to reproduce more cells of the same type.

27.6 Draw a simple diagram showing the life cycle of yeast.

This division into diploid and haploid phases is present in other plants such as mosses and ferns. The life cycle of a moss involves two different plants. One is a leafy plant which produces gametes (the diploid stage) and is called the **gametophyte generation,** and the other is a spore-producing plant (the haploid stage) which is called the **sporophyte generation.**

27.7 (a) What is the name given to a life cycle in which the gametophyte generation alternates with the sporophyte generation?
(b) Draw a simple diagram illustrating the life cycle of a moss plant.

Flowering plants appear to have a less complicated life cycle than those of mosses or ferns. Only one stage is visible but the diploid and haploid stages are still present.

27.8 (a) Draw a simple diagram of the life cycle of a flowering plant.
(b) Give three examples of flowering plants which have this type of life cycle.

28 Growth and Development

After fertilisation of the egg, **growth** and **development** take place. The zygote starts to divide and then further cell divisions rapidly take place.

28.1 Draw a simple graph to show the increase in the number of cells with time. Use the vertical axis to denote the number of cells and the horizontal axis to represent equal time intervals.

Growth can be measured in many ways.

28.2 List three ways of measuring growth.

It is not easy, however, to measure growth accurately. In some organisms, different parts of the body develop at different rates.

28.3 Give one example of differential growth in humans.

After fertilisation, there is first an increase in the number of cells (growth) which is followed by cells becoming specialised in order to take on different functions of the body (**differentiation**).

28.4 List six different types of cell in the human body and state their functions.

The control of differentiation is still largely unknown. It is related to how DNA works. In some organisms the zygote becomes dormant after fertilisation. Suitable conditions are necessary for further growth and development to take place. A good example is the seeds which are dispersed from flowering plants. Certain conditions are necessary for the seed to **germinate.**

28.5 (a) Write down a simple description of germination.

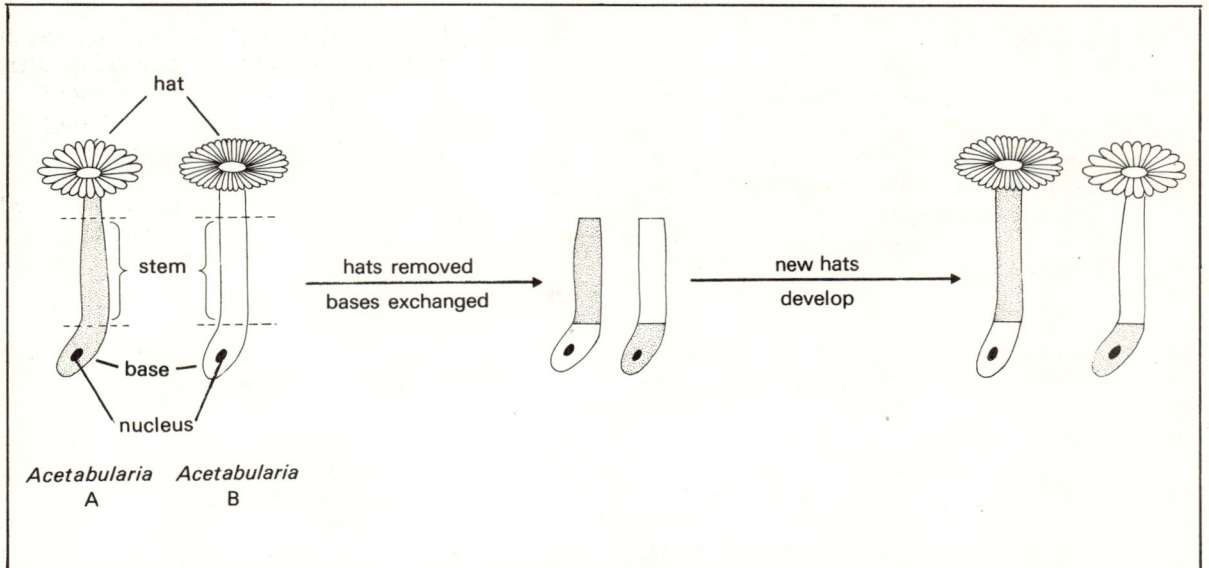

Fig. 28.1

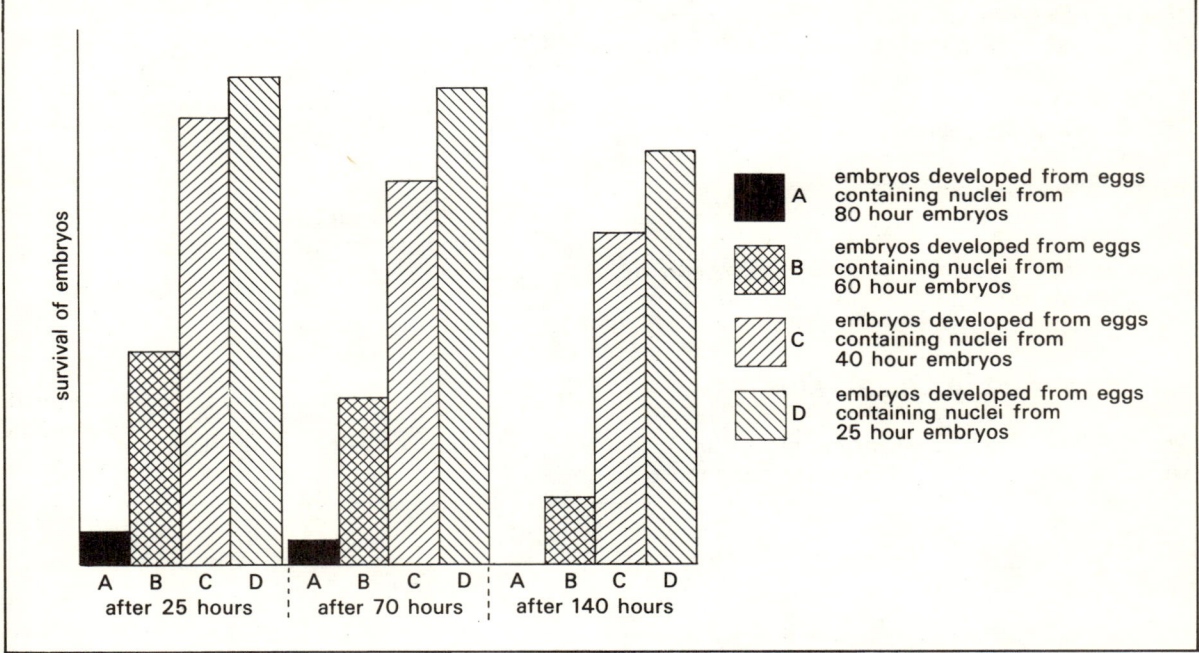

Fig. 28.2

(b) What basic conditions are necessary for seeds to germinate?

Other factors besides inheritance may affect the development of an organism.

Consider the following experiments.

(i) *Acetabularia* is a single celled plant. It has a long stem with a nucleus at the base and an umbrella-like hat at the top. Two different species of *Acetabularia* were used in the experiment illustrated in Fig. 28.1.

28.6 What do you conclude from this experiment?

(ii) Nuclei from frogs' eggs may be transplanted from embryos several hours old to newly fertilised frogs' eggs. One experiment involved transplanting nuclei from eggs at different stages of development (i.e. after 25 hours; 70 hours; 140 hours) into recently fertilised eggs. The results of the experiment are summarised in Fig. 28.2.

28.7 **(a)** What happens to the survival of the embryos after (i) 25 hours (ii) 75 hours (iii) 140 hours?
(b) What do these results suggest?

(iii) A third experiment involved tobacco seeds. One mutant variety is albino (cannot produce chlorophyll in their leaves). The gene for albinism is recessive. If the seeds are taken from a heterozygous (one green gene and one white gene)/heterozygous cross and then grown on black agar, two types of tobacco plant are seen on the agar.

28.8 What two types would you expect to see on the agar?

The two types are a result of inheritance. But **environment** may influence the colour of the leaves. Suppose the experiment is repeated but this time in the dark.

28.9 What colour would you expect the seedlings to be?

Chemicals may affect the development of organisms.

28.10 (a) Describe an experiment to investigate the effect of different concentrations of hormone (**auxin**) on the growth of cress seeds.
(b) Draw a sketch graph of the results you would expect.

Hormones are also important in controlling development in animals.

28.11 Name the hormone which induces **metamorphosis** in frogs.

29 Dispersal in Organisms

Most plants remain fixed in one place during the whole of their life cycle. Therefore there must be some means whereby plants can distribute their offspring so that new habitats may be **colonised**. Plants have developed many ways in which species may **disperse** themselves into new areas.

29.1 List four agents or vectors of dispersal.

Some plants such as mosses and ferns have a mobile phase in their life cycles.

29.2 What structure in a seed would enable it to be dispersed in water?

One agent of dispersal is man.

29.3 (a) List three ways in which man may disperse organisms.
(b) Devise an experiment to investigate one way in which man may disperse organisms.

Many plants have special adaptations for dispersal. Units of dispersal are called **propagules**.

29.4 (a) Refer to Fig. 29.1 which shows various fruits and seeds and write down for each seed the method of dispersal (air, water, animals or self dispersal).
(b) What is a fruit?

Dispersal is often haphazard. One way to overcome this problem is for the plant to produce a large number of seeds.

29.5 Name two species of plants which produce large numbers of seeds.

A few plants are able to move. These types of plants are called flagellates. One flagellate is called *Euglena*.

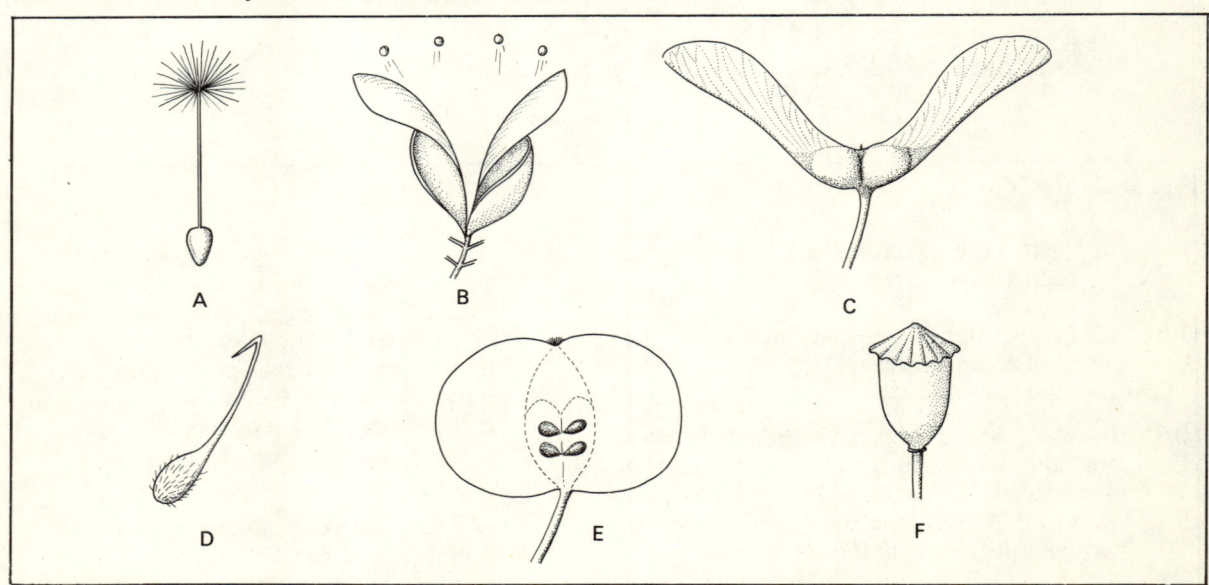

Fig. 29.1

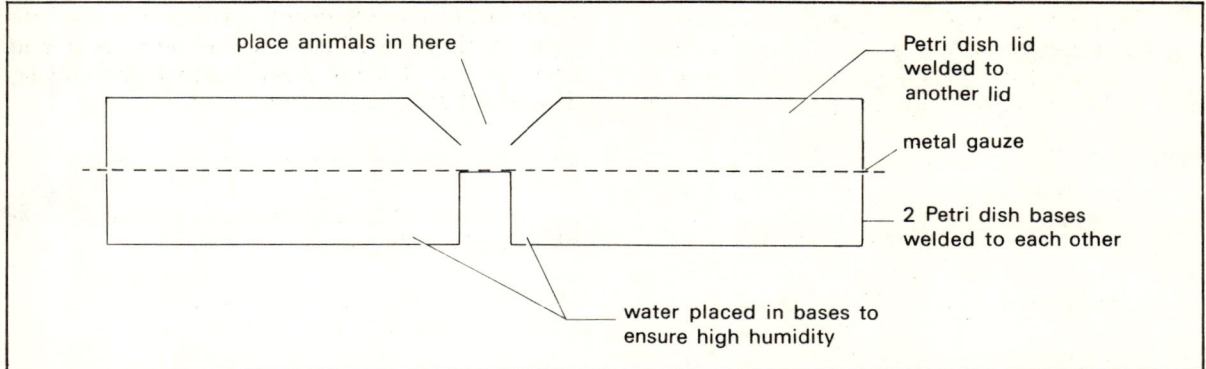

place animals in here

Petri dish lid welded to another lid

metal gauze

2 Petri dish bases welded to each other

water placed in bases to ensure high humidity

Fig. 29.2

29.6 What structure enables *Euglena* to move?

Most animals are **mobile** and can reach other habitats on their own. However, some animals are fixed in one place (they are **sessile**). Examples of this type of animal are mussels, limpets and barnacles. In these animals the egg or larval stage is mobile so that the animal can disperse to new areas. Other animals may simply be carried from one place to another by the medium in which they live. Jellyfish, for example, are moved from one place to another by sea currents.

Land animals search for a place to live. Many factors may influence their choice of habitat.

29.7 (a) Devise an experiment to investigate whether blowfly larvae (maggots) (i) like a particular type of food (ii) prefer light or dark conditions. Use the apparatus illustrated in Fig. 29.2.

(b) What must you do to be sure that the responses of the maggots which you observe are not simply due to chance?

30 Soil

Many animals and plants rely on soil as a source of food or shelter. Man himself is very dependent on what the **soil** provides.

30.1 (a) How is soil formed?
(b) How can man change the soil's fertility?

The composition and structure of the soil varies with depth. The soil can be divided into **topsoil** and **subsoil.** Some of the differences between them may be found by digging a **soil profile.**

30.2 Explain what is meant by a soil profile.

The structure of the soil can be investigated in a number of ways.

30.3 Describe how you could estimate the organic content of a sample of soil by heating it.

The size of particles varies in the soil. A simple way of showing this is to place a soil sample in water, mix it, and then allow the particles to settle. This is shown in Fig. 30.1.

30.4 What size of soil particle would settle first, then second, then third, and so on? (Do not give actual soil sizes.)

30.5 (a) List the differences between topsoil and subsoil in their air content, temperature, illumination, dampness and particle size.
(b) What are the advantages to plants if organic material (**humus**) is added to the soil?

Soil may also be classified according to particle size. An experiment illustrating this difference is shown in Fig. 30.2. Three samples of soil, one **clay,** one **sandy** and one **loam** were placed in the apparatus. Water was placed separately in the funnel and the time was recorded for it to flow through.

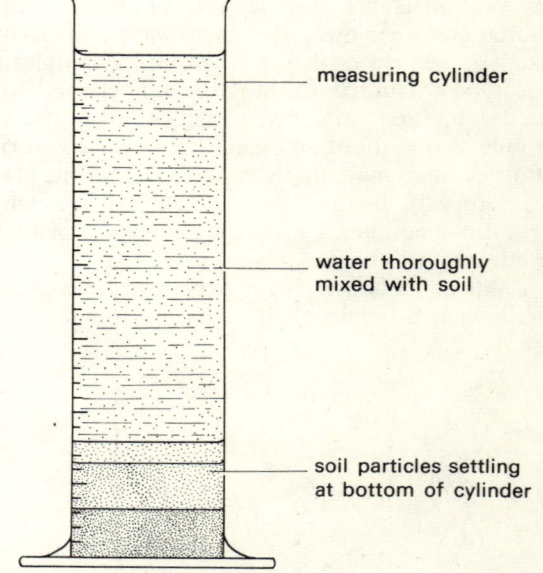

measuring cylinder

water thoroughly mixed with soil

soil particles settling at bottom of cylinder

Fig. 30.1

30.6 (a) In which soil sample would the water flow through (i) fastest (ii) slowest?
(b) List the differences between clay, loam and sand soil in (i) particle size (ii) air content (iii) water content.

Soil organisms may be extracted using a **Tullgren funnel** (illustrated in Fig. 30.3).

30.7 Explain how a Tullgren funnel works.

The apparatus can be used to determine the types and number of small soil organisms in different soil habitats.
One of the most familiar soil animals is the **earthworm.**

30.8 (a) Write down the names of the structures in the earthworm labelled A–D in Fig. 30.4.
(b) In what ways do the activities of the earthworm benefit the soil?

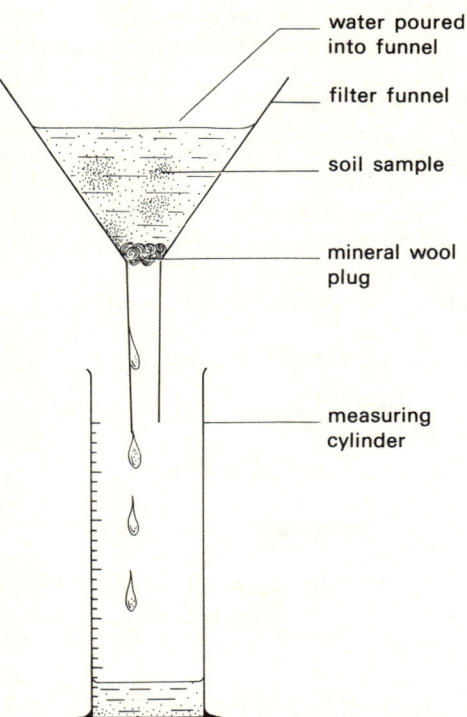

Fig. 30.2

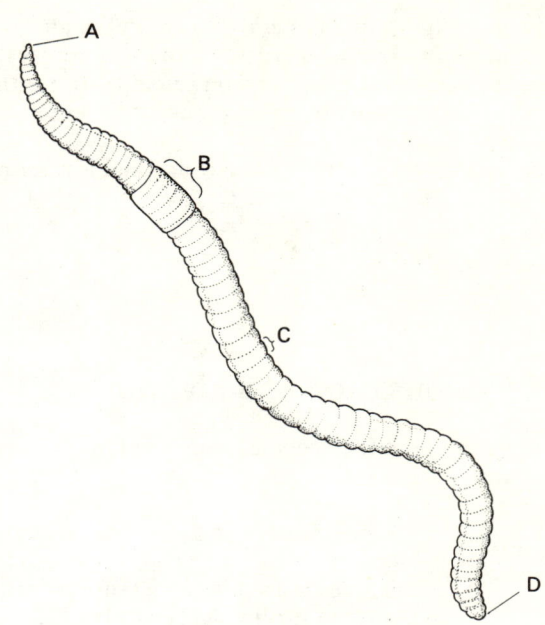

Fig. 30.4

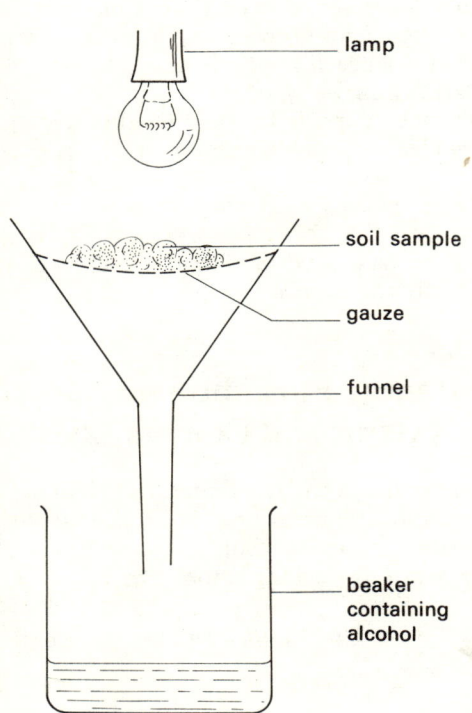

Fig. 30.3

30.9 Construct a simple food web of soil organisms from the following list: springtails, mites, leaf litter, earthworm, carnivorous beetles.

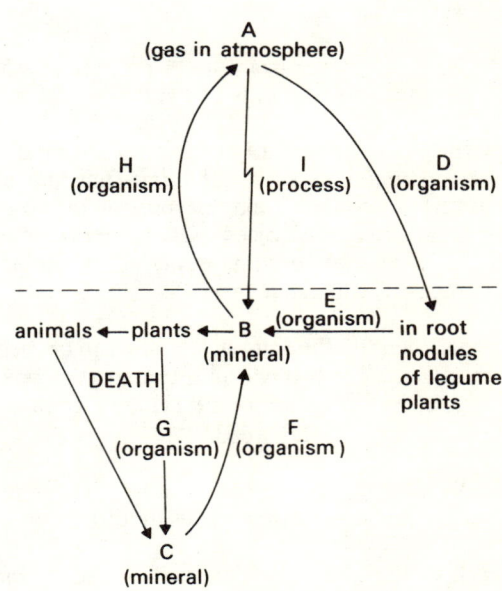

Fig. 30.5

Plants depend on the soil for **mineral ions.** For example, plants take up **nitrogen** in the form of **nitrate** from the soil.

30.10 (a) Where do nitrates come from? List three ways in which nitrogen may reach the soil.
   (b) Copy Fig. 30.5 of the nitrogen cycle into your books and complete the diagram by filling in the parts labelled A–I.

Other important minerals (e.g. **phosphorus**, **sulphur** and **carbon**) are recycled in a different way. Green plants take up carbon dioxide from the atmosphere by the process of photosynthesis.

30.11 (**a**) By what process is carbon dioxide released into the atmosphere?
(**b**) Draw a simple diagram of the carbon cycle.

31 Colonisation of a Habitat

All organisms must become established in a **habitat** in order to survive.

31.1 (**a**) Describe clearly what is meant by a habitat.
(**b**) List the needs a habitat must supply for an organism to survive successfully.

Habitats vary in shape and size. Habitats may be spread out over a large area such as a bird's **territory** (e.g. robin) or a small area such as a dead carcass (e.g. a sexton beetle).

31.2 Give one other example of an animal which occupies and defends a territory.

More than one species can live together in a habitat. Organisms which arrive at a habitat first may alter the conditions so that it may become favourable for other organisms to colonise it. Over a period of time one organism may become replaced by another. This process is called **succession.**

An experiment to illustrate succession can be carried out by placing fresh bread in a transparent box. A few days after setting up the experiment, mould can be seen growing on the bread.

31.3 What happens to the bread? (Give a more detailed answer than "goes mouldy".)

If freshly dug soil is left for some weeks, many varieties of plants will germinate. There will not be enough nutrients or space in the soil for all the plants to survive, and there will be a struggle for nutrients and space as the plants grow.

31.4 (**a**) What is the biological name given to this struggle for existence?
(**b**) What features of a plant will help its survival?
(**c**) Plants compete for nutrients and space. What other things do plants have to compete for?

One or more plants will become successful in the end.

31.5 What do you think is the meaning of the term "success" in an environmental situation?

Man has a slow reproductive rate, as compared with other animals. He is successful because his population number is enormous.

31.6 Why is man successful in terms of his enormous population number?

It takes many years to study such changes in the environment. After succession has taken place over many years a **climax** is reached.

31.7 (**a**) Which plant will usually dominate in the end?
(**b**) What would you expect to happen if a piece of land was left free from man's interference for many years?

Some communities may not be allowed to reach a natural climax; grazed grassland is an example of a **sub-climax.**

31.8 What animal will naturally graze grassland and prevent the environment reaching a natural climax?

The most common form of climax community is a wood. However, different types of trees influence other organisms growing under them. When leaves unfold in a beech wood, the canopy inside the wood is dark. In an oak wood the canopy is more open and therefore more light reaches the undergrowth. Beech leaves decay less rapidly than oak leaves.

31.9 If you examine the two types of wood you will find that more species of plants grow in an oak wood than in a beech wood. Explain this difference.

32 Energy Flow through Ecosystems and Communities

A **community** consists of interdependent plants and animals in a single habitat. Feeding relationships of animals are complex but we can trace the path of energy flow by looking at **food chains.**

32.1 What type of organism always begins a food chain?

A **food web** gives a better picture of what happens in a community.

32.2 The following organisms were found in a stream: bacteria, protozoa, rotifer, stickleback, algae. Construct a food web to show the feeding relationships between these organisms.

At each **feeding level** of organisms, i.e. plant→herbivore→carnivore etc., the number of them is less than at the previous level.

32.3 How does the total mass of **consumers** compare with **producers?**

To obtain an over-all picture of the numbers of organisms in a food chain or web, the model of a **pyramid** can be used.

32.4 Fig. 32.1 shows a food pyramid which represents the food web in a woodland area. Write down the letter which corresponds to each of the following organisms: robins, vegetation, caterpillars, sparrow-hawks, aphids.

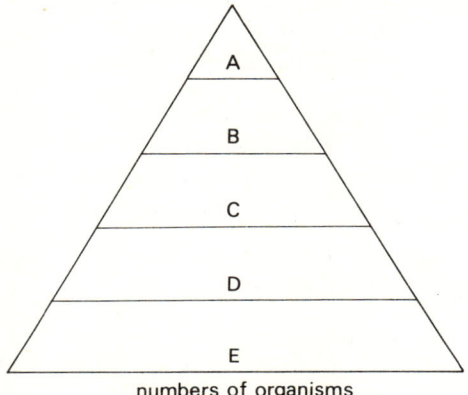

numbers of organisms

Fig. 32.1

Sometimes the **pyramid of numbers** can be misleading. For example, one oak tree may support many animals.

32.5 Which of the pyramids illustrated in Fig. 32.2 would illustrate an oak tree supporting a large number of animals?

Remember that the feeding relationships of communities exist below the ground as well. These organisms generally break down dead plant and animal material into minerals, so that mineral ions can be recirculated. The organisms which carry out this breakdown are called **decomposers.**

32.6 Draw a decomposer food web using the following groups of organisms: green plants, decomposers, carnivores, herbivores.

33 Man and the Environment

Man exerts a considerable influence on his surroundings in many ways.
(i) Man has destroyed climax communities by clearing woodland and grassland. This results in dead plant and animal material not being returned to the soil.

33.1 **(a)** When man removes trees, the soil may become exposed to harsh elements of the weather. What features of the weather would tend to remove soil from fertile farmland?
(b) What is the name of the process in which soil is washed or blown away, sometimes leaving bare rock?

(ii) When man grows food crops, weeds may reduce the **productivity** of these crops. Man may remove weeds by sowing crops, such as wheat, very closely together.

33.2 What would be the disadvantage of sowing crops very closely together?

(iii) Man may affect his surroundings by smoke or atmospheric **pollution** which involves the release of carbon particles and gases such as carbon dioxide and sulphur dioxide.

33.3 What effects on the environment take place with this type of atmospheric pollution?

(iv) Rivers can be polluted by sewage. Organisms such as bacteria feed on sewage and this activity lowers the level of oxygen dissolved in the water.

33.4 What effect would a lower oxygen level have on organisms (e.g. fish)?

(iv) Man applies weed-killers and pesticides to kill off undesirable organisms in his food crops. Although the pests may be controlled, poisonous chemicals may still remain in the soil. Some of these poisons may be passed through other organisms along food chains.

33.5 What effect might this have on animals at the end of food chains?

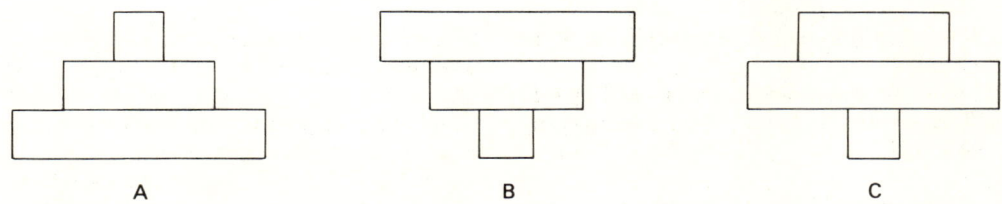

A   B   C

Fig. 32.2

(**vi**) Some organisms colonise areas altered by man, e.g. waste places.

33.6 List four animals which colonise areas altered by man's activities.

34 Associations between Organisms

Living things colonise a variety of habitats and there are a number of organisms which colonise other organisms. One such group of organisms is called **epiphytes.**

34.1 (**a**) What is an epiphyte?
 (**b**) Give an example of an epiphyte.

The same type of situation may be found among animals. These are called **epizoites.**

34.2 (**a**) What is an epizoite?
 (**b**) Give an example of an epizoite.

Some organisms may obtain their food in solution from other living things which have died. This type of organism may be a **saprophyte** (if it is a plant) or a **saprozoite** (if it is an animal).

34.3 (**a**) Give one example of (i) a saprophyte (ii) a saprozoite.
 (**b**) Describe briefly how saprophytes and saprozoites feed.

Some organisms live directly off the tissues of other living organisms (called the **host** organism).

34.4 (**a**) What is the name given to this type of organism?
 (**b**) What type of conditions would an organism expect to find when living inside a gut?
 (**c**) Why would you not find green plants living inside the gut?
 (**d**) What types of food would an organism expect to find in various sections of the human gut?

The host may suffer as a result of this type of colonisation.

34.5 (**a**) List special features you may find on **parasites** which enable them to remain on the host.
 (**b**) Give two examples of (i) animal parasites (ii) plant parasites.
 (**c**) How can man control parasites in himself?

Other associations may be beneficial to both organisms who participate in them. One example of a beneficial association is a lichen. This is a fungus with algae living inside it.

34.6 (**a**) What is the scientific name given to this beneficial association?
 (**b**) How does the association between the fungi and algae benefit both?
 (**c**) Give two other examples of this kind of beneficial association, explaining how each organism benefits from the other.

35 Mutation and Variation

For centuries many people living in the tropical and sub-tropical areas of the world have suffered from malaria.

During the mid-1940s the use of an insecticide, DDT, controlled the spread of the disease, by killing the mosquitoes which carried malaria. However, in the 1950s DDT became less and less effective in controlling the mosquito. Somehow the insects were becoming resistant to it. A new strain of mosquito had appeared.

35.1 What name do we give to the sudden appearance of a new strain of an organism?

New characteristics can be studied more easily by using micro-organisms such as bacteria.

35.2 (**a**) Suggest one problem in using micro-organisms.
 (**b**) Briefly outline the transfer of bacteria from a culture to a nutrient agar in a Petri dish.
 (**c**) List the precautions you would take when transferring bacteria from a culture to the nutrient agar.

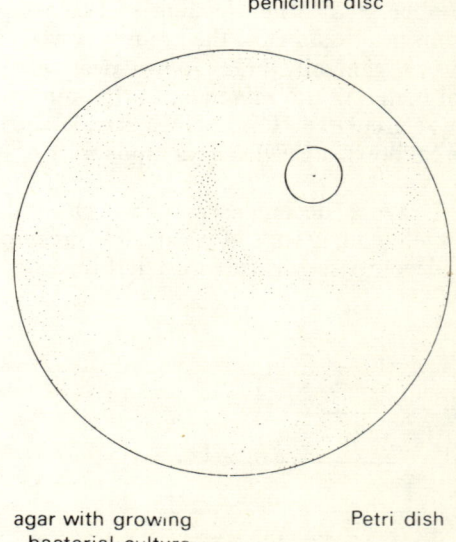

penicillin disc

agar with growing bacterial culture

Petri dish

Fig. 35.1

Suppose a penicillin disc is placed on the agar plate containing the bacterial culture, and the Petri dish incubated for about 48 hours as in Fig. 35.1. When the Petri dish is examined, a clear area where no bacteria have grown is seen around the disc.

35.3 (a) Explain the cause of this clear zone around the penicillin disc.

(b) What would you conclude if you found some bacterial colonies growing on the clear area?

Mutation is infrequent. A new characteristic arises approximately once in a million organisms, but this can vary with the organism and the gene.

35.4 Mutation can arise in three ways:
(a) **Chromosome rearrangement.**
(b) **Chromosome multiplication.**
(c) **Gene mutation.**
Explain briefly what is meant by each of these forms of mutation.

Mutation shows one form of **variation,** in that individuals with new characteristics may suddenly appear and differ from others of the same species. Variation can also occur in ways other than mutation, in that new individuals, produced by sexual reproduction, are not identical to their parents.

35.5 (a) Explain briefly why children are not identical to their parents.

(b) (i) How much would individuals produced from asexual reproduction differ from the parent organism? (ii) Why is this so?

The environment may also cause variation in the way the genes are expressed. For example, growth may be stunted in an oak tree if it survives at a high altitude.

36 Selection

Many organisms produce a large number of eggs but (after they have developed) few offspring survive to maturity.

36.1 Suggest reasons why many offspring do not survive.

Moth collectors in the nineteenth century kept careful records of the peppered moth, *Biston betularia*. This moth is usually greyish-white with black markings but occasionally dark-coloured moths were found (see Fig. 36.1). In Manchester the following observations on the moths were recorded.

1848 First dark specimen found.
1895 About 98% of the specimens were dark.

Fig. 36.1 (a) *Peppered moths on the bark of a tree in a rural area.*

Fig. 36.1 (b) *Peppered moths on the bark of a tree in an industrial area.*

A further investigation in 1960 by Professor H. B. D. Kettlewell showed that most of the dark-coloured moths were found in the heavily populated areas of England while most of the light-coloured moths were found in rural areas.

36.2 (a) Name one type of organism which might be a predator on the peppered moth.

(b) What would be the condition and colour of the bark of trees, and would there be any growth of lichen, in (i) a heavily populated (industrial) area (ii) a rural area?

(c) How would the colour of the peppered moths (both the dark- and light-coloured varieties) show up against trees in (i) heavily populated (industrial) areas (ii) rural areas?

(d) Suggest an explanation for the distribution of the light- and dark-coloured moths observed by Professor Kettlewell.

(e) What special name do we give to the ability of an animal to blend in with the environment?

The peppered moth illustrates the important biological process known as **selection**. Selection occurs when organisms which possess favourable characteristics, such as the ability to run faster, are able to survive because they are able to escape predators. Those organisms that cannot run so fast are less likely to survive. Consequently, they are selected out.

Another example of selection involves man and disease. Some people in the world possess abnormal red blood cells. These cells are sickle shaped (see Fig. 36.2 (a) and (b)) and are less efficient at absorbing oxygen. The name of this disease is called **sickle celled anaemia.**

The following genotypes for red blood cells occur:

Hb^A Hb^A	normal red blood cells (Hb represents the haemoglobin gene and ^{A} represents the normal red blood cell gene).
Hb^A Hb^S	some sickle cells but the person does not suffer from anaemia.
Hb^S Hb^S	sickle cells, person suffers from anaemia, usually fatal at a young age.

36.3 What is the general name given to the genotype of a person possessing the Hb^A Hb^S genes?

It has been found that persons with sickle cells are resistant to malaria.

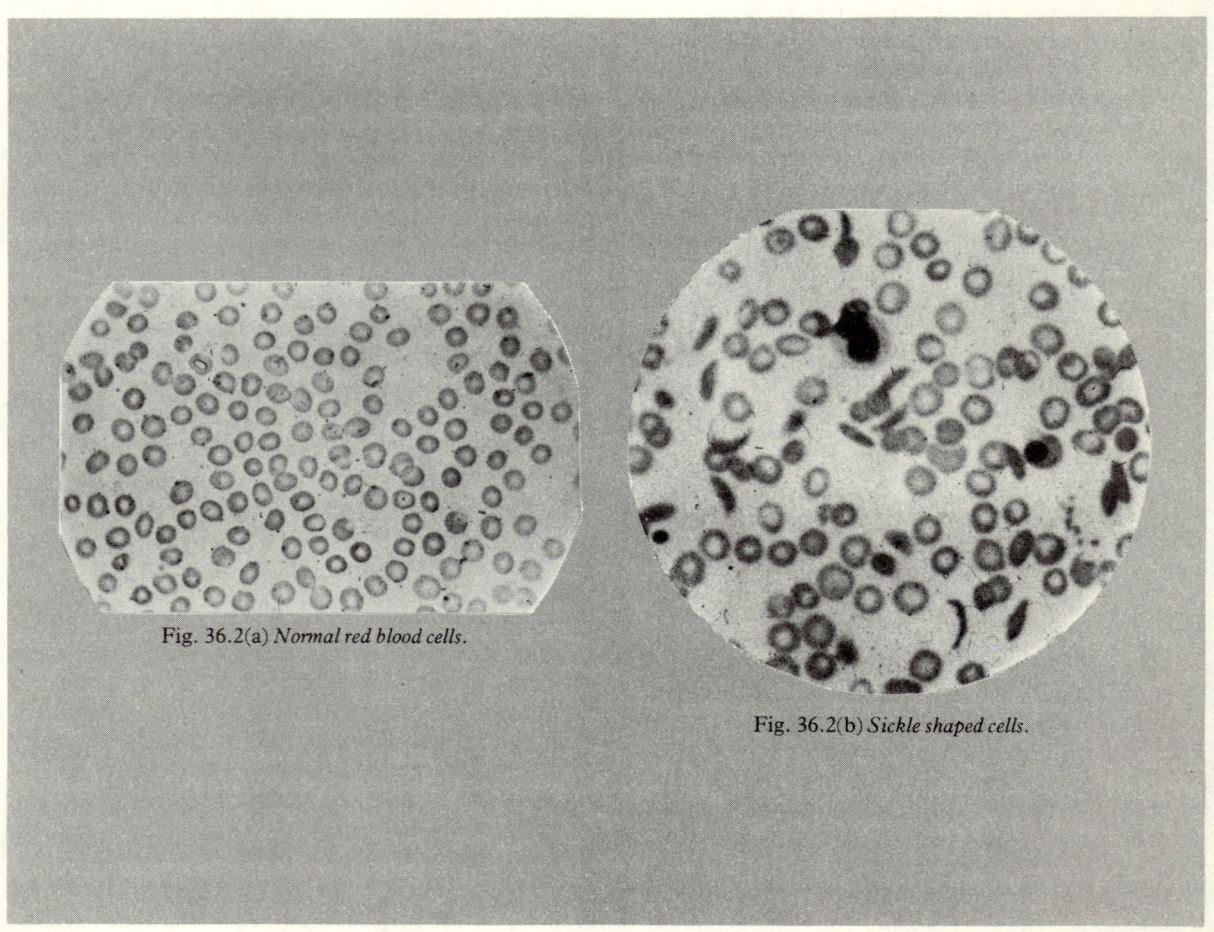

Fig. 36.2(a) *Normal red blood cells.*

Fig. 36.2(b) *Sickle shaped cells.*

36.4 If the sickle celled anaemia is fatal, which genotype allows the sickle celled gene to remain in the population?

36.5 Explain why the (harmful) sickle cell gene remains in the population. What factor is selecting for it?

36.6 By careful breeding, man may produce new varieties of organisms which have certain desirable features. This type of selection is called **artificial selection**. Give two examples of artificial selection used by man.

37 Evolution

Charles Darwin (1809–1882) was one of the first scientists to produce modern ideas concerning **evolution**. The main points of Darwin's theory are set out below as a series of exercises.

OBSERVATION 1
37.1 What do you notice about the quantity of eggs produced by the different organisms in Table 2?

OBSERVATION 2
The population of most species remains approximately the same over a lengthy period of time (once they are established in their environment).

37.2 Suggest reasons why the population remains approximately constant.

Darwin concluded that if the population numbers remained constant then there must be a struggle for survival.

37.3 Suggest reasons why some organisms may survive whilst others may not.

OBSERVATION 3
Darwin also noticed that there was variation within a given species (see Chapter 35). Offspring may differ slightly from their parents.

37.4 Name two ways in which such variation may arise.

OBSERVATION 4
Some variations were passed on from generation to generation.

OBSERVATION 5
Some of these variations were favourable to the species, others were not.

37.5 Give three examples of favourable variations in named organisms.

Darwin called this process of selection **"survival of the fittest"**. Favourable variations would persist in the population and be passed down to succeeding generations. With the process operating over many generations (for millions of years, perhaps) new species would arise. Darwin called this process **"evolution by natural selection"**.

Animal	Approx. no. of eggs produced at one time
cod	3×10^6–7×10^6
herring	3×10^4
frog	$1 \cdot 5 \times 10^3$
crocodile	50–80
pheasant	14

Table 2. Numbers of eggs produced from various species of animals.

37.6 Describe briefly one example of evolution by natural selection.

In 1809 a French biologist called Jean Baptiste Lamarck put forward a different theory of evolution. He suggested that new characteristics were **"acquired"**. The best way to explain this is by use of a simple example. Lamarck stated that the giraffe developed its long neck by stretching for food. Therefore, offspring from the giraffe would have longer necks and so on.

37.7 A man developed large muscles by strenuous exercise. His children did not have particularly big muscles. Does this support Lamarck's theory?

Much evidence has been discovered in recent times to support Darwin's theory of evolution.

37.8 List four major categories of evidence which are given in support of Darwin's theory of evolution.

Answers

1 Classifying Living Things

1.1 *Fucus vesiculosus.*

1.2

(i)(a) Possesses legs .... *see* (ii)
   (b) Does not possess legs .... *worm*

(ii)(a) Has six legs .... *see* (iii)
   (b) Has more than six legs .... *see* (iv)

(iii)(a) Body separated into three main sections
        (head, thorax, abdomen), one pair of
        wings .... *fly*
    (b) Body seen as two separate sections (head,
        thorax and abdomen in one section,
        wings enclosed by wing case) ... *beetle*

(iv)(a) Round body, legs similar in length, eight
       legs .... *mite*
   (b) Body visibly segmented, more than eight
       legs .... *see* (v)

(v)(a) Body length greater than its width, many
      segments and legs .... *centipede*
   (b) Body length about twice as long as width,
      fewer segments and legs, "armadillo-
      like" .... *wood-louse*

1.3 Kingdom: Animal
     Phylum: Vertebrata
     Class: Mammalia
     Order: Primate
     Family: Hominidae
     Genus: *Homo*
     Species: *H. sapiens*

1.4 (a) *Drosophila.*
     (b) *melanogaster.*

2 Animal and Plant Cells

2.1 To magnify objects.

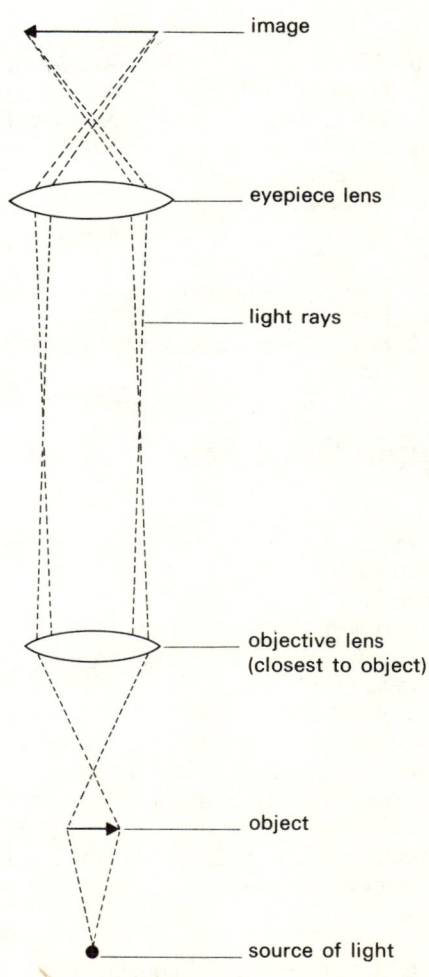

49

2.2 (a) It keeps the cells moist.
   (b) To stop the tissues drying out.
   To protect the high power objective (stop it getting wet).
   To keep the tissues flat.
   (c) By using a stain.

2.3 (a) A = cell membrane – it "encloses cell" and allows substances to pass in and out of the cell.
   B = mitochondrion – it makes ATP.
   C = nucleus – it controls cell processes.
   D = cytoplasm – this is where cell processes take place.
   E = cell wall – this is a rigid outer covering for plant cells.
   F = cell membrane – see A.
   G = vacuole – this is a large structure in plant cells which contains water and mineral ions. It is important in osmosis.
   H = nucleus – see C.
   I = chloroplast – this is the site of photosynthesis and where starch is made.

Differences

(b) *Plant cell*	*Animal cell*
Has a cell wall	No cell wall
Has a vacuole	No vacuole
Has chloroplasts (therefore can make its own food)	No chloroplasts

Similarities

Both have a nucleus
Both contain cytoplasm
Both have mitochondria

3 Simple Organisms (Unicells)

3.1 Ability to respire.
Reproduction.
Sensitivity.
Feeding.
Excretion.
Growth.
Movement.

3.2 The movement of molecules (as liquid or gas) from a region of high concentration to a region of low concentration.

3.3 Mainly carbon dioxide, but amino-acids and other complex compounds may also be produced.

3.4 Light, temperature, chemical, (O_2, CO_2).

3.5 A "plant-like" unicell.

3.6

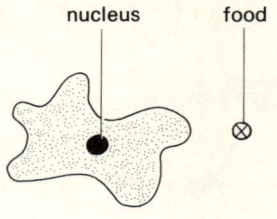

nucleus   food

Amoeba

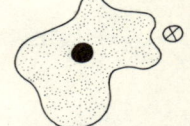

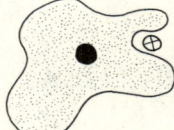

food vacuole

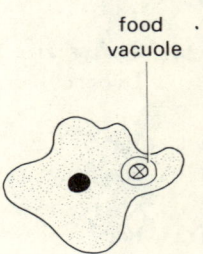

3.7 (a) *Amoeba*.
   (b) *Paramecium*.
   (c) *Euglena*.

3.8 C D B A E.

4 Gas Exchange in Animals

4.1 (a) (i) The candle goes out after a short period of time (approximately 10 seconds). (ii) The candle goes out almost immediately.
   (b) That exhaled air does not allow the candle to burn; therefore there must be a difference between atmospheric and exhaled air.

4.2 (a) Bubble a gas sample through a reagent (such as lime water or bicarbonate indicator) which detects carbon dioxide.
   (b) The lime water turns a milky colour much more rapidly in exhaled air than in atmospheric air.

4.3 (a)

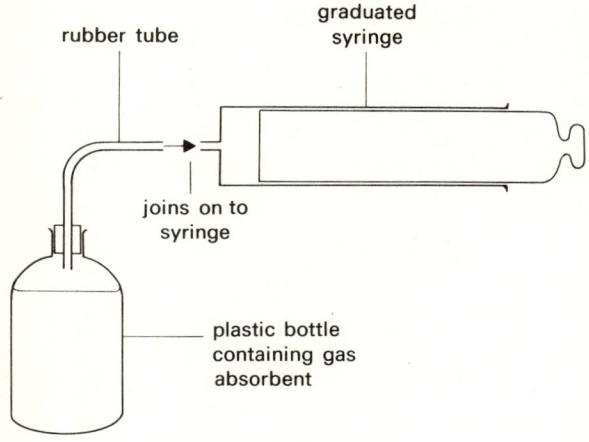

(b) These reagents are mixed with the gas sample. Potassium hydroxide will absorb the carbon dioxide and potassium pyrogallate will absorb the oxygen.

(c) Since potassium pyrogallate will absorb BOTH carbon dioxide and oxygen, potassium hydroxide has to be used FIRST.

(d) % CO_2 = 100 – 96 = 4 mm³, 4/100 (total volume) × 100 = 4%
% O_2 = 96 – 80 = 16 mm³, 16/100 × 100 = 16%
remaining gases = 80%

(e) Nitrogen.

(f) Exhaled air.

4.4

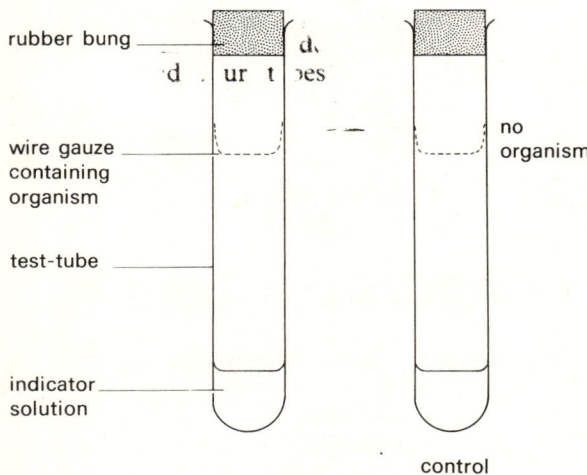

4.5 Test your breath with cobalt chloride paper. If water vapour is present then the paper will turn from blue to pink.

4.6 (a) Rate and depth of breathing will increase because the muscles are using up much oxygen and you need to take in more air to replace that which is used up.

(b) Rate and depth will increase because there is much less oxygen in the atmosphere.

4.7 (a) Pharynx, glottis, larynx, trachea, bronchus, bronchiole, alveolus.

(b) A = rib (section)
B = bronchial tree
C = pleural layer
D = intercostal muscles
E = diaphragm
F = space occupied by heart
G = diaphragm muscle
H = bronchus
I = lung
J = trachea

4.8 Mainly to raise the ribs.

4.9 (i) The diaphragm sheet moves downwards.
(ii) The chest volume increases.

4.10 (a) The volume increases and the pressure decreases.

(b) The atmospheric pressure is now greater than that of the space inside the bell-jar so the air rushes in.

(c) The movement of the ribs and diaphragm cause the pressure inside the chest cavity to decrease and therefore the air moves into the lungs.

4.11 (a) The ribs move down. (ii) The diaphragm sheet moves up.

(b) The volume is reduced.

(c) The pressure inside the chest cavity is now higher than that of the atmosphere so the air is pushed out.

4.12 The lungs would not inflate.

4.13 (a) In order to find the volume of your lungs, breathe in as deeply as you can and then blow out as much as possible of the air you have inhaled into the bell-jar via the tube.

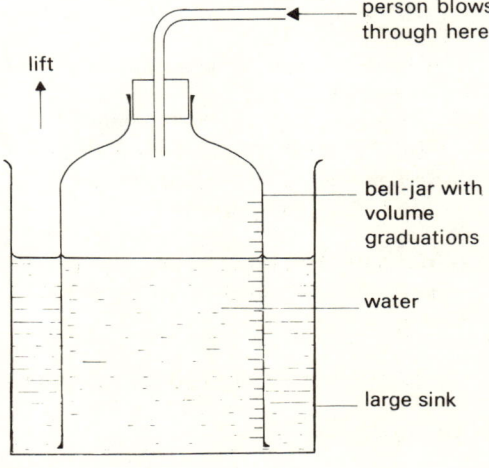

(b) No, there is always a volume left in the lungs called the residual volume which cannot be expelled by breathing.

(c) Tidal volume.

4.14 (a) So that the gases do not have far to move across to the bloodstream.

(b) By diffusion.

4.15 (a) Large surface area.
Good blood supply to gas-exchange organ.

(b) Gill.

4.16 Oxygen travels down each of the tracheae and enters the tissues by diffusion.

5 Respiration

5.1 See answer to Question **4.5**.

5.2 (a) The mass of the water (or the volume).
The temperature of the water before and after the experiment.
The mass of the peanut.

(b) Since 4.2 joules of energy are required to heat 1 gram of water through 1 °C the following calculation can be made: 1 gram of water raised 1 °C = 4.2 joules.
The volume of water is known and the temperature difference of the water is also known. Multiply the two values together along with 4.2 joules and you have the amount of energy given out by a particular peanut. Adjust the value for a particular mass of peanut.

(c) Not all the heat from the burning peanut heats the water.
Some of the heat is used to heat the test-tube itself.
The peanut burns inefficiently.
Heat is lost from the water through the test-tube wall.
The experiment can be improved by:
Surrounding the peanut by the vessel containing the water.
Using a vessel which transmits the heat more efficiently.
Burning the peanut in oxygen.
Insulating the container.

(d) $40 \text{ cm}^3 \times 31 \text{ °C} \times 4.2 \times 1/0.1 = 52\,080$ J or 52.1 kJ/g of peanut.

5.3 In the cell.

5.4 Aerobic respiration.

5.5 $C_6H_{12}O_6 + 6O_2 \rightarrow 6CO_2 + 6H_2O + \text{energy}$.

5.6 In the mitochondria.

5.7 Anaerobic respiration.

5.8 Lactic acid.

5.9 (a) Alcohol (ethanol) and carbon dioxide.

(b) To make sure that the yeast respires without oxygen.

(c) The lime water should turn milky indicating the presence of carbon dioxide.

5.10 (a) $C_6H_{12}O_6 \rightarrow 2C_2H_5OH + 2CO_2$

(b) Wine-making; bread-making.

6 Feeding Mechanisms in Animals

6.1 (a) Incisors, canines, premolars, molars.

(b) Incisors = cutting.
Canines = gripping and tearing.
Premolars and molars = crushing and grinding.

6.2 A = crown
B = root
C = nerves and blood vessels
D = bone of jaw
E = cement
F = fibres supporting tooth in socket
G = pulp cavity
H = gum
I = dentine
J = enamel

6.3 (a) Reasonably strong, though small, incisors, but prominent canines for gripping. Sharp premolars and molars for cutting off chunks of meat.

(b) Carnassal teeth.

(c) Up and down only to make the cutting action most effective. Notice the large surface area for muscle attachment at the top of the jaw bone.

6.4 (a) Incisors on lower jaw only, which cut against pad on upper jaw.
A large space (called the diastema) where the grass is collected before grinding.
Large flat but ridged premolar and molar teeth for grinding.

(b) From side to side.

6.5 (a) A = labrum
B = mandibles
C = maxilla
D = labium

(b) Mandibles cut and grind the grass.
Maxillae guide the grass in and cut to a lesser extent.
The labium and labrum stop the grass falling out and protect the mouthparts.

6.6 Saliva is secreted on the food. The enzymes in the saliva digest the food and the large proboscis "soaks up" the food (in liquid form) which then reaches the gut by the pumping action of the muscles in the proboscis.

6.7 **(a)** See diagram given for the answer to Question **3.6**.
(b) Small animals are pierced by stinging cells in the tentacles. The food is then directed into the mouth.
(c) The mosquito has a sharp proboscis which pierces the skin of the victim and obtains blood.
(d) Its long proboscis is specially adapted to "suck up" nectar in flowers.

7 Food

7.1 For energy, growth and replacement.

7.2 Carbon, hydrogen and oxygen.

7.3

one glucose
molecule

O = oxygen atom

Starch consists of many glucose molecules joined together.

7.4 **(a)** Add iodine (I_2/KI) solution to sample of starch.
(b) The starch turns a blue-black colour.

7.5 **(a)** To test for reducing sugars, add food sample to blue Benedicts solution and heat.
(b) (i) A green colour. (ii) A yellow colour. (iii) An orange-red colour.

7.6 By boiling food sample with two drops of acid before carrying out the Benedicts test. *and neutralising.*

7.7 Carbon, hydrogen and oxygen.

7.8 Fat in food leaves a translucent stain on paper.
Dissolve fat in ethanol then add water. A milkiness occurs (an emulsion).

7.9 **(a)** Carbon, hydrogen, oxygen and nitrogen (sometimes phosphorus and sulphur).

(b) Amino-acids.
(c) Because the different amino-acids can be arranged in different combinations.

7.10 **(a)** Add blue Biuret reagent to a food sample.
(b) The solution should turn a violet colour.

7.11 **(a)** Vitamin D.
(b) Meat, fish and fats.
(c) Refer to a textbook.

7.12 **(a)** These substances are incorporated into:
(i) Red blood corpuscles. (ii) ATP and DNA. (iii) Bones and teeth.
(b) (i) Liver. (ii) Any protein products. (iii) Milk and milk products.

8 Getting Food to the Body

8.1 **(a)** The starch test and the glucose test. See answers to Questions **7.4** and **7.5**.
(b) Glucose is found in the beaker of water.
(c) Glucose can get through the tubing but the starch cannot.

8.2 A partially permeable or semi-permeable membrane.

8.3 **(a)** Saliva.
(b) Starch is broken down to reducing sugar.

8.4 When starch is eaten, it is broken down to reducing sugar by the enzymes in the alimentary canal to produce reducing sugars. These smaller molecules are then able to enter the body through the gut wall.

8.5 Enzymes work under specific conditions of temperature and pH (acidity/alkalinity), and on specific food substances. Each enzyme has its own specific set of conditions.

8.6 Starch.

8.7 A = salivary gland
B = oesophagus
C = stomach
D = pancreas
E = duodenum
F = ileum
G = rectum
H = appendix
I = large intestine or colon
J = bile duct
K = gall bladder
L = liver

8.8 **(a)** Peristalsis.
(b) Contraction of the circular muscles makes

the lumen (space inside the gut) smaller while contraction of the longitudinal muscles makes the lumen larger.

8.9 **(a)** (i) Food becomes acid due to the secretion of hydrochloric acid by the stomach; pepsin, which digests proteins, is also secreted. (ii) The food is now alkaline because of bile (secreted by the gall bladder). All the enzymes necessary for the completion of digestion have been secreted by the pancreas and glands in the wall of the duodenum.

(b) Salivary amylase – acts on starch.
Pepsin – acts on protein.
Pancreatic peptidase – acts on protein.
Pancreatic amylase – acts on starch.
Lipase – acts on fats.
Intestinal peptidase – acts on polypeptides.
Maltase – acts on maltose.
Sucrase – acts on sucrose.

(c) Mainly glucose, amino-acids, fatty acids and glycerol.

8.10 There are many villi (finger-like structures containing blood vessels) which give the gut a large surface area. This enables the food to pass into the blood system rapidly and efficiently.

8.11 There are small organisms, such as bacteria, living in the gut which can digest cellulose to give glucose.

9 Transport in Animals

9.1 **(a)** (i) 3:1 (ii) 2:1.
(b) The ratios are becoming smaller.

9.2 The alimentary canal, the lymphatic system and the breathing system.

9.3 **(a)** Red blood cells, white blood cells, platelets, plasma.
(b) The red blood cells carry oxygen.
The white blood cells act as a defence against disease.
Platelets help to form clots when the skin is broken.
The plasma is the main transport medium for food, waste products, etc."

(c)

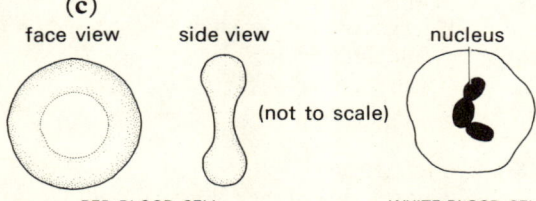

RED BLOOD CELL   WHITE BLOOD CELL

(d) In the bone marrow.

9.4 **(a)** 1 = arms, head and upper body
2 = lungs
3 = heart
4 = liver
5 = intestines
6 = rest of body including kidney, reproductive organs and legs

(b) A = pulmonary artery
B = vena cava
C = hepatic vein
D = hepatic portal vein
E = hepatic artery
F = dorsal aorta
G = pulmonary vein

9.5 **(a)** (i) The whole blood system with the exception of the intestine and liver blood supply. (ii) Hepatic and hepatic portal system.

(b) (i) Waste products from one organ do not interfere with the workings of another.
Fresh oxygen supply to each organ.
Fresh food supply to each organ.
Restriction in the flow of one organ does not interfere with the flow of another.
(ii) Substances entering one organ can be processed by another before release into general circulation, e.g. products of digestion are processed by the liver.

9.6 **(a)** A = pulmonary artery
B = semi-lunar or artery valves
C = vena cava
D = right auricle or atrium
E = tricuspid valves
F = right ventricle
G = central muscle wall of heart
H = left ventricle
I = tendinous cords
J = bicuspid value
K = left auricle
L = pulmonary vein
M = dorsal aorta

(b) Auricles only have to pump blood into the ventricles while the ventricles have to pump blood around the lungs or body.

(c) The right ventricle pumps blood to the lungs only and therefore it is less muscular than the left ventricle which pumps blood around the body.

(d) To make the valves effective, i.e. stop the flaps "flapping" back.

(e) A goes to the lungs.
C brings blood back from the body.
L brings blood back from the lungs.
M takes blood to the body.

9.7 **(a)** Artery.
(b) Thick wall of elastic fibres to withstand pressure.

9.8 (a) Vein.
    (b) Thin walls (no pressure problems) and valves to ensure one-way flow of blood.

9.9 (a) Capillary.
    (b) Very small and the walls of the vessel are one cell thick.

9.10 (a) Oxygen and carbon dioxide.
    (b) Both are carried by the red blood cells, combined with haemoglobin; carbon dioxide is also transported in the plasma.

9.11 (a) By the muscles of the leg and arm. These vessels also have valves.
    (b) The subclavian veins.

9.12 White blood cells accumulate here in preparation for invasion by micro-organisms.

10 Photosynthesis

10.1 The carbon dioxide is being absorbed by the green vegetation.

10.2 (a) Place a green leaf in a test-tube containing a suitable indicator. Make sure that the leaf is not submerged in the indicator unless it is a water plant. The control is the test-tube plus indicator but no leaf.

(b) The indicator should show a lowering of carbon dioxide in the test-tube containing the green vegetation.

10.4 (a) The plant is able to produce a substance or substances which are able to keep the mouse alive.
    (b) Refer also to answers to Questions **4.2** and **4.3**.

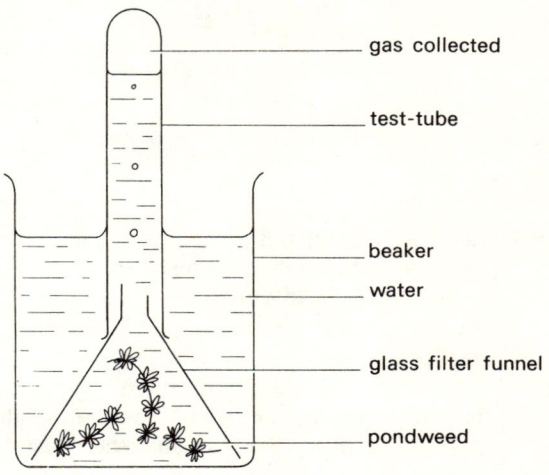

gas collected

test-tube

beaker

water

glass filter funnel

pondweed

(c) Oxygen.

10.3

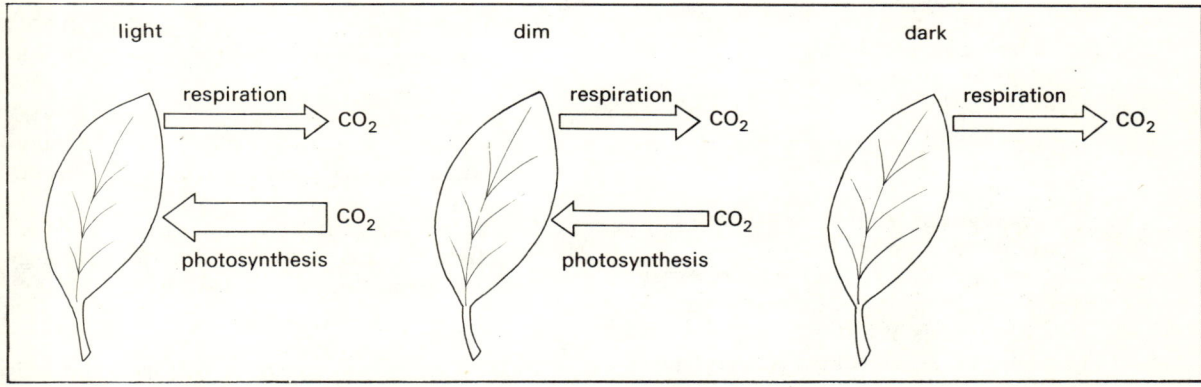

10.5

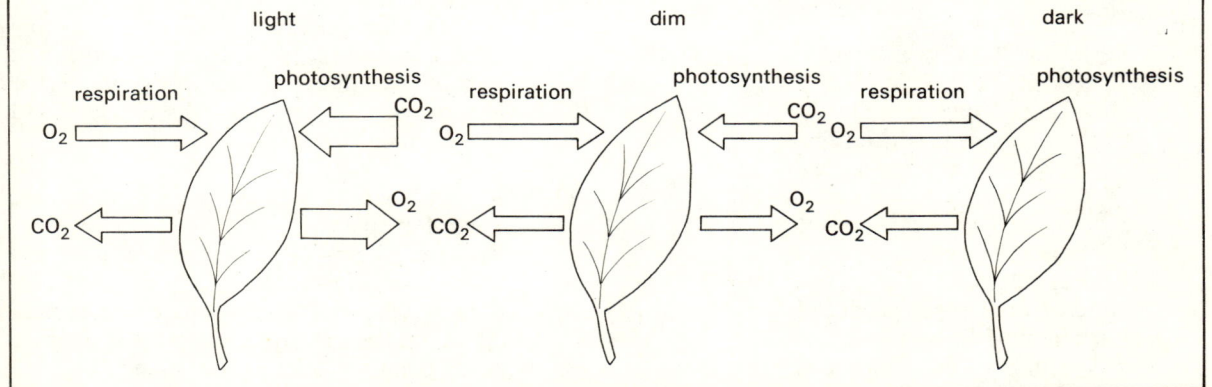

10.6 (a) In boiling water.
(b) Because it would obscure the chemical test at the end of the experiment.
(c) By boiling in ethanol.
(d) Use I_2/KI solution.

10.7 (i) Place one plant in the dark and one in the light and then after a time, test for starch.
(ii) Place one plant in normal air and another where CO_2 is removed and then after a time, test for starch.

10.8 $6CO_2 + 6H_2O \rightarrow C_6H_{12}O_6 + 6O_2$

10.9 (a) All the spectrum except for red and blue.
(b) That chlorophyll absorb red and blue light for photosynthesis.

10.10 Use a variegated leaf (one which is green but has white patches or strips). Expose to light. Make a map of the leaf and then test for starch.

10.11 (a) The cells on the upper surface of the leaf.
(b) A = upper epidermis
B = palisade mesophyll
C = spongy mesophyll
D = lower epidermis
E = a guard cell of a stoma
F = a stoma
(c) The upper epidermis is the outer covering and prevents water loss.
The palisade mesophyll is where photosynthesis takes place.
The spongy mesophyll is the gas reservoir.
The lower epidermis contains stomata.
The guard cells of a stoma and the stoma regulate the passage of gases in and out of the leaf.

10.12
Respiration
Performed by all organisms
Energy released
Glucose and oxygen used
Carbon dioxide produced
Takes place in mitochondria.

Photosynthesis
Performed by green plants only
Energy stored
Glucose and oxygen produced
Carbon dioxide used
Takes place in chloroplasts

10.13

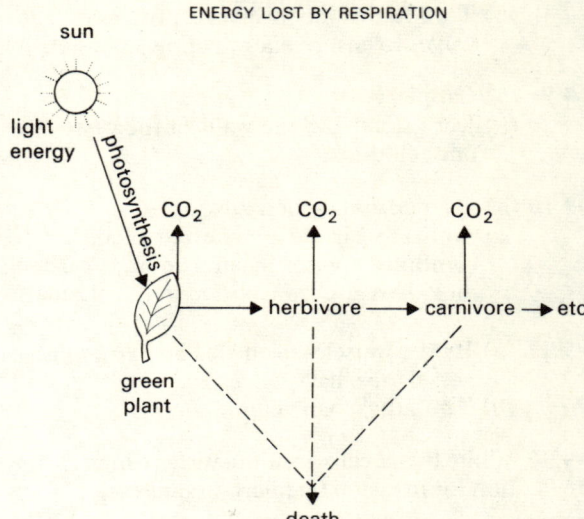

11 Transport in Plants

11.1 (a) Place the leafy shoot in the dye solution. After a period of time, cut sections of the stem and examine under a microscope.
(b) C.
(c) Xylem.

11.2 (i) To make the chlorophyll molecule. (ii) To make proteins. (iii) To make ATP and DNA.

11.3 Place several plants in a nutrient culture solution but omit a different ion in each solution.

11.4 The transport of ions into the plant is an active process requiring energy. (Energy from respiration of carbohydrate.)

11.5 (a) It dies.
(b) That tissue has been removed which is essential for the plant to live.
(c) Phloem.

11.6 If a plant is ringed then food cannot be transported around the plant. Notice also that food is transported mainly to the young leaves which cannot provide themselves with enough food from photosynthesis.

11.7 A = phloem – transports food substances around the plant.
B = cambium – cells divide to produce new xylem and phloem.
C = xylem – transports water and mineral ions from the root upwards to the aerial parts of the plant, particularly the leaves.

D = epidermis – outer covering of stem and helps with support.

11.8 Much more dead tissue in the form of xylem at the middle of a woody stem. Also the phloem forms a continuous ring on the outside of the stem.

12 Water and the Organism

12.1 (a) The whole apparatus would lose weight.
(b) To make sure water is not lost by direct evaporation from the flask.

12.2 (a)

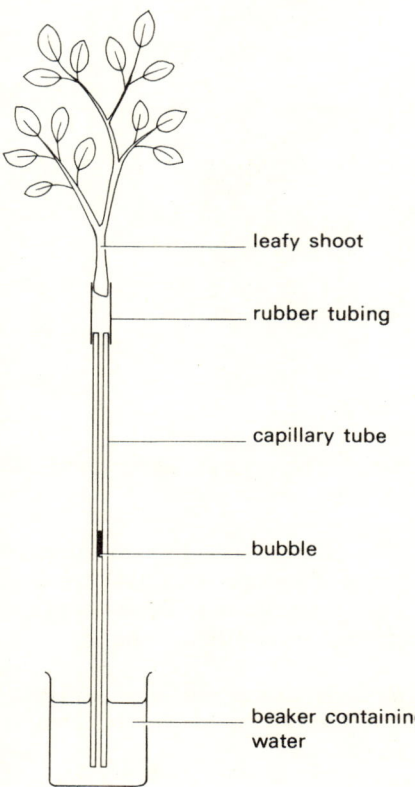

leafy shoot

rubber tubing

capillary tube

bubble

beaker containing water

(b) Place the potometer in each of the conditions listed. Wind, high temperature, light and low humidity increase water loss. Water loss is reduced if there is no wind, low temperature, high humidity and dark.

12.3 (a) Stomata.
(b) If the stomata are open then water loss from the plant is increased and vice versa.
(c) Control passage of air in and out of the leaf.

12.4 (a) The tubing in experiment 1 swells while the tubing in experiment 2 shrinks.
(b) Fluid enters the tubing in experiment 1 and leaves the tubing in experiment 2.

12.5 A semi-permeable membrane.

12.6 (a)

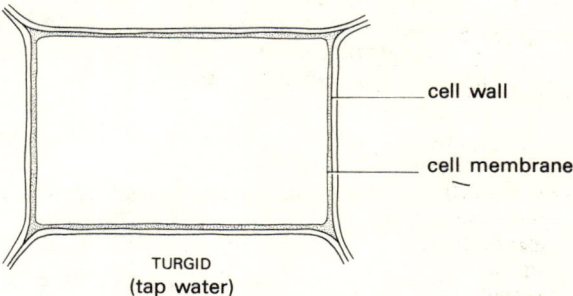

cell wall

cell membrane

TURGID
(tap water)

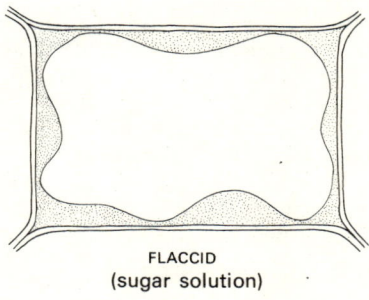

FLACCID
(sugar solution)

(b) See answer to Question **12.4**.

12.7 (a) Turgid.
(b) Flaccid.

12.8 Osmosis is the net flow of water from a weaker solution to a stronger solution through a semi-permeable membrane.

12.9 (a) (i) They would burst. (ii) They would remain normal. (iii) They would shrink.
(b) See answer to Question **12.4(b)**.

12.10 (a) Into the *Amoeba*. Because the cytoplasm of *Amoeba* is more concentrated than the water in which it lives.
(b) Contractile vacuole.

12.11 (a) Into the fish. Because the body fluids of the carp are more concentrated than the water in which it lives.
(b) Mainly by producing much urine.

12.12 (a) From the cod to the sea. Because the sea-water is more concentrated than the body fluids of the cod.
(b) Drinks sea-water, secretes salt, produces little urine.

13 Steady State Mechanisms

13.1 Homeostasis.

13.2 (a) Amount of heat produced by the body.
Heat lost by conduction, convection and radiation.
Amount of insulation.
The environmental temperature.
(b) By increasing insulation and moving to a warmer place.
(c) Increases metabolic rate.
Increases insulation.
Use of clothes in man and raising of the hair layer in mammals.
Decreases blood supply to the skin (vaso-constriction).

13.3 (a) You reduce insulation (take off clothes).
You sweat.
Blood supply to the skin is increased (vaso-dilation).
(b) Sweat on skin could not evaporate due to the humidity.

13.4

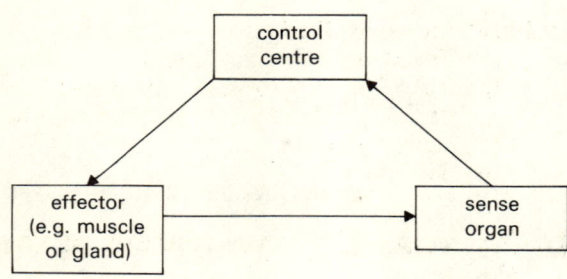

13.5

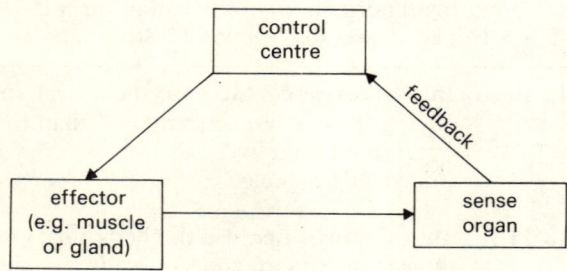

13.6 (a) They both increase.
(b) You continue to breathe rapidly.

13.7 An increased level of carbon dioxide.

13.8 (a) Insulin.
(b) It lowers the blood sugar level.
(c) Diabetes.

13.9 Produces heat.
Regulates blood sugar.
Regulates amino-acids and proteins.
Stores vitamins and minerals.
Purifies blood.
Produces fibrinogen.
Excretes bile pigments.

14 Excretion and Osmoregulation

14.1 (a) A = aorta
B = kidney
C = ureter
D = bladder
E = renal vein
F = renal artery
G = vena cava
(b) By a ring of muscle (sphincter) at the base of the bladder.
(c) Pressure in the bladder.

14.2 A = Bowman's capsule
B = Glomerulus
C = 1st convoluted or proximal tubule
D = Henlé's loop
E = 2nd convoluted or distal tubule
F = collecting duct
G = blood capillary

The Bowman's capsule and the glomerulus allow substances to pass from the capillary to the nephron.

14.3 They will allow through most molecules except the largest. White blood cells, red blood cells and platelets do not pass into the nephron, in addition to the large proteins.

14.4 (a) C, 1st convoluted or proximal tubule.
E, 2nd convoluted or distal tubule.
(b) Glucose, water and certain mineral ions.

14.5 (a) Water.
(b) To carry soluble waste outside the body.
(c) Water is being absorbed.

14.6 (a) A large amount of urine would be produced because the blood will contain excess water.
(b) A small amount of urine would be produced, because the amount of solutes in the blood increase in concentration.

14.7 Ammonia is extremely soluble in water and can be washed away easily in water.

15 Defence against Disease

15.1 (a)

(i) micrococci

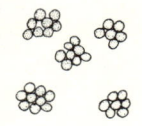

(ii) diplococci

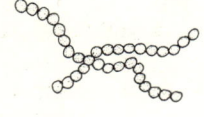

(iii) staphylococci

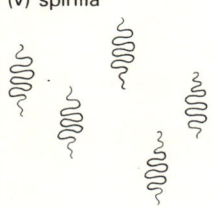

(iv) streptococci

(v) spirilla

(vi) bacilli

(b) E.g. tuberculosis, leprosy, cholera, diphtheria, pneumonia, typhoid.

15.2 E.g. chicken-pox, measles, common cold, poliomyelitis, influenza.

15.3 By droplets from coughing and sneezing.
Contaminated water and food.
Direct contact.
Via animals.

15.4 Efficient sewage disposal.
Clean water supplies.
Efficient rubbish disposal.
Personal cleanliness.
} All these prevent accumulation of harmful bacteria.

15.5 Protection of the skin.
Mucus in respiratory passages.
Acid and enzymes in digestive system.
Bleeding and the formation of clots.
White blood corpuscles (phagocytes).

15.6 (a) Antibodies or antitoxins.
(b) Antigens.

15.7 (a) An organ from one human or animal is placed in another human or animal.
(b) When an organ ceases to work.

15.8 (a) A suspension of inactivated germs which stimulate the production of antibodies, after injection into a person or animal.
(b) Jenner gave his subjects cowpox – a related disease. However, this particular form of immunity is unusual. The situation described in (a) is most common.

15.9 (a) Inactivated germs are injected into an animal such as a horse. The horse produces antibodies. These are extracted from the horse and injected into a human to produce immunity.
(b) Diphtheria and tetanus.

15.10 (a) Alexander Fleming.
(b) From the *Penicillium* fungus.
(c) It is a chemical substance produced from a fungus which causes the death of growing bacteria.
(d) Bacteria.

16 Nervous Communication in the Body

16.1 (a) Afferent neuron or sensory neuron.
(b) Efferent or motor neuron.
(c) Intermediate or association neuron.

16.2 E.g. knee jerk reflex or touching a hot stove with your fingers.

16.3

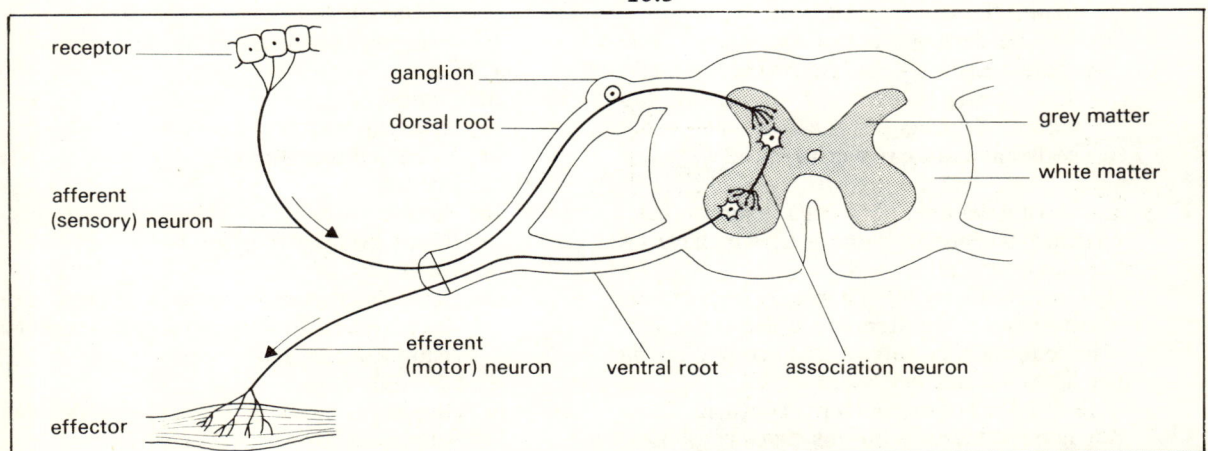

16.4 (a) A = dendron
B = nucleus
C = axon
D = fatty sheath
E = axon endings
F = cell body
(b) To insulate the axon.
(c) A connection between one nerve cell and the next.

16.5 (a) The centre of intelligence, memory and sensation.
(b) Balance and muscular co-ordination is processed here.
(c) Control of unconscious processes, i.e. blood pressure, temperature, etc.

17 Chemical Communication in Animals and Plants

17.1 Hormones.

17.2 (a) A = pituitary
B = thyroid
C = islets of Langerhans
D = adrenal
E = ovary
F = testes
(b) Growth hormone, thyroid stimulating hormone, anti-diuretic hormone and gonadotrophic hormones are produced in the pituitary gland.
Thyroxine is produced in the thyroid gland.
Insulin is produced in the islets of Langerhans.
Adrenalin is produced in the adrenal gland.
Gonadotrophin is produced in the ovary.
Testosterone is produced in the testes.
(c) A general increase in the metabolic rate. If the human is still developing then there is an over increase in size.
(d) When an emergency occurs or the body is under stress. Adrenalin increases the heart beat, breathing rate, blood supply to muscles and blood glucose level.
(e) (i) The development of secondary sexual characteristics – breasts, wide hips, etc. The uterus is prepared to receive and maintain the egg. (ii) Deeper voice, more body hair, more powerful muscles.

17.3 In the first set of experiments it shows that a chemical is secreted from the tip which causes the shoot to bend.
The incision cuts off the supply of hormone to the rest of the stem from the tip. Light also reduces the amount of hormone facing the light.
The third set of experiments confirms that a hormone is responsible for plant responses.

17.4 (a) Lay a broad-bean seed which has simple shoots and roots and lay it with the shoot and root in the horizontal position in the dark. As a control use the apparatus shown in Fig. 17.3 (page 25).
(b) The shoot bends up whilst the root bends down. The control does not bend.
(c) A klinostat.

18 Receptors in Animals

18.1 (a) Light, sound, chemical, pressure, temperature.
(b) Eyes, sensitive to light; ears, sensitive to sound and balance; tongue, sensitive to taste; nose, sensitive to smell; various receptors in the skin, sensitive to touch, heat, etc.

18.2 (a) In the nose and tongue.
(b) Salt, sour, sweet, bitter.

18.3 Travels in straight lines.
Can be reflected, refracted and diffracted.

18.4 Two eyes; they move in unison; need time to adjust from light to dark and from dark to light; eyes can be short-sighted or long-sighted; they can move from side to side and up and down; surface of eye is wet, smooth and curved; they are housed in bony sockets; our field of vision is restricted; eye has a white body, coloured inner ring (the iris) and a black centre (pupil); some of us need spectacles; some of us cannot distinguish colour.

18.5 A = muscle which moves eyeball
B = sclerotic
C = choroid
D = retina
E = yellow spot
F = blind spot
G = optic nerve
H = vitreous humour
I = ciliary muscles
J = lens
K = suspensory ligaments
L = iris
M = pupil
N = cornea
O = aqueous humour
(a) Cornea.
(b) Pupil.
(c) Iris.
(d) Lens.
(e) Retina which contain rods (detect low light intensities) and cones (daylight vision and colour).
(f) Choroid.
(g) Optic nerve.
(h) Sclerotic.

18.6 (a) The lens is naturally elastic and bulges when the suspensory ligaments place no stress on it; it therefore focuses close objects. Under this state the ciliary muscles are contracted. When the ciliary muscles relax the suspensory ligaments are under tension, the lens is pulled thinner and objects a long way away can be focused upon.

(b) The vitreous humour.

18.7 Two ears; can detect souce of sound; can detect high pitch and low pitch sounds; can detect loudness and softness; each ear has an external flap; colds can cause mucus to accumulate and cause temporary deafness; changes in altitude cause detectable changes in pressure within the ears; people tend to lose their sense of hearing as they get older.

18.8 A = outer ear or pinna
B = hammer bone
C = anvil bone
D = semicircular canals
E = sacculus
F = utriculus
G = auditory nerve
H = cochlea
I = stirrup bone
J = Eustachian tube
K = ear-drum (or tympanic membrane)
(a) Pinna.
(b) Ear-drum.
(c) Bones of the ear.
(d) Eustachian tube.
(e) Receptors in the cochlea.
(f) Auditory nerve.

18.9 (a) Hearing would be impaired because the movement of the ear-drum would be restricted. Air pressures in the middle ear would not be able to adjust to the atmospheric pressure.
(b) Impaired hearing because there would be no movement of the ear-drum.

18.10 (a) When you move a pressure is exerted on the hairs by the motion of the fluid.
(b) To cope with the three dimensions of movement.

18.11 Prevention of access of micro-organisms. Protects the underlying tissues from mechanical injury. It contains sense organs which can detect temperature, touch, pain and pressure. It regulates temperature by sweating, or by dilation or constriction of the blood capillaries in the skin.

18.12 (a) A = hair
B = epidermis
C = dermis
D = touch receptor
E = pressure receptor
F = sebaceous gland
G = hair erector muscle
H = sweat gland
I = blood capillary
J = sweat pore
K = hair follicle
(b) The touch receptor, the pressure receptor and the temperature receptor.

19 Structures Which Do Things (Effectors)

19.1 See answers to Questions 17.2 (a) and (b).

19.2 By contracting.

19.3 (a) Tendons.
(b) The force exerted in position 1 would be greater than in position 3.

19.4 So that it can exert maximum force to move the soil away.

19.5 By having a set of two muscles.

19.6 The biceps are the flexors, and the triceps are the extensors.

19.7 Antagonistic harmony.

19.8 (a) ATP (synthesised by the respiration of glucose and oxygen) and oxygen.
(b) Carbon dioxide and lactic acid (if the muscles are working vigorously).

19.9 (a) A = hard bone
B = soft bone
C = cartilage
D = ligament forming a capsule (containing synovial fluid)
E = synovial fluid
(b) The hard bone and the soft bone make up the rigid structure on which movement can be made possible.
The cartilage is shock absorbing.
The ligament connects one bone with another.
The synovial fluid ensures that the joint is well lubricated.

19.10 Diagram (a) = joint at neck
Diagram (b) = joint at foot and ankle
Diagram (c) = arm joint at elbow

20 Movement and Support

20.1 In search of food.
In search of a place to live.
In search of a mate.
Migration.

20.2 Speed; muscular action is more extensive in running and limbs tend to touch the ground less.

20.3 Horses, deer and similar animals; large cats such as lions, cheetahs, etc.

20.4 Horses, frogs, kangaroos. They jump by making powerful contractions of their hind legs.

20.5 Its body is supported by water.

20.6

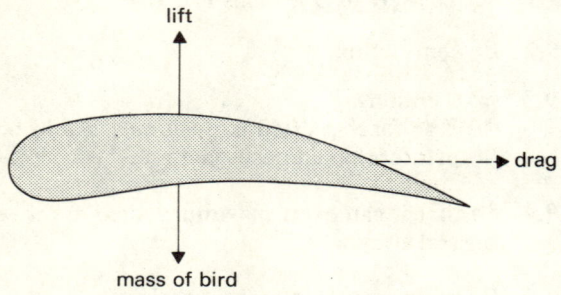

20.7 (a) Drag.
(b) Streamlining.

20.8 (a)

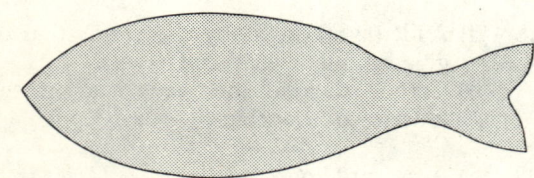

(b) The tail or caudal fin.
(c) Dorsal, ventral and lateral fins.
(d) Make different shapes out of plasticine and drop them into a tall tank of water to see how they "fall" in the water.

20.9 (a) Wind, rain, snow and hail.
(b) A firm stem which can be flexible without breaking. The leaves and stem providing least wind resistance. Water can fall off the leaves easily. Root system provides anchorage in soil.

20.10 The one in water would be firm whereas the one without water would be limp.

21 Behaviour

21.1 Broken eggshells are more conspicuous to predators.

21.2 Place house-flies into a long glass tube. Blacken off half of it. Place flies into the tube and observe where they accumulate.

21.3 Migration of animals and birds; spiders spinning webs; birds building nests; birds incubating eggs.

21.4 The baby is able to make the correct response to enable it to feed.

21.5 A conditioned response.

21.6 (a) Its mother.
(b) The mother is able to look after the chick and protect it.
(c) It would follow the man.

21.7 (i) The hen would try to get through the wire but would not succeed. It lacks the intelligence to go around the wire. (ii) The dog would first try to get through the wire, then look around and eventually run around the wire to the food. Dogs can work out problems more effectively than hens. (iii) The child is likely to run directly around the wire. Its intelligence enables the problem to be worked out quickly.

21.8 Working well at school with praise from teacher; winning at competitive sports; monetary rewards (bribery); the offer of a university place if high enough A level grades are achieved.

21.9 Tasks for the benefit of all can be shared around. Large numbers mean greater protection for individuals.

22 Cell Division

22.1 Cut a small length (about 2 mm) off the end of a root. Transfer to a mixture of hydrochloric acid (separates the cells) and dye (acetic orcein) to make the nucleus show up more clearly. Transfer tip to a microscope slide and place on more dye. Heat the slide for about five seconds, then place on a cover slip and and squash.

22.2 (a) To contain the instructions for the making and reproduction of cells and organisms.
(b) So that new cells contain the same instructions.

22.3 B, D, A, E, C.

22.4 $2n \rightarrow 2n$

22.5 Half the number of chromosomes are produced as compared with the original cell. The daughter cells are haploid.

22.6 (a) Dissect out the testes. Place on a microscope slide with acetic orcein and heat for about five seconds. Squash testes with a cover slip and then observe under a microscope.
(b) Nuclei and chromosomes.

22.7 When fertilisation takes place the haploid cells combine to form a diploid cell with the normal number of chromosomes.

22.8 (a) Growth and replacement of cells and organisms.
(b) Mainly to produce gametes.

22.9 Mitosis $= 2n \rightarrow 2n$
Meiosis $= 2n \rightarrow n$

23 Asexual Reproduction

23.1 (a) Asexual and sexual reproduction.
(b) Asexual reproduction.

23.2 The chromosomes are duplicated exactly.

23.3 Because in asexual reproduction the process of cell division provides the daughter cells with a set of chromosomes identical to those of the parent cells, and thus the genetic instructions are repeatedly duplicated.

23.4

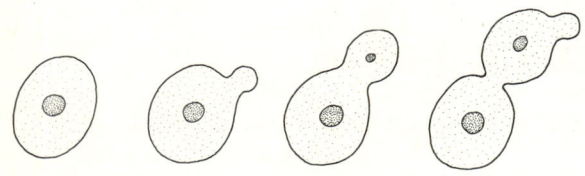

23.5 Root tubers, e.g. dahlia.
Stolons (from stems), e.g. blackberry.
Stem tubers, e.g. potato.
Runners, e.g. creeping buttercup.
Suckers, e.g. chrysanthemum.
Rhizomes, e.g. iris.
Corms and bulbs, e.g. gladiolus, tulip, daffodil.

24 Sexual Reproduction

24.1 (a) Male = sperm; female = egg (or ovum).
(b) Male = pollen; female = ovule.

24.2 A = cell membrane
B = cytoplasm
C = nucleus
D = sperm nucleus
E = tail or flagellum

24.3 (a) 23.
(b) 46.
(c) Zygote.

24.4 Fish and amphibians.

24.5 Internal fertilisation.

24.6 A = bladder
B = ureter
C = prostate gland
D = seminal vesicle
E = urethra
F = penis
G = testis
H = epididymis
I = sperm duct
J = scrotum

24.7 A = ureter
B = oviduct
C = funnel of oviduct
D = ovary
E = vagina
F = vulva
G = urethra
H = bladder
I = uterus

24.8 During one menstrual cycle:
The egg is released (ovulation) on approximately day 14 of the cycle.
The fertile period is from day 11 to day 17.
Graafian follicle in the ovary produces oestrogen (a hormone).
One egg develops in the Graafian follicle.
A uterus lining develops to receive the egg.
If conception has not taken place by day 28, menstruation begins and the uterus lining is rejected.

24.9

Male	Effectiveness
Condom (sheath)	Very effective if used carefully, and is undamaged.
Vasectomy (sperm duct severed)	Totally effective after a period of six months after the operation. Normally irreversible.

Female

The "pill" Very effective but very slight risk of blood clots.

Diaphragm (cervical cap) Quite effective especially if used with spermicidal creams.

The coil (inter-uterine loop) Effective but may be displaced.

Abortion Effective but moral problems involved in killing an unborn human.

Sterilisation (Fallopian tubes tied off) Totally effective almost at once, but irreversible.

24.10 By the wind or via insects.

24.11 To increase the prospect of new genes being incorporated into the daughter seeds.

24.12 (a) A = petal
B = anther
C = filament
D = stamen
E = stigma
F = style
G = ovary wall
H = carpel
I = sepal
J = receptacle
(b) (i) H. (ii) D.

24.13 Pollen lands on stigma. The pollen bursts open and grows into the stigma forming a pollen tube. Nourishment is obtained from the stigma. The nucleus moves down the pollen tube and fertilises the embryo sac which contains the egg nucleus.

25 Mendelian Genetics

25.1 Small, easily identifiable features, short life cycle, large numbers of offspring.

25.2 Place *Drosophila* flies into an etheriser from the culture bottle. Place a little ether in the etheriser and remove flies when anaesthetised.

25.3 An organism which has a characteristic which breeds true over several generations.

25.4 (a) One with small wings.
(b) A normal winged fly.

25.5 (a) + +.
(b) + vg.
(c) One of + +, two of +vg, one of vgvg. 1 : 2 : 1.
(d) One of +vg, one of vgvg. 1 : 1.

25.6 Because it may contain the recessive vg gene.

25.7 XY (male) × XX
X or Y   X   gametes
XX   XY   i.e. 1 : 1 or 50 : 50

26 The Material of Inheritance

26.1 The DNA from the normal bacteria, when placed with the mutant bacteria, allows the mutant strain to grow on the agar plate, i.e. the normal DNA is necessary for the mutant bacteria to be able to use the normal medium.

26.2 The genetic instructions are reproduced exactly.

27 Life Cycles

27.1 All the stages in the life of an organism from the egg to the adult, which in turn produces more eggs.

27.2

adult → egg (female)
sperm (male) → egg (female)
egg → zygote
zygote → cell division → embryo → adult

27.3 (a)

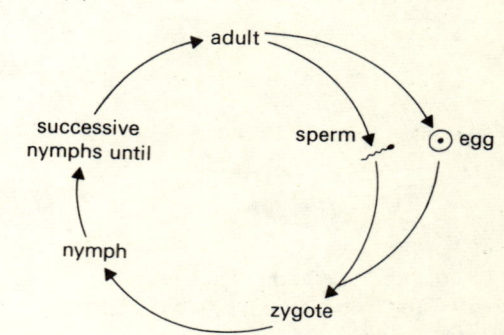

adult → egg
sperm → egg
egg → zygote
zygote → nymph → successive nymphs until → adult

(b) Dragon-fly; cockroach.

27.4 Metamorphosis.

27.5 (a)

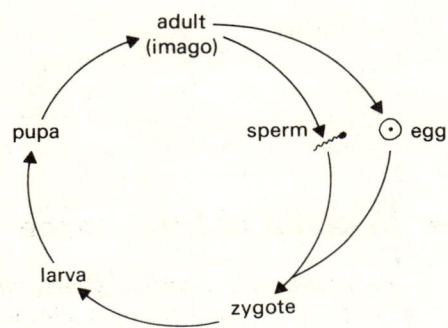

(b) Moths, flies and bees.

27.6

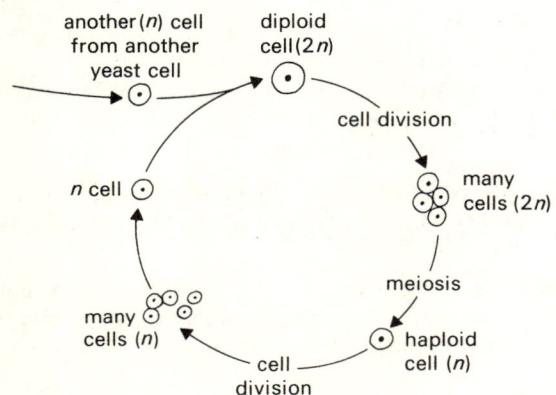

27.7 (a) Alternation of generations.
(b)

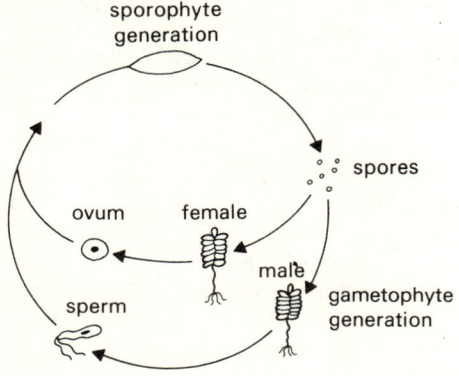

27.8 (a)

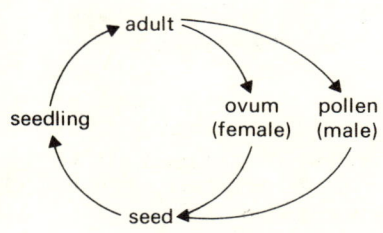

(b) Any flowering plant – buttercups, dandelions, chickweed, trees, bluebells, anemones, grasses, celandines, poppies, clover, thistles, parsley, etc.

28 Growth and Development

28.1

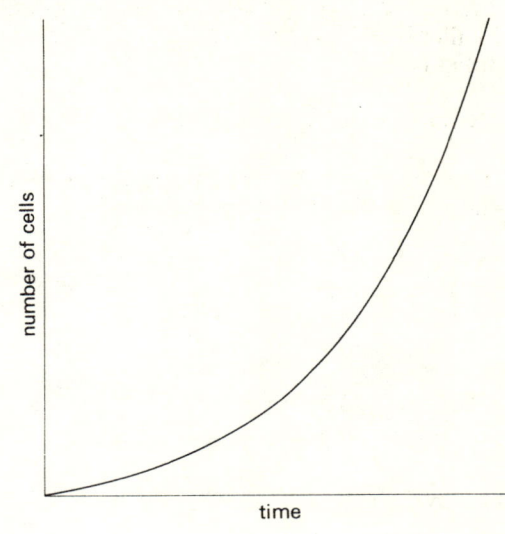

28.2 By measuring any increase in mass, length and volume.

28.3 Development of the brain. Development of the reproductive organs.

28.4 Muscle – cells which contract so that limbs may move, heart can beat, food can be moved along the gut, etc.
Nerve – conducts electrical signals in the body from one part to another.
Skin – provides a hard-wearing outer covering for the body.
Gland – produces substances such as hormones and enzymes.
Connective – binds organs and tissues together.
Lung – allows gas exchange to take place.
Absorptive cells – absorb molecules.

28.5 (a) The seed becomes activated to produce new shoots and roots.
(b) Water, correct temperature, oxygen.

28.6 That the nucleus determines development.

28.7 (a) Generally the survival of the embryos decreases as time passes. The later the nucleus is implanted the less the chance of survival of the embryos.

(b) That the nucleus determines development and that the influence of the nucleus decreases with time.

28.8 Green and white tobacco seedlings.

28.9 White.

28.10 (a) Place the same number of seedlings in Petri dishes which contain discs of filter paper and very dilute hormone. There is a different concentration of hormone in each Petri dish.

(b)

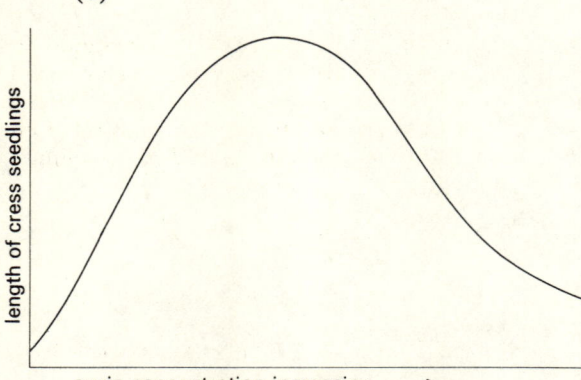

28.11 Thyroxine.

29 Dispersal in Organisms

29.1 Wind, water, animal, self-dispersal.

29.2 Either it is very light or it possesses buoyancy aids such as hairs or large air spaces within the seed.

29.3 (a) By seeds becoming attached to him.
By seeds being carried alongside other seeds that man deliberately wants to plant.
By man eating fruits.
(b) There are a number of possible experiments so check your answer with your teacher.

29.4 (a) A = wind
B = self
C = wind
D = animal
E = animal
F = wind and self
(b) A fruit is the ovary wall and the enclosed seed.

29.5 Most trees. Willow-herb, dandelion, bulrush.

29.6 A flagellum.

29.7 (a) Use a choice chamber. Place the blowfly larvae in the central opening. (i) Put the particular type of food in one chamber and none in the other and observe which chamber the maggots are attracted to. (ii) Make one chamber dark and the other light and observe which chamber the maggots congregate in.
(b) Use a large quantity of maggots and repeat the experiment a number of times.

30 Soil

30.1 (a) By erosion of rock. Dead organic material may be mixed with this.
(b) Man can increase the fertility by adding manure and fertiliser.
Man can decrease fertility by over-cultivation.

30.2 A vertical section through the soil.

30.3 Heat soil (which is dry) to quite a high temperature, weighing beforehand. At the end of the experiment heat until there is no further decrease in weight.

30.4 The largest particle would settle first, followed by the next largest particle and so on until the smallest particle had settled.

30.5 (a)

	Topsoil	Subsoil
Air content	High	Low
Temperature	More variable	More constant
Illumination	Lighter	Dark
Dampness	Variable	Generally damp
Particle size		Both variable

(b) Soil does not become waterlogged.
Humus provides air spaces which allow oxygen to the roots.
Humus retains moisture.
Humus absorbs minerals from the soil.
Humus binds the soil together and prevents particles from being blown away.

30.6 (a) Water flows through the sandy soil fastest and the clay soil slowest.

(b)

	Clay	Loam	Sand
Particle size	Very small	Mixture of clay and sand	Quite large
Air content	Almost none	Good	Very good
Water content	Waterlogged	Drain well	Dries out quickly

30.7 The lamp heats up, and so dries and illuminates the soil. The animals try to get away from this.

30.8 (a) A = head
B = saddle
C = segment
D = posterior end
(b) It aerates the soil by burrowing.
It turns over soil by passing it through its digestive system.
It drags leaves into the soil to provide humus.

30.9

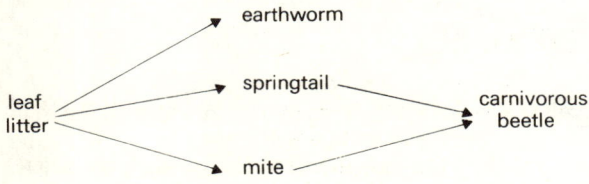

30.10 (a) From lightning.
From nitrogen-fixing bacteria.
From decay of dead organisms.
Nitrates already existing in soil.
(b) A = nitrogen
B = nitrate
C = nitrite
D = nitrifying bacteria.
E = bacteria
F = bacteria
G = bacteria
H = denitrifying bacteria
I = lightning

30.11 (a) Respiration.
(b)

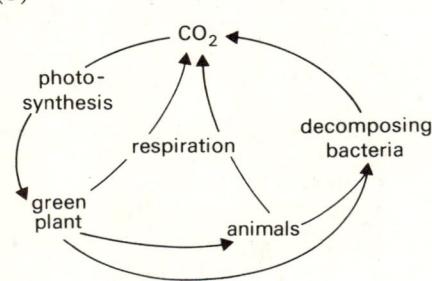

31 Colonisation of a Habitat

31.1 (a) A particular area of the environment which contains its own community of organisms.
(b) A place to breed, obtain food, and to shelter.

31.2 An owl; a badger; a robin; a rhinoceros; a stickleback; a lizard.

31.3 A few species of mould develop on the bread, but over a period of time new species are seen developing and the old species die out.

31.4 (a) Competition.
(b) Rapid growth, large leaves, effective reproductive capacity.
(c) Water and light.

31.5 An organism is able to colonise a habitat and able to reproduce over many generations.

31.6 Because of lengthy parental care.

31.7 (a) The tree.
(b) A forest would eventually emerge unless prevented from doing so by unfavourable soils or climatic conditions. Deserts, tundra and savannah are examples of one form of sub-climax called a climatic climax.

31.8 Rabbits; sheep; goats.

31.9 The leaves on an oak tree allow the light in far more effectively than beech leaves.
Oak leaves have a higher nutritious content than do beech leaves.

32 Energy Flow through Ecosystems and Communities

32.1 A green plant.

32.2

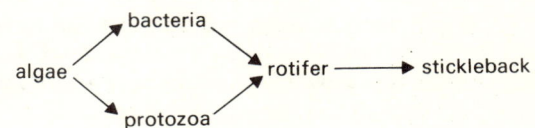

32.3 The total mass of producers far exceeds that of consumers.

32.4 A = sparrow-hawks
B = robins
C = caterpillars
D = aphids
E = vegetation

32.5 C.

32.6

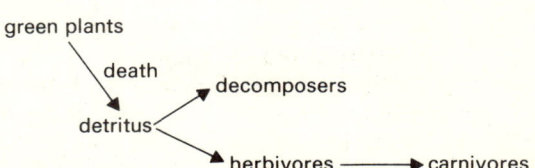

33 Man and the Environment

33.1 (a) Wind or rain.
(b) Erosion.

33.2 Competition between the crop plants.

33.3 The growth of plants is inhibited. Lichens, in particular, suffer.

33.4 A number of fish would die.

33.5 The poisons would be concentrated in the organisms at the end of food chains.

33.6 Many invertebrates such as wood-lice, spiders, flies and beetles. Also some mammals such as foxes, grey squirrels, rats and mice. Birds include sparrows and starlings.

34 Associations between Organisms

34.1 (a) A plant which lives on the surface of another plant.
(b) Pleurococcus, ferns, moss.

34.2 (a) An animal which lives on the surface of another animal.
(b) A sea anemone on the shell of a hermit-crab; barnacles on shells; vorticella on water-fleas.

34.3 (a) (i) Bacteria and fungi. (ii) The house-fly.
(b) Enzymes are released by the organism directly and externally on to a food source. The food is reduced to a liquid which is absorbed back into the body of the organism.

34.4 (a) Parasite.
(b) Warm, dark, damp, full of nutritious liquid, enzymes.
(c) Lack of light.
(d) Stomach: partially digested food. Small intestine: products of digestion such as glucose and amino-acids. Large intestine: largely indigested waste products.

34.5 (a) Means of access, e.g. teeth or boring organs.
Means of remaining on the host, e.g. hooks and suckers.
Protection against the host's defences, e.g. tough outer covering.
Other features include lack of sense organs and phenomenal reproductive capacity.
(b) (i) Disease-causing organisms such as bacteria and fungi, tapeworms or flukes.

(ii) Dodder, mistletoe.
(c) By drugs.

34.6 (a) Symbiosis.
(b) The fungus uses some of the food produced by the algae whilst the fungus supplies water and minerals to the algae.
(c) Bacteria in root nodules of leguminous plants. The bacteria supply the plant with nitrogen while the plant supplies the bacteria with food and a place to live.
Honey-bees and flowers. The bee pollinates the flower and the bee obtains nectar.
Cleaner birds and crocodiles. The bird cleans the crocodile's teeth and the crocodile gives the bird protection against predators and allows the bird to obtain food from its teeth.
Damselfish and sea anemone. The fish removes digestive wastes whilst the anemone provides protection to the fish.
Wood-lice in ants' nest. Wood-louse obtains food in the form of ant waste, whilst the ants provide protection for the wood-louse.

35 Mutation and Variation

35.1 Mutation.

35.2 (a) The problem of preventing other organisms contaminating the experiment.
(b) Flame innoculation loop. Flame top of culture bottle. Cool loop in sterile water and then scrape a little of the bacteria on to the loop. Transfer bacteria on loop quickly to the Petri dish of nutrient agar, opening the lid for as little time as possible. Flame the loop to kill residual bacteria.
(c) To make sure that all apparatus and surfaces are sterile.
Transfer organisms quickly to avoid contamination.
See information in (b).

35.3 (a) Bacteria cannot grow on this clear zone.
(b) A new strain of bacteria is able to grow in the presence of penicillin.

35.4 (a) Pieces of chromosome have been rearranged in a different order.
(b) The number of chromosomes have increased to above that which is normal.
For example, an organism with $2n = 4$ could mutate to $2n = 8$.
(c) Pieces of the DNA have been broken off, rearranged or added to.

35.5 (a) Because they have inherited genetic information from both the mother and father.

This information will have been passed down through parents and children over many generations.

(b) (i) Very little. (ii) Because of cell division and reproduction by mitosis.

36 Selection

36.1 Lack of food, but the majority are eaten by other organisms.

36.2 (a) Birds.
(b) (i) Dark and grimy, little lichen growth. (ii) Covered with lichen.
(c) (i) The light-coloured variety would show up more clearly than the dark variety. (ii) The opposite to that in (i).
(d) In rural areas the light-coloured moth is better disguised against predators than the dark variety, whereas the opposite occurs in industrial areas.
(e) Camouflage.

36.3 Heterozygous.

36.4 The heterozygous genotype.

36.5 The sickle cell gene confers a resistance against malaria.

36.6 Different breeds of dogs. Selection of cattle and grain crops.

37 Evolution

37.1 A large number of eggs is produced.

37.2 Not all the offspring survive to maturity.

37.3 Some are better able to survive by possessing favourable features, e.g. they are stronger, they can escape from predators more quickly.

37.4 Mutation and by sexual reproduction.

37.5 Possessing camouflage, e.g. stick insect.
Tall plants such as trees.
Ability to run fast, as in deer.
Possession of strength, claws and fangs.
Aggressive behaviour.
Brilliant plumage in birds.
Ability to produce a large number of offspring.

37.6 For example, the Galapagos finches. One species of finch arrives from the mainland to the Galapagos islands. They reproduce and rapidly increase in numbers until there is competition for food. Most die off but a few survive because they possess favourable beak features which enable them to take advantage of new food opportunities. This situation operating over many generations and a long period of time has led to many species of finch on the different islands.

37.7 No.

37.8 Fossils, comparative anatomy, selection in nature, study of embryos, artificial selection, biochemical tests (immunology).

Index

Page numbers in brackets indicate that the actual word can be found in the answer section even though the word does not appear on that page.

Doing Bombers off the Jetty!

for our own children—Belinda, Anna, Alexander, Lucy, Lachy, Molly and Emily

Doing Bombers off the Jetty!

Models for Writing Poetry

Peter McFarlane &
Rory Harris

MACMILLAN

First published 1996 by
MACMILLAN EDUCATION AUSTRALIA PTY LTD
627 Chapel Street, South Yarra 3141
Reprinted 1998

CONTENTS

To the student

Doing Bombers off the Jetty! is a book of voices, some old and some not so old. The young voices collected here have read, listened to, responded to, and written their own poems by way of modelling. We invite you to do the same. That is, hang your ideas on to the forms and styles described in this book.

Your tasks are to read, write and experiment. There is no right or wrong, only successful or less successful poems — those that move you and those that don't quite hit the mark. When you've got it right, someone will tell you. You may even get that shiver as you write and know you are on to something worth continuing with. Then, when you have finished a poem, begin the next one. There is always another poem.

Doing Bombers off the Jetty! is also a book to read out aloud and perform from, not once but many times. There's a line from an old poem called 'The Rain Stick' by Seamus Heaney that reads 'Through the ear of a raindrop. Listen now again.' What is wonderful about this line is its many meanings. Raindrops with ears, raindrops which hear, wet ears, ears shaped like raindrops, raindrops shaped like ears . . . the list is almost endless. The exciting thing about the poem is that the poet tells the reader to 'Listen'.

We invite you to write not once, but again and again until you get it right, until your reader will want to 'Listen now again.'

To the teacher

Doing Bombers off the Jetty! is designed to be used with classes in the middle years of secondary school, but it has applications elsewhere, and can be readily adapted and used by anyone interested in writing poetry.

The book contains a wide range of poetic forms and styles, with models varying from the traditional to the innovative. Each of the models is examined in a separate section, and within each of these is a simple series of steps that students can follow to produce poems of their own.

At the end of each section there are specific suggestions for students to create a poetry collection of their own. We recommend that you implement these suggestions either by working through the book from beginning to end or by working across the text.

As the examples from young writers in this book indicate, all of the material has been successfully trialed in the classroom. A few sections are a bit more demanding than others but in most cases, students and their teachers have used them and experienced that instant success that is so important to building confidence in themselves as writers.

Success in writing comes also from the reading and sharing of our work with others. This is particularly so in the case of poetry. It is important to read poems well. If we as teachers let our students hear the power in their own poems, then they will take on that power. The best way of doing this is to have informal performances in the classroom, but these can be heightened if in some cases the students rehearse their poems and give them a more public performance.

Breath length poems

The long line is a very commonly chosen poetic form, usually with poets using a beat word or phrase such as 'School is' or 'I love' at the beginning to get it going. Breath length poems rely on a rush of words. As the lines of the poem accumulate each one adds meaning to the others, adding to the poem's force and impact.

> I love walking along the beach
> with the wind in my hair
> I love eating chocolate at night
> when I'm alone
> I love . . .

⚡ Writing your own

Keeping the features of the breath length model in mind, take five or so minutes to write a love poem of your own. Don't worry if you don't finish your poem in this time. With your teacher's direction, and taking it in turns, select one line from your poem and read it around the class so that in effect the class is reciting its own 'I love' poem. This was how Sharon Slade's 'I Like Doing Bombers off the Jetty' initially began

> I like doing bombers off the jetty
> I like the minister's son
> I like riding my bike in the rain
> I like . . .

After she had written this poem Sharon was invited to transform it into a new and special form by lengthening each line to a breath length the way the American poet Allen Ginsberg did in his long poem, 'Howl'.

from 'Howl'

> I saw the best minds of my generation destroyed by madness,
>   starving hysterical naked,
> dragging themselves through the negro streets at dawn looking for
>   an angry fix,
> angelheaded hipsters burning for the heavenly connection to the starry
>   dynamo in the machinery of night,
> who poverty and tatters and hollow-eyed and high sat up smoking
>   in the supernatural darkness of coldwater flats floating across the tops
>   of cities contemplating jazz,
> who . . .
> who . . .

Ginsberg went on for another eight pages, forcing the readers to take deep breaths as they returned to each beat word or phrase ('who' in Part I, 'Moloch' in Part II, and 'I'm with you in Rockland' in Part III), but Sharon Slade was satisfied with simply using the beat words 'I like' and only writing one typed page.

To get some idea of the importance of the breath length and what it is saying, Sharon's poem needs to be read out loud with everyone joining in on the title and the references to the minister's son, and individuals chosen by your teacher reciting each stanza. After a quick rehearsal even the first stanza can be read in one breath.

I Like Doing Bombers off the Jetty

I like doing bombers off the jetty when the tide's right & the day's hot & the
     water's cold & a small school of white bait has just swum under the jetty &
     into the sun so I can land on top of them & scatter all the fish & when I bob
     up all I can see through lids closed to keep out the salt sea sting is white
     froth and bubbles everywhere.
I also like the minister's son.
I like riding my bike in the violent slashing rain & coming home cold & wet to
     burn the roof of my mouth with hot HOT HOT milo & then go all-out-piggy
     on heavenly tasting shop-bought biscuits with cream (YUM!) centres.
I also like watching lightning with the minister's son.

I like spending my weekly paycheck on dangling silver jewellery & the latest *Dolly*
      magazine & (begging Mum) I just HAVE to get that gorgeous batik print
      material from Rita's Rags & I do want to get the next book in the Mallorean
      series: pity it's not published yet.
I also like buying a Valentine's card for the minister's son.
I like Saturday mornings on holidays in Adelaide when I can spend hours in
      bookstores & then not be able to decide which of those seventeen books I
      like the look of I will actually buy.
I also like reading books with the minister's son.
I like clean white pages just begging for me to scribble a poem on them & now
      I've gone and messed this one up 'cos I simply can't resist a new page.
I also like writing letters to the minister's son.
I like the subtle symmetry I find in poetry & the way the right words to use flow
      from my mind to my fingers & down onto the paper where they look so real
      not at all like the stubborn whimsical & elusive things they really are.
I also like kissing the minister's son.
I like lying in bed with my head & shoulders propped up with big fluffy pillows &
      watching the sun get up behind my pink curtains through lazily half-closed
      eyes & wondering what the day ahead has in store for me.
I also like day-dreaming of the minister's son.
I like all of these things because I am me & they symbolise all that I am was & will
      be & without them I would not be me & with them I am a complete person
      for they are me & I like that.
But the minister's son likes my pink curtains and I DON'T!

Sharon Slade

After listening to this, go back to the 'I love' poem that you wrote and try blowing out each of your lines to a breath length. Feel free to change the pattern. It's good if each breath length shows variation, and if your final poem surprises the reader as Sharon's did (there was only one reference to the minister's son in her original poem).

Amy Spiers first wrote an 'I love' poem called 'I love my room'. Her expanded version becomes

I love my room: the blue walls, the pre-Raphaelite posters, the Botticelli
Venus, MC Escher, and my grandmother's cupboard which I got to keep
when she died

Will Mooney's 'I Love Walking Through the Wilderness at Morning' becomes

> I love walking through the wilderness at morning when the sun's first light casts glorious shadows and reveals tiny plants sparkling with fresh dew

Melinda Tew's 'I Love Being in Bed' becomes

> I love being in bed on a stormy night, hearing the melodic beat of the rain against my windows and the gentle swoosh of the cars over the wet road outside

David O'Donohue's 'I Love Drinking Ice Cold Coke' becomes

> I love drinking ice cold coke on a steaming hot day in the summer where the drink slowly splashes down my throat cooling it splash by splash

Claire Spiers's 'I Love the Winds and Waters' becomes

> I love the winds and waters when I utterly convince myself I could tame the waves and the winds make me think of wolves and subtle stupid things

You may not need to expand your opening lines. Morgan Vaudrey's first attempt was perfect

> I love the wooden chair that sits on my verandah and moves in the wind as though someone is there

Chad Farr's opening line 'I love watching the sun's reflection' required only a little expansion

> I love watching the sun shine and reflect off the sea waters of a morning and birds hovering around schools of fish and passing trawlers going out to the deep blue sea

The total effect comes when you put all of your lines together. Ian H's 'I love playing soccer, I love watching soccer, I love going home from school, I love writing stories about the forest' develops real force when its expanded version is read as one poem.

> I like playing soccer when the temperature is just right and the ground is
> muddy and I can fall over and get as muddy as I want
>
> I like watching soccer on a warm day seeing the players in their strips
> watching all of them doing what I would love to do one day
>
> I like going home from school and all the worries of school work are left
> behind
>
> I love writing stories about the forest and jungles because it makes me feel
> like I'm there and doing all the things that are fun and not boring like here

When you have finished, or after you have had enough time to write something significant, repeat the performance that you did earlier — with each of you reading one of your lines in turn around the class. Your class could join in on key words, or develop responses to some of the things said.

> I love watching my sister explode with anger
> *Wicked*
> I love watching my brother bounce off the walls
> *Yeah*

All of the poems will be different and will very much reflect the personalities and interests of the writers.

Sophie Harrison took the opportunity to use her imagination and have some fun with the things she liked.

I Like to Run on the Banks of the Creek

> I like to run on the banks of the creek with my toes digging into the sand,
> my hair flying loose over my shoulders and the sweet sound of
> running water filling my ears, then down into the cool, fresh water
> rolling up my jeans, slipping into the water and then getting up
> again, laughing, brushing myself off and on along the stream.
> I like to sit tall on a stool in the eventful kitchen and enjoy my family who
> proceed to ditch pots, pans and wooden spoons at me as I run
> laughing from the kitchen and up a tree where I am a spectator to the
> diversion I have made as Dad comes in to find my mother screaming,
> the soup boiling over, the dog barking, my sister shouting insults at
> me, and me, myself, laughing.

I like to sit cosy on the hearth in front of the fire while the wind blows
    strong outside, playing with the trees, snow billowing down, flakes
    falling from the wind-blown gums, the moon shining through and a
    fog setting in, frosting the window panes.

I like to play in autumn as the leaves tumble down and the wind tosses the
    trees and I fall deep in a pile of crackly, stiff leaves and toss them up
    in a shower above me, leaves and twigs attaching themselves to my
    hair and woollen jumper as I laugh and play on the leaves.

I like to go to the beach on a hot summer's day when the sun shines bright
    and the sand burns bare feet as umbrella stands scatter and bodies lie
    like slabs of meat on a counter and young kids and dogs splash and
    swim in the water and mothers sit sipping champagne under $400
    shade tents.

I also like to write poems that sound good but may have nothing to do
    with me.

Sophie Harrison

Julian Reichl took the opportunity to write a self-portrait.

I Like Surfing at the Beach

I like surfing at the beach when the sun's coming up and when the sun's
    going down and I like walking up the beach after a big storm.

I like playing cricket in the summer when it is very hot and hockey in the
    winter when it is very wet and muddy and I like beating people that I
    don't like.

I like all sorts of food but especially spaghetti bolognaise and fish and
    chips because they are my favourites and licking a drippy icy pole on
    a very hot day when no-one else has any.

I like girls on the beach with bikinis and I like dogs on the beach chasing
    seagulls.

I like all animals but especially my dogs when the sun's going down on a
        hot day and there's about to be a thunderstorm.
I like riding a horse all day and taking lunch and tea with me so that I
        don't have to come home until I feel like it.
I like going to the cricket when the crowd's fired up and there are lots of
        big sixes being hit and Merv and Warnie are taking lots of wickets.
I like waking up in the holidays really early to the sound of surf and
        paddling out before the sun's come up and no-one else is out.

Julian Reichl

 ## Looking at other poems

The possibilities for breath length poems are endless. Look at other American writers such as Kenneth Koch and Walt Whitman who used the long line extensively in their poetry, and try their methods. Or try using other beat words such as 'Why?'

Why?

Why is it that every time I decide to use the hair drier, I step outside and it is pouring and I have to walk all the way to school in the rain and by the time I get there my hair is wet again?

Dance competition's in three weeks.

Why is it that any time I feel like having toast for breakfast there's no bread and I end up having cereal instead?

I wonder if Mum's got all my costumes finished.

Why is it when you are so small and innocent you always want 'boobies' but by the time you are old enough to have them you don't want them any more?

What will my hair look like, I wonder?

Why is it that when you kiss someone you always worry about what they'll think and you hope that you're doing it right because you don't want them to laugh about you to their mates?

I really need to practise that last step.

Why is it that when you walk into a classroom and you see clean desks you always want to write rude words and draw disgusting pictures all over them but you know the teacher is going to tell you off anyway?

I bet I'll be against that girl who always wins!

Why is it that your knickers drawer is always the top drawer and whenever your friends are in your room going through your drawers they always open the top drawer first and right in the middle are the bright red knickers with little mushrooms on them that your gran gave you for Christmas last year?

I'll probably get too excited and fall off the stage.

Why is it that when you go to the beach everyone else is slipping on shirts and slapping on hats and slopping on sun cream and you are wearing nothing and piling on tanning lotion and at the end of the day everyone else goes home tanned and you are still as white as a sheet?

My legs always look fatter than everyone else's.

Why is it that when you say something really funny no-one listens and you are the only one laughing and whenever you say something really stupid and wish you had never opened your mouth, everyone laughs at you?

I might win. Stranger things have happened!

Bianca Millard

Another way is to try to focus on an issue of importance or concern to you, and give yourself a restricted time limit of thirty seconds to a minute to write each long line of 'breath'.

Placed and Forgotten

They don't understand, they don't want to, they don't have time, they're all too busy, caught up in their own lives. Perhaps I'm a shadow, a darkness in the corner, always lurking, never revealed.

Perhaps I should change, shed light on myself, summon attention, colour my blackness. What if I was loud, unavoidable and interrupting?

What if I did this and I was noticed, if I came forward and was laughed at, if I was loud and was told to be quiet, or worse, if they didn't notice me and my efforts were in vain?

I'd retreat back into darkness, to lurk in the corner, to relapse to a shadow. I'd stay to ask myself forever the eternal question, why I can't live in a world where everyone is treated as equals and no-one is placed and forgotten.

Kellie Wheatcroft

You may want to do as Donna Gross did—read Allen Ginsberg's 'Howl', and write your own poem in a similar style in which you express your own concerns about the future of your friends, 'the best minds of your own generation.'

Dear Friends

Dear friends who peel the orange until its heart is free to roam amongst
    the buttercups

    who ride in carriages moving through thought to reach a destination
    of emptiness

    who pray for dreaming because reality is such a shrivelled rose from
    an ex-lover shining dullness over existence

    who soak in the blood of homo-sapiens just for the sake of getting
    turned on

    who slide across give-way signs, half deliberately, half because they
    were drunk

    who wander solitary through laneways at dusk searching aimlessly for
    past purities and dealer's houses

    who fall deep into vicious circles of drug abuse, physical abuse,
    emotional abuse until they break

    who are terrified of smiling in case someone becomes offended by
    lack of teeth due to high levels of sugar intake

    who scream the screams of those in pain because they are afraid of
    silence

    who have unrealistic ideas and are under the impression that talk will
    change the world although no-one wants to listen

    who feel like nobodies because too many comparisons are made and
    lonely minds get twisted into bruised mushrooms consigned to the
    bin

who cry until tears dehydrate the muscle of mind and sleep only to wake with salty moisture issuing from eyelashes again

who stay or leave or laugh or cry or dream or fear or sleep or become insomniacs

who hate silence

To all those revelling in simplicity, reaching the point of blankness and mingling colours until all life becomes brown

those drifting on the perimeter, turning circles and becoming lost in waves of dizziness

those laughing at the world's denigration because otherwise there will be 'lemming' suicides

those playing 'midst the debris after the atom bomb of realisation has fallen

those pruning flower bushes on starry nights to watch the evil shadows of the clippers on the naked lawns

those dancing through the oceans of never-ending luscious dreams, drowning in the nightmares

those calling to the valleys just to witness echo and smile at their own voice talking to them

those lying in corners hoping for added comfort, therefore rest but the luminescent light of interrogation ceases to disconnect

those whose stomachs moan, calling for solidity before the body disintegrates

those on the verge of drug addiction, suicide, fame, depression as well as already there

those small fragments of creatures in human form lingering on the outskirts of the onion skin craving any escape

To all those beneath, away from, or on the face of the planet
Don't fall!

Donna Gross

Starting your collection

It is important that you look back over the diverse range of poems you have written during the year to see what you have achieved. The best way of doing this is to collect all of your poems on disk and keep hard copies in a folder or a book. In this way, you will be taking poetry seriously and doing what all poets do when they start out — making a first collection of their poetry. Start your collection by using any of the poems you have written as part of this unit (or photocopies of poems by other writers that you particularly like).

The moment of taking writing seriously occurred for Rory Harris when he bought a sixty-five dollar Adler typewriter. Before owning the machine he'd written long rambling journals and poems on loose leaf sheets and collected them in folders. Owning the typewriter made the print 'real' — the poems looked professional. The typewriter liberated him from pen and folder, and validated what he was writing. The dots on the pages took on a new meaning.

By the end of the year, he had collected about thirty edited and typed poems. He produced ten copies of the manuscript on a photocopier, called the collection *over the outrow*, and gave it away for Christmas presents. Printing the collection ten times meant that he had a book out. Years later, he used the same title again for his first major poetry collection.

When Peter McFarlane started writing he collected all of his poems in a ring binder. The ones he was happiest with he posted off to see if a magazine, journal or newspaper was interested in publishing them. Usually they were rejected, but every now and then he received the good news that a poem had been accepted. When that happened, he obtained copies of the published poem, and added the acceptance to a list in the front of his collection.

Once he had enough 'finished' and published poems, he titled the collection *My Grandfather's Horses* after a line in one of the poems, then had it published as a book.

Speed writing poems

Speed writing is a marvellous way of getting rid of writer's block, of tapping into the subconscious, and coming up with witty and uninhibited poetry. It involves selecting a topic and writing anything you like about it within a given time limit.

 ## Getting started

Begin by selecting a word, object or idea and speed write about it for one minute. Write in sentences, but allow your ideas and words to associate freely. Don't worry if your writing is ungrammatical or if your words and ideas do not make sense. Don't stop writing. If you can't think of anything new to write, just continue writing the word you are on until the writing frees up and more words tumble out. When you have finished, count up the number of words you have written. You could get fifteen or even more.

Now read your piece to your writing partner. If you heard a piece that you think others would enjoy hearing, ask the poet to read it aloud to the rest of the class.

Select another focus and write for three minutes. Aim at trebling the number of words that you wrote in one minute. Read your work to your writing partner and read out a few poems in class.

Look at Ania Walwicz's poem 'Big Time' and listen while it is read aloud by your teacher or a member of the class. Notice how Ania allows her thoughts to range widely and skip in playful everyday language.

Big Time

Wanted some good moments. Some hot times. Some sharp things that I couldn't forget. Hotter than life to feel like that. Something great. And proud. More or less like that. No small time low down. No just so and so. I was after bull's eye. And perfect. So it couldn't be more taut. That it was in the right spot. Want to be a star. Not the fourth girl in the back line of the chorus. But centre forward. Had enough playing half-back. Don't want to be half-back anymore. So I wanted to be right there in the front. And not necessarily strong.

But feeling a lot more than most. Be the doer or have it done to. Didn't matter. I can play any role. As long as there is this one big moment for me there. As long as there is. I was looking for anything and everything to make me more than I was. And I was only small. And not much. Hardly anything. So I had no choice but to go looking for some good times. And something stronger than lemonade. And brighter than cream. And louder than a whisper. And warmer than lukewarm. And bigger than my room that was too small. And better. I knew I would get better. For sure. You just know these things. Deep down. There was this pearl for the diver. Gold for the finder. Silver for the girls. Sparklets for the mister. Red for the bull. Big time moments for me. Fireworks for this girl. That lived at night. Ate chocolate.

Ania Walwicz

Walwicz's first collection of poetry, *Writing*, contained fifty-four poems written in this style. The poems varied in length from fifty words to 500, they varied in their moods and rhythms according to the topic that she chose to write about, but they were all similar in that they were all presented as blocks of words.

A good way of writing with some of the wit, inventiveness and originality of Walwicz's poetry is to speed write for a longer time, say five minutes. Select a focus of your own, some object or idea that is important to you. If you can't think of anything, select a colour, or write about something that is in the room such as a window or a clock. Don't worry about grammar or spelling — these can be tidied at the end, or the piece can be put in lower case and left unpunctuated like Kate Sheehan's 'eyes'.

eyes

open shut them open shut them clap clap eyes soft green can be blue witches' eyes are purple my eyes are my eyes I kiss your lips and close my eyes take me away to your place for tea you say I have beautiful eyes like the sea you say the sea maybe but I know much and knowing much let you see through your eyes I see the world big round square no oblong shapes eyes back to eyes tell me what else you see I say he says I see you are sad I am not sad I say not very sad but you wouldn't marry me I cry through my eyes my eyes are full too full so they close open shut them shut I am not here you are gone you are not here I cannot see you I cannot see only with a stick I see I can touch but not see I cry I cannot see you you cannot say I have beautiful eyes I love you please come out of the dark out of the shadows come here I need you I need you you need me I need you I can't see don't you understand?

Kate Sheehan

Eyes

Eyes. Her eyes were a deep blue, deeper than any blue I've ever seen before, almost like an ocean, that's what her eyes reminded me of, the ocean. Tumbling waves, crashing onto the sandy shore, salty water stinging her eyes, fish, the colourful fish that swim beneath the surface of the water, in another world, in their own world, a world where only they can swim, swim far away until they reach the sunset, swim down amongst the seaweed, shells and sharks, the whole bang lot all cramped into the deep blue sea, the bottom of the deep blue sea, all alone in their world, a world of their own.

Naomi Martin

Chaos

Chaos. People running. The whole world rushing. Late for school. Late for work. People crashing into each other. Yelling, shouting, screaming. Got to go where I want to go. Late. Have to hurry. Have to keep up with the ever moving world. Get to school. Crowded. Noisy. Hot. Cold. Running to class. Drop my books. Everyone laughs. No-one cares. Pick them up and keep on going. Have to go. Have to keep on going. Never like to sleep or rest. Work. Work. No playing around. Work. All work no play. School work. Housework. Always worrying. Go to bed. Wake up. The world is still in a mad rush. No-one waits for anyone or anything. Everyone hurrying. Not caring about what is happening. Only thinking about themselves, no-one else.

Nadia Berezansky

Clock

Time oh no, oh no, oh no I'm always late. The time is approaching oh dear, let's go, right now, off we go this very instant. Watches, clocks, especially my clock. It goes so fast. Hurry hurry hurry, speed speed speed. Quickly now, out the door, I think I've made it. Frazzle dazzle hurry it up, can't be late all the time. What's the time? What's going to happen now? It's all a daze, a dream rushing by. I need a rest, a holiday to relax and be free. Oh well hurry, hurry off I go, on and on, all the time. Time time time time. What is the time? It comes and goes like a flash, in, out and gone just like that. In a flash, flash, flash, that's all it takes, it's gone and can never be found. Clocks, clocks, oh so many, tick tock, tick tock.

Wendy Harriss

Black

Black is the colour I feel. Black, Black, Black, Black, Black, Shiny Black Bracelet I wear always to keep my blood flowing. The power of the crystal, Black, Black, dark, evil peel away the tender parts, dig down inside, lies. Black that tattoos a soul. Black that fades in and out of my mind, Black the colour of my pupils as they observe you. Watching. Black desire, Black pain. Black, the colour that's not a colour. Black spider, Black eye, Black shadow.

Lucy Tucker

Adding to your collection

Over the next ten days write ten speed writing poems of your own in the Ania Walwicz style. Write about anything that interests you. Vary your time limits from five to fifteen minutes. What you write may surprise and amaze you.

Minimalist poems

Minimalist poems get their effect by using very few words — they are reduced to their simplest elements.

Let's begin

To begin to write a minimalist poem, you could write an 'I love' poem of a few lines:

> I love my dog
> I love my cat
> I love the water
> I love the beach
> I love girls
> I love sleeping in
> I love watching movies
>
> *Tim Retrot*

Then expand each line by repeating the exercises you used in 'Breath length poems'.

> I love my dog even though it runs into poles and things. It's a bit stupid it is. I'm quite ashamed of it. I'm scared to say that my dog is just dumb and will always be that way.
>
> *Tim Retrot*

> I love watching the cold icy waves crash up against the soft coloured brickwork at the end of a hot day trying to watch each wave crash at the same time until I become dizzy.
>
> *Katrina Lynch*

I love to discover people's inside beauty by searching through their souls and imagining what they are thinking. You can't judge a person by what they look like.

Melanie Rottier

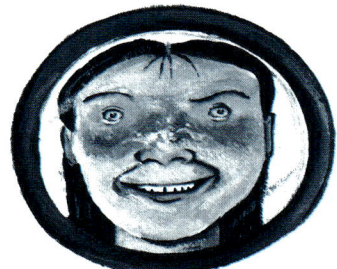

I love the hot sun playing on my face
then going home to watch my nose peel
and my red face grimacing back at me.

Morgan Vaudrey

I love slowly walking along a deserted beach with the warm sun shining down on my back.

Katherine Gray

I love entire emptiness when thoughts come easily and loneliness seems friendly and I dream about subtle stupid things like being a hermit nun.

Claire Spiers

Examine your poem and see if you can find a simple, clearly drawn poem within your lines. You will need to look beyond the rush of words and the accumulation of lines in your breath length poem, and reduce it to its simplest elements.

Katrina Lynch ran her words down the page

cold
icy
waves
crash
on
brickwork
try to
watch
them
all
at
once

Tim Retrot simplified his

my dog
runs
into poles
stupid it is

Melanie Rottier deleted the first sentence, centred
the poem and chose particular line breaks

You can't

judge

a person by

what they

look like

Morgan Vaudrey looked for key words and added a new ending

hot sun
days
lying
baking
burnt
peeling
ahhh now where is the
aftersun lotion?

Katherine Gray simply rearranged her lines,
letting her breath determine the line breaks

I love
slowly walking
along a deserted beach
with the warm sun
shining down
on my
back

Claire Spiers deleted the words 'I love' and
changed the line breaks

Entire emptiness
when
thought comes easily
and
loneliness seems friendly
and
I dream about subtle stupid things
like
being a hermit nun

Will Mooney's poem from page 4
became

Shadows
rise and fall
in the wake of the sun

⇣ *Using speed writing poems*

Speed writing poems can also be used as the basis for minimalist poems. Select a topic that is important to you, or just something that you like (an object, a place, a colour, a person or a word), and write about it for two minutes. Aim to write as many words as you can. Leave the pen on the paper at all times. If you run out of things to write, repeat the last word until your ideas free up again. Here are some examples from students who wrote about faces.

Face is One of a Friend

Face is one of a friend the face of someone who is. A face of a clock ticking slowly on and on as time goes by each day. Face is that of an enemy, the face of someone else. The clock drowns out everything else, the face of a window looking at you.

Vanessa Harmon

If my Face was a Giraffe

If my face was a giraffe I'd shave it. Face goes to dust, dust goes to nothing. Faces give feelings, show feelings. My face sees fear in me. Fear of not being able to keep it forever.

Miles Jordan

Gaping Holes Spoken From Words

Gaping holes spoken from words uttered in a splash or flow like a river the expressions moving or always changing never the same but always a face looking out of the face into everything which lies everywhere trying to make sense.

Joel Zika

Work out how many words you have written in one minute and multiply it by five to get the target you should aim for over five minutes of speed writing. Now select another topic and see if you can reach your word count target as you speed write for five minutes.

My Dog Gizmo

Puppy dog my little fluff cute little wizzy chase your ball go to your bed say sorry naughty girl drop that silly little fluff. You want to go outside? Where did you think you were going puppy? No you can't have any ice cream, it'll make you sick. Get away from the frozen peas that's disgusting do you feel sick poor little puppy. Oh tummy scratch isn't that nice! Come here come on eat all your dinner. Is that all? Get out of the curtains wizz you're messing them up go away I'm trying to practice. Will you stop sniffing. Niff, niff I wish you'd get lost. Get off my bed you stink! Little 'mell, hop down puppy you're making me uncomfortable. Stop being such a grouch or you'll get a smack, naughty! She was only saying hello. Where's grandpa? Go see grandpa. Wizzy stop sitting on my foot I'm trying to put on my shoes!

Alyssa George

The Old Chair

There's an old chair in my room. It is scruffy where the cats have sharpened their already sharp claws and it is faded where the sunlight's claws have scraped away the colour. When I sit on it, it groans, and down the sides are treasures, old pens, small coins, my second favourite ring, old notes and stories written in cat hair and dust. It is strange the stories. They tell of times passed and notes passed; little smiles or giggles that mean everything to someone and nothing to everyone else. But they still had a meaning. I don't know what it was. She smiled at me across a classroom and I can't see why, but now we are friends. Did she know that already at the time? I don't know if she did. I didn't. When he raises his eyebrows I blush and the old chair groans when I relive it in the afternoon sun, gentle through a dusty messy window. I watch other people and wonder what it is they think about. Maybe they relive things as well.

Nicola Riley

As Light Gentle Bubbly Sand

As light gentle bubbly sand like a small wing made of shiny plastic flashing colours send visions of other worlds into my mind the smoke rising in little streams like a quiet brook in a secluded valley how can I get into this world of dreams pack it, block the hole, suck, breathe, ahhhhh…it's open now let me in, let me in, I can see a new world of fantasy, fantastic fantasy, fantasy fantasy the water murky a rotting pool smells drift up from the bubbly mind grasses of bright and new colours that you have never even imagined before my mind is open to all new thoughts and they slowly drift in as if I am in a dream I can't think straight or what we call straight anyway little furry so soft and smooth, not furry, hypo colours mixed in swirls.

Alice Liddell

Friends

Friends come and go but the real friends will stay forever with you in your heart and mind. I had a friend and he died but I still see him everyday. I can imagine what he looks like, how he sounds, how he smells. The little things. Friends change like the seasons. They come into your life like a fresh spring breeze, fall out of your life like a leaf off a tree or melt away like snow. Friends don't have to be human. My friend is my cat. My happy medium as I like to say. Whenever I'm stressed he will calm me down. I couldn't live without a friend because they know me inside out.

Jess Radford

Fear

Fear is the emotion which rules us all, we fear the day, we fear the night. We fear the night because dark comes, but what is in the dark to fear? No eyes are looking at us. Nothing. We fear dark, always the darkness in a hole. Dark. Because we cannot see. Blind people must spend their whole life in fear. Dark is also safe. A dark tunnel in which we can curl up and cry can be thought of as safe. Safe. Are we ever safe? Safe from what? Safe from death? Never. What is the fear in dying though? It's because we don't know. Don't know what will happen and we fear the unknown. But why must the unknown be feared? It's only unknown and what is unknown we will never know so we will forever fear. Forever. But is there really a forever, for when we die we cease to exist, so therefore nothing can go on forever because we will not be there to observe it.

Alice Proctor

These rushes of words can exist in their own right as poems, prose poems or poetic prose. But they can also be looked at as source material that can be compressed and refined to make minimalist poems. Look at the work of these young writers and see how they have extracted minimalist poems from their speed writing pieces. Do the same with your own speed writing work.

My Dog Gizmo

Silly little fluff.
Get away from the frozen peas.
Get out of the curtains, Wizz.
Will you stop sniffing?
Niff, niff.
Sooky 'bub.
My little 'mell.

Alyssa George

The Old Chair

The cats have sharpened their
already sharp claws
and the chair is faded where the sunlight's
scraped the colours away.
The sides are treasures
old things, small coins and
stories written in cat hair and dust.

Nicola Riley

A Slight Bubbly Sound

A slight bubbly sound
A small window into my mind
And visions of other worlds
Let me in, I can see a new world
Colours never imagined before
My mind is open
And I am in a dream.

Alice Liddell

Friends

I had a friend and he died
But I still see him. Every day.
I can imagine what he looks like.
How he smells, how he sounds.
Little things.

Jess Radford

Fear

What is the fear in dying?
We fear the unknown.
But why must the unknown be feared?
For the unknown is unknown
and will be forever unknown.
So what is there to fear?

Alice Proctor

👁 *Looking at more minimalist poems*

Minimalist poems use as little ornamentation and elaboration as possible. They get their resonance from being reduced to their simplest elements even though they might be considering the most complex of issues.

Look at the way the minimalist poets, Miroslav Holub and Lily Brett make us think about the existence of evil, and how Mike Ladd and Tadeusz Rozewicz make us consider our relationship with the universe. Holub's 'grass', 'grain', 'fire', and 'rocket' connected with giving a hand 'to some people' makes us think about creation and responsibility; Brett's simple questions force us to consider the Holocaust and its implications for both murderer and victim; Harris puts a 'salty' edge on innocence; and Ladd's picture of people against spare lines, jagged and otherwise, and Rozewicz's 'grass' and piece of rope make us think about our existence and our place in the world — past and future.

The Questions

the questions
that tormented
my mother

were
the same questions
every day

did she do
anything
at anyone else's

expense
to save
herself

did
her mother know
she'd have preferred

to go
with her
to the ovens

did
her sister hear
her crying

did
her niece
die quickly

another question
that tormented
her

was
why was she
saved

why
was she
spared

she wasn't sure
she was
saved

she wasn't sure
she was
spared.

Lily Brett

Beach Theory

Coastlines are infinitely jagged,
jagged with a jaggedness
that can't be measured —
it's all a matter of scale.

The horizon is a broken bowl
pulled into line
by its own endlessness.

Here at least
we stand out —
this is why we love the beach.

Mike Ladd

A Hand

We gave a hand to grass —
    and here is grain.
We gave a hand to fire,
    and here is a rocket.

Slowly,
hesitating,
we give a hand
to people —
    to some people.

Miroslav Holub

picnic

the string
of lights

along the
jetty, sparklers

burn underwater
my children

in the squeaking
playground, lick

salt from
their fingers

& swing
into the fish

& chip night

Rory Harris

The End

the beginning

a face
tightened
gnarled
convulsed

twisted into a single
coil
a knotted rope
or cord

slowly
it starts to unwind
loosen
fall
in the silence

it hung down

collapsed
and sagged

into fear humiliation
into the final defeat

into nothing
Tadeusz Rozewicz

Grass

I grow
in the bondings of walls
where they are
joined
there where they meet
there where they are vaulted

there I penetrate
a blind seed
scattered by the wind

patiently I spread
in the cracks of silence
I wait for the walls to fall
and return to earth

then I will cover
names and faces
Tadeusz Rozewicz

Adding to your collection

Repeat either the speed writing or breath length processes you have looked at in this unit and use the words you come up with to write another minimalist poem. Add your new poem and any others that you like from this unit to your collection.

A new look at haiku

The Japanese haiku is a poetic form widely used by beginner writers. It has three lines that contain seventeen syllables organised into a 5/7/5 sequence. The 'mood' of the haiku comes from its reference to the seasons, weather, or time of day. This form is ideally suited to clear and precise description. Most importantly, a haiku contains the element of wit, of seeing the world and experience in a unique way, and thus helps us to avoid clichés and stereotypes in poetry.

✿ Combining the ingredients

Look at the way in which the following writers combine the ingredients of a haiku. Discuss the clever comparisons they make.

Traffic

We pass demon eyes
The red glow in the grey dawn
The snake wriggles on.

Sarah Pearson

Quack!

Quack! Playing, acting,
reflecting afternoon rays,
seagulls fly, ducks swim.

Hilary Gold

Timetable

Electronic eyes
Changing expression and voice
Watch the people run.

Sarah Pearson

Births, Deaths, Marriages

It sits in turmoil
The musty smell of coldness
Diamonds of the past.

Sarah Pearson

Cat and Mouse

Red lights driving fast
in the mist of the morning
chase us to crossings.

Cassie Bentley

Window Seat

Lights coming our way
Them too with people aboard
pale glass-eyed zombies.

Cassie Bentley

Sunset

Sunset on the sea
drawing cold shapes on water
on wavy canvas.

Stuart Taylor

Market

At first I can smell
the sweetness of flowers, then
comes dead animal.

Kerri Smith

Aeroplane

It glides through the night
as calm as the silver lake
as swift as a dove.

Ingrid Ryan

Moonlight

Moonlight shimmering
on a cold, dark, winter night
in the sea of space.

Stuart Taylor

Waves

The waves charge the beach
An ocean war has started
Waves hit and retreat.

Michael Julius

 ## Looking at other poems

Haiku are clear and evocative pictures that have a precision, beauty and deceptive simplicity. Once this is realised and we see how the ingredients of nature, form and wit are combined, it becomes clearer why Japanese haiku poets such as Matsuo Bashō (1644–94) were so highly regarded in their time, and why contemporary Australian poets such as Robert Gray and Ernie Tucker have continued to write in this form.

Look at the following examples of haiku and discuss their ingredients. Bashō's *Narrow Road to the Deep North*, written in 1694, is one of the great works of Japanese literature; it contains about fifty haiku interspersed among the story of his journey through northern Japan to the sacred shrine of the sun goddess at Ise. 'Into the Sea', in which he describes the large river rushing westward into the sea, is one of the fifty haiku. 'On a Withered Branch', written earlier, was an important poem; its combination of two pictures in comparison with each other influenced many Japanese haiku poets that followed.

Into the Sea

Into the sea
it drives the red-hot sun —
the river Mogami.

On a Withered Branch

On a withered branch
a crow has settled —
autumn nightfall.

Look at these two poems by Robert Gray.

On this Peak, Alone

On this peak, alone;
in the wind, it feels as if my shirt
is trying to go back.

Two Swallows Skim

Two swallows skim
a long verandah, above cane chairs;
bodysurfing the breeze.

Here are some haiku by Ernie Tucker.

Fuming

Fuming
from a semi trailer,
spring rain.

At the Edge of the Bush

At the edge of the bush,
a figure freezes
nuzzling the dusk.

Through the Motel Window

Through the motel window
venetian blinds
separate the eucalypts.

In the Highest Leaves

In the highest leaves,
the moon sees
a koala.

The Last Drop

The last drop
poised on the leaf edge
threatens to fall.

Dribbling Down the Creek

Dribbling down the creek,
the canoe
disturbs the symmetry.

Wire Coat Hangers

Wire coat hangers
in a hotel wardrobe
jangle the music.

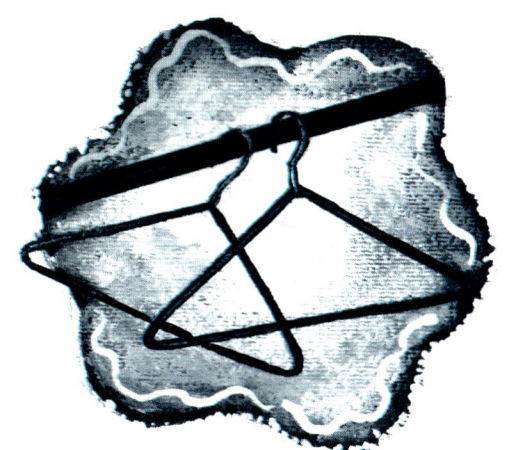

The Two Currawongs Chortle

The two currawongs chortle
on the front grass,
high cloud and dawn light.

By the Fibro Shack

By the fibro shack
the water tank
electroplates the dawn grass.

Detached in the Pavilion

Detached in the pavilion
the sage
travels to the pinnacles.

Adding to your collection

Look at the world around you, and write haiku about the things you see in it: insects, animals, objects, people and places. Remember to combine the ingredients of nature, clarity, precision, freshness and wit, and wherever possible remember to retain the 5/7/5 syllable structure. Add your haiku to your collection.

Simple experience poems

A lot of people think that the best subject for poetry is nuclear war, tragic death, unrequited love or the latest disaster shown on the news on TV. Poems that come from feelings of outrage or love, or from passionately held views on global or traumatic events, can have the potential to move us and make us feel extreme emotions, but poems made from the simplest things can move and affect us equally well. These are simple experience poems.

Everyone has simple experiences that are especially meaningful to him or her. William Carlos Williams's poem, 'The Red Wheelbarrow', contains a precise description of such an experience; his use of the word 'glazed' makes his description of the image that is important to him shine like a glossy photograph.

The Red Wheelbarrow

So much depends
upon

a red wheel
barrow

glazed with rain
water

beside the white
chickens

William Carlos Williams

Write your own poem

Choose a simple experience of your own and imitate Williams's poem, starting with his opening lines

so much depends
upon
. . .

Continue by trying to fit the visual details of your own simple experience into the same or similar form as Williams.

the lecturer's mark book

so much depends
upon

the lecturer's mark
book

spotted with red
wine

beside the student's
essay

Rory Harris

Our New Truck

So much depends
upon

our new
truck

with hay on the
back

wet with early morning
dew

Lee Mogg

That Green Fishing Line

So much depends
upon

that green fishing
line

wet with sea
water

pulling up
fish

Jason Scarabotti

A Champion Horse Racing

So much depends
upon

a champion horse
racing

with a black shiny
coat

beside a row of stands full of people
watching

Nichola Ross

Skateboard

So much depends
upon

a skateboard
glazed with lacquer

beside a brown wood
ramp

Michael Paynter

Extending the poem

Now look at 'The Red Wheelbarrow Extrapolations' by the Australian poet Nigel Roberts as he starts with the Williams poem and extends it. It is as if he is improvising on a musical instrument — like the trumpet he refers to in the poem. Roberts is playing variations on the original theme; he's having fun as he extends the ideas of the poem and comments on the influence of the poet William Carlos Williams, and the poem, 'The Red Wheelbarrow'.

The Red Wheelbarrow Extrapolations

1

So much depends
upon
   that trumpet
in its case
with a Harmon Mute
   For Sale
to that black kid
who dribbled
a basketball to the window
of the Eagle Loan.

2

I have started

              a poem with
                a line from
             Carlos Williams —
in response to
        the particulars
        of character
            time / place
& event
        as it occurred
& sang there
        outside the Eagle Loan.

       3

    Somehow
   the poem
  starts
as a projectile of breath
    to go
      to shape its
        own form
        & path in speech   all this / yes
         by what   wheelbarrows
   the ear has collected   kitchen sinks
      or the heart   & trumpets / do
   put down   constitute a revelation.

4

Outside the Eagle Loan
a poem starts while you are waiting
for a bus & checking out
the local *mise-en-scène*
the ant traffic
is no big event
& that street kid
pressed at eye level to a trumpet
in the window of the Loan
a detail
until you connect
the black & the brass

with Louis
Diz, Fats Navarro
Clifford Brown & Miles

which is no big deal
but again
is the root thing of a poem

& its priority
egg before chicken
chicken, before wheelbarrow.

5

No rain

& as for
white chickens

did you expect
at the intersection
of 18th & Castro

to find
free ranging chickens
there
outside the Eagle Loan?

6

Carlos

how many times
have I asked you

to get that barrow
& those chickens

in
out of the rain?

Nigel Roberts

👁 *Looking at other poems*

Look at the ways some other writers have tried varying the poem.

A Big White Duck

So much depends
upon

a big white
duck

that chases
the cats

when he's not
locked up

that looks at the bats

in the big
wide sky

then turns to
the duck

and waves
goodbye

then all he
does

is stare at
you

so you get
some almonds

and give him
a few

Luke McIntyre

for both of you

never
have i

spent
so much

time
in playgrounds

as with
you &

your mother
my wife

these wool
capped, coat

wrapped
autumn leaf

afternoons

Rory Harris

A Little Dog Shelter

So much depends
upon

a little dog shelter

keeping the dog
warm

down by the back
fence

and behind the back
fence

is
a main road

with traffic rushing
past

in peak hour

and all through
the night

along the road
go

cars
hundreds

pink, green and
yellow

all through
the night

overtaking the
cars

semis
the kings of the

road
from interstate

at the end of the
road

is a
sea

a rough, raging
sea

way past the
sea

is the
horizon

over the
horizon

is a land

a whole, new
land

so much depends
upon

a little dog
shelter

keeping the dog
warm

down by the back
fence

Tracy Hayes

Hair

So much depends
upon
hair
you can put it
up
or leave it down
the girl next door wears her hair in
shoelaces
they're all different
colours
she gets them from the
supermarket
where her mum buys
frozen peas and
lamb

my uncle has a
farm
and he has
lambs
he sells them to the
meatworks
where my mum buys
sausages
I have sausages with
frozen peas
my mum buys the frozen
peas
at the supermarket
where
the girl next door
buys her
shoelaces which
she puts in her
hair

Emma Lewin

Adding to your collection

Now it's your turn. Start with the poem you wrote based on the form of 'The Red Wheelbarrow' and try writing your own improvisation and/or extrapolation.

Telling lies

Poetry gives you the opportunity to use your imagination, to make up stories; it's not just about telling lies, but describing what you see and extending it. The person collecting firewood, the teacher walking across the quadrangle, the couple window-shopping, or the busker in the mall all have lives beyond what you can see. As a writer your task is to show those lives from the details they present. Where has the person come from? Where is she or he going? Sometimes truth has very little to do with it.

Finding a beginning

One day Rory Harris saw a woman throwing wood into a shopping trolley as she pushed it along the road. That night when he was at home making up poems, he began describing what he saw.

> she collects firewood along the roadside
> jams the branches into a shopping trolley
>
> her dress flaps in the wind

Then gradually he started to extend it, telling lies about this woman, being a creative liar as he added extra dimensions to the life he had seen.

she collects firewood

she collects firewood along the roadside
jams the branches into a shopping trolley

her dress flaps in the wind
like the threads of flags

a body hidden under printed cotton
like a country's borders we drive across

they made an attempt to adopt her
a half life in school

the rest a blur into middle age
& a husband who got lost on the way home from the pub

& her kids share a bedroom
with posters covering the holes where punches landed

where they weren't meant to
from uncles they stopped naming

& they tell their teacher stories about their dreams
& Mum snaps a branch across her knee

it shatters into splinters
she bends to recover the pieces

Rory Harris

Another time Harris saw a boy talking to a schoolgirl in a subway. By describing what he saw and then extending the lives of these two by 'telling lies', he invested the moment with all kinds of menace.

conversation as a monologue

she leans against the subway wall
her back contorts to take its shape

he leans over
one hand takes his weight above her

he does most of the talking
the wall drips

she cocoons her body
wraps her arms around her breasts

hides her school uniform in the darkness
his voice drops when people walk by

silence fills the gaps with expectations

Rory Harris

⬤ *Stretching the truth*

Think of people you have seen that you could write about: the man watering his garden, the solitary girl on the bus, the tourist, the street kid, the girl walking along with a bag over her shoulder, the preoccupied girl. The following poets have written about these subjects. Read their work and then write about a character of your own in the same way that they have. You might like to try disciplining your work by writing in two-line stanzas, running the lines on where you need to and writing it all in lower case, just as Rory Harris has.

Grenades

He throws balls of paper
like grenades

& can't stop laughing
when the teacher glares.

He wishes his father
was the target

wants to put a brick
through the back of his head.

Under the desk
his fists bunch more paper

Peter McFarlane

As he Waters his Garden

As he waters his garden
his pink dressing gown drags on the lawn

with his pink fluffy slippers showing.
His cat Ugly runs around in circles,

gets very dizzy after a while.
'Come here Ugly', he calls.

Ugly stops, goes to him.
Inside he gets changed,

comes out wearing schoolboy clothes.
He is forty-five.

Socks up to his knees, grey shorts
and a bright pink polka-dotted tie.

Neighbours crack up at him.
He goes inside.

Tanya Morgan

The Traveller

He takes out his map.
It's old, covered with red lines.

His hair is tied back,
A hat covers his face.

He has nowhere special to go.
Seen a lot, but remembers little.

He has a backpack.
It is covered with designs.

He plans his next journey
A felt-tip in his hand.

Angela Felton

he cycles up the bike track

he cycles up the bike track
puffing and panting and struggling

he puts down his bike
with a resonating smash

he makes his place at home
on the streets

as this is where he lives
now that his family is gone

the cold wind howls around him
and he shivers in the chill

his clothes provide no warmth
for his cold body and cold heart

Ron Frim

she carries her bag

she carries her bag
it hangs over her shoulder

walking past the same place
the time is the same

her dog no longer a puppy
follows her like always

trotting alongside her
as he always does

a faithful friend
her only friend

nobody stops to talk to her
she stops for no-one

the little dog is her only friend
she bends down

patting him softly on his head
he wags his tail, happy to be near her

she has on her orange coat
clashing badly with her shock of red hair

she stops at the shops
gets two loaves of bread

then leaves as usual
walking home with her little dog

his tail wagging
and his red collar standing out against his
    black coat of hair

she goes home
opens the door

the dog tries to sneak in
but he's held back by her leg as usual

she makes herself a buttered sandwich
with the small amount of butter she has

forget the butter, she says to herself
always forgetting something

the dog scratches at the door
he whimpers softly to himself

she's alone now
in her alone little world

where she doesn't have to remember the dog
remember the butter, buy a new coat

the dog is hungry

Lisa Notini

👁 *Looking at other poems*

You may prefer to change the form and write in a different way. It may not be a character that you write about: it may be an event like 'the rouge', the nineteenth century school dance that Brett Cawrse imagined; or a Victoria Cross winner from the First World War; or a period in the nineteenth century when an all boys' school admitted a solitary girl (or 'squish pot' as they used to call them) to its classes. Poems can tell lies about history as well as characters. The procedure is the same: start by describing what you see and then extend it with your imagination. Sometimes it is enough to keep to the facts, but often the facts can be restricting. Telling lies in poetry is a way of liberating you from these restrictions.

He Tiptoes into my Room

He tiptoes into my room.
The floor creaks beneath his feet.
He sits on my bed
watching me sleep,
stroking my hair and
brushing my cheeks.

He remembers the old days
when we used to be friends.
His hair unbrushed
and his clothes unchanged.
He doesn't know the pain he's caused
to me and her.
She's gone too,
vanished because of one horrible being.

I wake,
covered with sweat.
I check every inch of my room.
I'm left with the chilling memories,
memories of a man,
a man more evil than the rest.

Ingrid Ryan

the rouge

he stands nervously against the cold wooden wall
as people approach he sinks back into the hard pine

a friend comes along and offers a lady
he tries to decline with a shy shake of the head

the blond beauty pulls him roughly
they sway side to side in rhythm

his hand slides down her back

Brett Cawrse

Hugo Throssell

He stands before the stage,
with his award,
the Victoria Cross.

As he touches the award
his mind drifts in time
back to when he won it.

He was in the war
called World War I,
fighting for his country.

He dodged bullets,
dived for his trench,
watched his friends die.

Silence fills the hall.
A sneeze awakens him.
He says, 'Thank You', and leaves.

Back to his memories.

Adrian Liston

Girl at a Boys' School

'Hey, boys, check out the squish pot.'

    'Nice legs.'

'Yeah, but what's she doin' here?'

    'Maybe it's a boy?'

'Good one, Nick.'

    'Let's go talk to her.'

'OK, you go.'

    'No, you go.'

'No, you go.'

    'No, you go.'

Ryan Thomas

Adding to your collection

Add three new poems to your collection: one that tells lies about a character, one that tells lies about history, and another one that tells lies about a current event in the newspaper or on TV.

Object poems

Look into the bottom drawer or box of things you have kept, all the treasures you have never thrown away — postcards, medals, key rings. Look at them. Now write! Show the life of the person they belonged to. When you have finished you will have an object poem.

Taking a closer look

Rory Harris's 'airstrip' was first drafted during a student writing workshop. The guest writer prepared a collage of objects and placed them on a desk: an old photograph of a woman standing on an airstrip, a camera, a passport and a trophy. The task was to write about all or some of these artefacts and create a 'life'. It's a similar stimulus to writing that is prompted by an interesting photograph, rock crystals, or even a lit candle. The trick is to get inside the object and begin to interrogate it. Why this? Why that? How did it happen? How would you feel in a similar situation? Once these questions have answers you can begin to feel your way around the edges of the poem. 'airstrip' is of course a fiction. The poem describes an English woman returning 'home'.

airstrip

for Alan Laslett

miles from England
she walks out
a flat bared strip
of white conscience
twenty years of a colony upbringing
privileged beyond her years
her artefacts will arrive by steamer

Rory Harris

Three Razors

1958: Safety

What's
the attraction
Grade Two

crouched
behind the palm stump
I sweep my face

with Dad's
am amazed
when it is noticed

no slip
no cut
but seen.

1972: Cut-throat

Two AM
and an inheritance
from grandpa

hovers, vibrates
above my wrist
20, 30 seconds,

pounces,
expertly fashions a mouth
whiter than skin;

then toothless,
belching up blood . . .
Then

the arm-across-the-eyes explaining,
the face-to-wall
Casualty stitching.

1991: Electric

Untouched
10 years
I open it

to discover
a terrifying
black dust.

John West

The Myth of a Photographic Memory

The camera
Cannot recapture
What I feel
Remembering back
Thirty years
Or more

So perfect
The leave taking
Unreal

Like an
Unprinted negative
Ghostly
And insubstantial
The artefacts remain —
The trophy
Proudly won
The soapstone carving
Representing
A unity
That never was
The lens —
So exact —

Projecting on
Dusty bellows
Reaches out
To a distant
Fading image
I press the shutter
Nothing
Clicks.

Alan Laslett

 # Looking at other poems

Another way to write an object poem is to interrogate each object in a collection and write a line in response to each. In the following poem the objects were a glue bottle, correction fluid, a watch, some cards, a pencil and some glasses.

Alone

1. The glue bottle alone, next to Liquid Paper. The bottle is in a world of its own, it's powerful, sticking things together, husband and wife.

2. Liquid Paper covering things up so they can't be seen. The police covering up crime, covering the mistakes of our world, a cop fighting against murderers.

3. The clock tells us the time. What time? Who needs time? Who needs a clock? Timetables, schedules, too strict for me. Who wants a clock? Not me. A teacher would.

4. The cards are a casino ripping off people, the king, the jack, the queen. Playing cards can be fun till you start to bet. A game of charades or poker?

5. The pencil is a sign of school. With no pencil, no school, cool! Pencils are a drag, a four-inch-long stick, lead and wood, not my kind of life.

6. Glasses are good, helping short-sighted to see. The ones on the table are useless. No-one's looking through them. When someone wears them they are useful.

Until then the glasses lie unmoving on the table with the glue and Liquid Paper, the clock and the cards, the pencil and the glasses. Lying away, away from us and forgotten.

Thomas McNeil

Objects are accompanied by the lives of those who use them, or own them. In the following poem the objects were a Gladstone bag, a wooden cigarette box, a novel, a passport, beach shells, a crucifix, a cigarette tin, a newspaper and a wedding photograph. Search them for the life in them. Smell it, touch it, now write about it.

Moving to Australia

I was moving to Australia
With my wife as you know
It's a very sad thing
That she had to go
This photo means more
Now that she's dead
But I'm still going to Australia
Only with the bottle instead
I'm getting out a smoke
From my cigarette tin
When I see in the paper
'Smoking kills within'
I spark up the smoke
Once I've lit the match
I take a few drags
Then I flick the ash
On my wedding
My lady gave me three shells
Cause the two of us
Couldn't afford wedding bells
I have to forget
About my lady you know
So it's off to Australia
I have to go
It should be easy
To forget
But it may be harder
Not to regret
It's my fault she's gone
It's my fault she's dead
After the bullet meant for Skippy
Went straight through her head
I don't know how
I'll live without her love
I'll just slit my throat
And meet her above.

Aaron Paul

A Gladstone Bag

I walked along and saw the rush
Of all the mad workers.
Their clockwork movement to and fro,
Causes chaos to occur.
A big Gladstone bag,
Big and brown,
Crashes open in the stampede.
Look at its contents,
What does it contain?
A wedding photo
Of two old goats,
A copy of *The Times*
A cigarette case that smashes open,
An old passport with an ugly photo,
And would you believe
This mad idiot carried a sea shell.

Derek Bajer

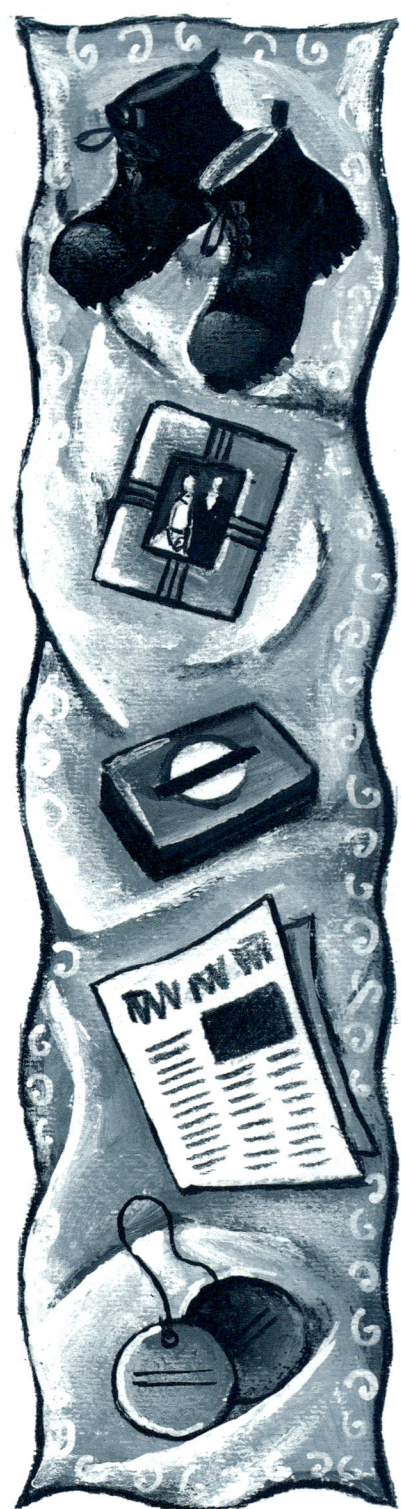

Dogtags

He walked over
To the tent
Black shiny boots
Charcoal stripes on flushed cheeks
Tags swinging
Catching
The afternoon sunlight
The smell of death all around
It was time
To collect up his belongings.

He walked inside
And sat on the rusty mattress
Looked up at the table
Saw the photo
From his wedding day
His wife
Unaware
Of her beloved one's fate.

The cigarette tin
Still full of stringy tobacco
The case sent for Jerusalem
A man's only joy
In these conditions.

His novel
Given to him
By his grandfather
Only half read
Never to be finished
Already collecting dust
The newspaper
Folded up neatly
The Australian Times
We made the front cover
'Our diggers coming home'
Sent only days before
From his mother.

Then he came
To his old bag
Smelling of leather and sweat
The worker's companion
But alas, no more.

And hidden away
In the front drawer
Were the shells
Screaming memories
Of a child's innocence
That he kept with pride.

The man put his head
Into his hands
And touched the crucifix
Feeling the pain
Of a lost brother.

Olivia Groufsky

It was my Life

It was my life that I had
The life that I breathed
The life that I felt
The life that I held
It was there with me and in the air
My life
My wife
And my death

Matthew Jacka

Adding to your collection

Prepare a collection of artefacts that are particularly evocative for you. Smell them. Touch them. Find the life in them by writing your own object poem and adding it to your poetry collection.

Building detail and the twist

To write a poem that builds on detail, you should first find a situation where there is action. Think of a scene involving action, a bodyboarder on a wave for example. Describe it detail by detail, layer by layer until the action has developed in front of you. Do not be concerned about anything else except the action.

A boy at a bus stop

> He stands at the station
> walkman headphones plugged in
> a magazine in his hand . . .

Someone flying a kite in the park

> Out in the park
> flying a kite
> the sky is blue
> the clouds . . .

Adding a twist

Harris's 'she came in from the terminal' describes a woman in a railway station cafeteria. She is revealed to us like a developing photograph. This build up of clinical detail is then given a twist when the cup becomes a sparrow and all that being a sparrow falling 'from a height beyond memory' signifies.

she came in from the terminal

> she came in from the terminal
> walked into the railway cafe
> slid a tray the entire distance
> around the counter
> stopped
> bought a metallic pot filled with tea
> carried it back

to a single dustless table
setting everything down
with fragile care
as if it would shatter of its own purpose
poured the liquid
into the white china cup
sipped at it carefully
then hunched forward
as if to drink with more ease
wrapped her hands cautiously
around the warm whiteness
as if it were a sparrow
having fallen from a height
beyond memory

Rory Harris

Rome

In the early
morning sun the birds
are singing on the
sunbreak on Rome. The
coffee machine is
ringing. The pigeons are
digging in the dirt, girls
and boys are
flirting. The smell of
coffee is around the
cafes. The Pope is
talking from the
Vatican window while
robbers are
lurking, stalking by
walking round and
round the eager crowd.

Mario De Ionno

Coffee Shop Blues

She seemed to be walking towards me
stopped a few yards in front
looked as far as eternity
then looked at me
turned
bought a coffee
walked back
looked restless
sipped her coffee
burnt her lips
and wiped them
walked towards me
I thought to myself
fancy my chances
getting ready to speak
but then she walked straight up to
the geek behind me

Andrew Woolman

he waits at a bus stop

he waits at a bus stop
walkman headphones plugged in
a cigarette in his hand
he is fixed
on what he hears through his headphones
unaware of what is happening
in the outside world
imprisoned by hypnotic music

the cigarette burns to a butt
he throws it to the ground and steps on it
after checking his watch, he crosses the road
out of nowhere a car zooms past him
he drops his headphones, and finally wakes up

awake to the real world

James Kumar

Soccer Ball

The black and white checkers
Spin around and around
Propelled forward by the boy's foot
Up into the air
                        Up and a
            Up   w
        Up   a
    Up   y

Into the goal

Andrew Woolman

Adding to your collection

Write your own poem where you build details layer by layer and give them a twist. You could describe a person washing dishes, a person chopping wood or setting a fire in a grate, someone enjoying a meal, someone waiting for someone else and growing impatient. As you write, the greater implications will become apparent. This is the twist. Don't worry about trying to predict it. In most cases the twist will come naturally out of what you write.

Dramatic monologues

Dramatic monologues can come in a variety of forms, from the rhyme and formal metre of someone like Robert Browning's 'Porphyria's Lover' or 'My Last Duchess' to the prose poetry and conventional speech rhythms of Elizabeth Young's 'They're Looking at Me'.

They're Looking at Me

They're looking at me I can feel it. Staring at me. I bet they feel sorry for someone like me. I was always a chubby child. Always teased. Fatso they would yell. I hated all those skinny girls. Flat stomachs, thin long legs, small pear-shaped faces. That was never me. Of course I tried losing weight. It's too hard. If I had a dollar for every time I ate something with more than ten grams of fat I would be rich. I've always wanted to be thin. They're still looking at me. I can feel it. It is so humiliating being in a fabric shop and asking for five metres of material just to make a skirt. They're still looking at me. They look away quickly, but as soon as I turn my back they're staring again.

Elizabeth Young

Imagine you are someone else

The trick is to imagine a character and then let the thoughts of that character come out as if she or he is talking. Think of a bag lady and write a line of her speaking

> It makes me chuckle when I see people snatch a look at me and then quickly look away.

> This damn trolley! It's gettin' too old, bumpin' into things and jammin' up.

Or a mother who has just noticed something in the room of her runaway daughter

> She never did pick up after herself . . .

56

Or you could be a star footballer

> Mate, it has been the worst game I've ever played in me life. Things ain't easy when you've got the coach on your back . . .

> Funny how they're your mates when you're kickin' 'em good, but it all changes when you're not . . .

Imagine you are someone in a crisis and develop a dramatic monologue of your own. Start by imagining your character talking to someone. Give yourself a time limit (five or ten minutes) and treat the exercise as an opportunity to develop your speed writing.

I Used To Have a Real Handbag

I used to have a real handbag you know, a soft one made of leather, it wasn't always plastic bags from Sydney. You wouldn't think it to look at me though. I suppose you wouldn't believe I was pretty once either, never beautiful mind you, but I didn't look like this. Now the council's trying to get me to move on. Young councillor come up to me the other day, smarmy young fellow, told me I'll have to move on now. You understand that. Now they're trying to make this a posh suburb they don't want the people like me around, think we might spoil the tourists' view. Don't know where I could go though. Besides I've got a right to stay here, I was born in that big house there. You don't believe me do you? I've lived here longer than any of the councillors on that stupid council. Now you're walking away from me. Why? Do you think I'm senile? Just a crazy old hag?

Helen Dowling

I Can Feel my Lip Throbbing

I can feel my lip throbbing. It's going to be big this time. I hate it when he hits my face. It's so difficult to come up with excuses for my bruises. I would be so humiliated if people knew I was so bad a wife that my husband had to hit me to keep me in line. It's not as if I don't try hard. I just forget things at times. He doesn't ask much of me. All he wanted was dinner on the table when he got home, but I was talking to mum on the phone and I lost track of time and the next thing I knew he was walking through the front door. It's like dad always used to tell me — I'm hopeless. And now, as I sit here crying with my nose running and hands shaking, I know dad was right. I just hope James doesn't come in and see me like this. It always makes him more angry when he sees me cry. If I wait a few more minutes, he will have calmed down and I'll be able to go and apologise to him. That's one of the best things about James — he's so forgiving.

Tanya Lintzens

Now write a monologue as if the audience is privy to all the thoughts in your character's head. Once again give yourself a time limit and do it as a piece of speed writing.

Finding Shirley's Smile

I've been sitting here in this cursed room for fifteen minutes now, waiting for someone to come in and tell me what the hell is going on. No-one seems to think it matters if they tell me or not. Mum and Dad went out to talk to the doctor in front of my precious little sister. Don't get me wrong, I love her and everything and she is quite cute with her blond ringlets and freckly nose. But ever since she got sick she has been the only one of us two daughters that ever existed.

It's not the first time I've had to traipse down here with Shirley, Mum and Dad, this week in fact is the third. Each time I ask if I can stay at home but I'm told that my sister needs me. WHAT FOR???? They drag me down here to an old hospital filled with hundreds of sick people, put me in an office somewhere, and then keep me in the dark about what's going on. I'm not a kid or anything. I am sixteen for god sakes. I can understand adult language, even Shirley can understand the special language they have been talking lately. 'I'll only be five minutes', sure Mum, it's now been twenty and I'm busting to go to the toilet. I should leave this damn hospital and catch the bus home! Hey? Then again I might never find out what's wrong with Shirley. It's just that I'm fed up, that's all. I wish I was the child that was sick and getting all of the attention. Maybe then Mum and Dad would buy me presents and Shirley would have to wait in this room that absolutely stinks of mothballs and has pictures of bones and germs on the walls.

I guess I should stop being so selfish, I suppose I could be grateful that I don't have to go to school this morning. Maybe I should be more considerate towards Shirley. I just hate being kept in the dark. I love my sister and I want to know what's wrong with her. I just need to know what made her stop smiling because until I see that smile again I won't be happy. I guess the tears I shed don't matter at the moment, all that matters is getting Shirley's smile back.

Carolyn Ramsey

Pete

I hate Bruce. You should've seen what he did to me today at kindy. I was just swinging on the swing when he came and pushed me right off and I got into trouble because it was his turn on the swing. Well I thought it was a good trick telling him it was snack time so when he ran in, I jumped on the swing.

I hate my teacher too. Mrs Ryan. She told me I had to go and sit in the corner for stealing the swing when it wasn't my turn and now I can't have a cake at snack time. I only get crackers and water. It's not fair. All those goody-goody girls that stand next to her all laughed at me when I got into trouble. I hate them too.

I hate my mum. She said I can't watch TV at all today because I tipped my corn flakes on my little baby sister this morning. I only did it to stop her crying so much but it didn't work.

I hate my little sister, she always has pooey nappies, she smells horrible, and she always cries. After she eats her stinking food she throws up.

So now I have to sit here in the corner and stare at the wall until Mrs Ryan says I can go. I hate looking at the wall. And I'm not eating my crackers and water at snack time either. I think that after I go home from here, I will go and beat up those goody-goody girls because I hate them.

Therese Crisp

Reading your monologue aloud

Read your monologue to the person next to you. Their reaction will tell you how successful you have been in catching the distinctive voice and movement of your character and bringing out his or her crisis. Finish by having a class reading of some of the dramatic monologues. They need to be heard!

Chaucerian poems

In the prologue to Chaucer's *The Canterbury Tales*, we meet thirty or so characters on a pilgrimage to Canterbury in England. In addition to the three examples that follow, there is a knight, 'a most distinguished man', his squire, a yeoman, two nuns and three priests, a monk, a friar, a merchant, an Oxford cleric, a reeve, a sergeant-at-the-law, a landowner, a haberdasher, a dyer, a carpenter, a weaver, a carpet-maker, a ship's captain, a doctor, a parson, a plowman, a manciple and a papal pardoner with his

. . . hair as yellow as wax
Hanging down smoothly like a hank of flax
In driblets fell his locks behind his head
Down to his shoulders which they overspread;
Thinly they fell, like rat-tails, one by one.

Read our three examples taken from Nevill Coghill's translation of *The Canterbury Tales*: the Cook, the Wife of Bath and the Miller.

They had a Cook with them who stood alone
For boiling chicken with a marrow-bone,
Sharp flavouring-powder and a spice for savour.
He could distinguish London ale by flavour,
And he could roast and seethe and boil and fry,
Make good thick soup and bake a tasty pie.
But a great pity, as it seemed to me,
Was that he had an ulcer on his knee.
As for blancmange, he made it with the best.

A worthy woman from beside Bath city
Was with us, somewhat deaf, which was a pity.
In making cloth she showed so great a bent
She bettered those of Ypres and of Ghent.
In all the parish not a dame dared stir
Towards the altar steps in front of her,
And if indeed they did, so wrath was she
As to be quite put out of charity.
Her kerchiefs were of finely woven ground;
I dared have sworn they weighed a good ten pound,
The ones she wore on Sunday, on her head.
Her hose were of the finest scarlet red
And gartered tight; her shoes were soft and new.

Bold was her face, handsome, and red in hue.
A worthy woman all her life, what's more
She'd had five husbands, all at the church door,
Apart from other company in youth;
No need just now to speak of that, forsooth.
And she had thrice been to Jerusalem,
Seen many strange rivers and passed over them;
She'd been to Rome and also to Boulogne,
St James of Compostella and Cologne,
And she was skilled in wandering by the way.
She had gap-teeth, set widely, truth to say.
Easily on an ambling horse she sat
Well wimpled up, and on her head a hat
As broad as is a buckler or a shield;
She had a flowing mantle that concealed
Large hips, her heels spurred sharply under that.
And knew she the remedies for love's mischances,
An art in which she knew the oldest dances.

The Miller was a chap of sixteen stone,
A great stout fellow big in brawn and bone.
He did well out of them, for he could go
And win the ram at any wrestling show.
Broad knotty and short-shouldered, he would boast
He could heave any door off hinge and post,
Or take a run and break it with his head.
His beard, like any sow or fox, was red
And broad as well, as though it were a spade;
And at its very tip, his nose displayed
A wart on which there was a tuft of hair
Red as the bristles in an old sow's ear.
His nostrils were as black as they were wide,
He had a sword and buckler at his side,
His mighty mouth was like a furnace door.
A wrangler and buffoon, he had a store
Of tavern stories, filthy in the main.
His was a master-hand at stealing grain.
He felt it with his thumb and thus he knew
Its quality and took three times his due —
A thumb of gold, by God, to gauge an oat!
He wore a hood of blue and a white coat.
He liked to play his bagpipes up and down
And that was how he brought us out of town.

Notice that there are four stressed beats to each line, with the voice naturally emphasising certain syllables as the lines are spoken

> The míller was a cháp of síxteen stóne,
> A gréat stout féllow big in bráwn and bóne.
> He did wéll out of thém, for hé could gó
> And wín the rám at any wréstling shów.

Notice also that the poems are written in rhymed couplets with each two lines rhyming. Try writing two similar lines about a character of your choice.

> A fóotballer there wás, óne of huge síze
> Who had shórts near búrsting ón his thíghs.

In this case the stressed beats are: 'foot', 'was', 'one' and 'size' in the first line, and 'shorts', 'burst', 'on' and 'thighs' in the second line. Note that 'thighs' and 'size' rhyme at the end of each line.

 Looking at other poems

Now imagine a bus trip to the Gold Coast and, using the Chaucerian style, fill your bus with more wondrous characters of your own as the following poets have done.

Suddenly I Noticed Quite a Fuss

> Suddenly I noticed quite a fuss,
> Towards the middle of the bus.
> There was a lady there (I think),
> Who'd obviously been on the drink.
> She resembled closely an old worn tyre,
> And clearly was no object of desire.
> Her face reminded me of something grey,
> The dog sicked up yesterday.
> Her ears resembled cauliflowers,
> And her nose looked like the Eiffel Tower.
> Her legs were that of a grisly bear,
> Covered thick with dark brown hair.
> Of Byronesque features she had none,
> Of a horse's features she had some.
> The driver seemed oblivious to the thunder,
> That started as she began to chunder.

> *Osman Mewett*

There Was a Punk

There was a punk who gazed around the bus interior,
You could tell he thought he was far superior.
There were very few passengers actually sober,
And the punk even looked to be in a coma.
His name was Dave and he was very cool.
He enjoyed making people look the fool.
His hair was green and stuck up high,
His luggage was spread out like a pigsty.
In his hand he held a dirty beer bottle,
And the man next to him, he loved to throttle.

Nicholas Barnes

Reading the original

You may want to read the original Chaucer. Here is Chaucer's original description of the Wife of Bath and a modern parody of it by Meg Wanless.

A good WYF was ther of biside Bathe
But she was som del deef and that was scathe.
Of clooth makyng she hadde swich an haunt
She passed hem of Ypres and of Gaunt.
In al the parisshe wyf was ther noon
That to the offrynge bifore hire sholde goon,
And if ther dide, certeyn so wrooth was she
That she was out of alle charitee.
Hir coverchiefs ful fyne were of ground,
I dorste swere they weyeden ten pound
that on a Sonday weren upon hir heed;
Hir hosen weren of fyn scarlet reed
Ful streite yteyd, and shoes ful moyste and newe.
Boold was hir face and fair and reed of hewe.
She was a worthy womman al hir lyve:
Housbondes at chirche dore she hadde fyve
Withouten oother compaignye in youthe,
But therof nedeth nat to speke as nouthe.
And thries hadde she been at Jerusalem;
She hadde passed many a straunge strem:
At Rome she hadde been and at Boloyne,
In Galice at Seint Jame and at Coloyne;

She koude muche of wandrynge by the weye:
Gat tothed was she soothly for to seye.
Upon an amblere esily she sat
Ywympled wel and on hir heed an hat
as brood as is a bokeler or a targe,
a foot mantel aboute hir hipes large
And on hir feet a peyre of spores sharpe.
In felawshipe wel koude she laughe and carpe;
Of remedies of love she knew par chaunce,
For she koude of that art the olde daunce.

Geoffrey Chaucer (1340?–1400)

Ye Housewyf

Ther was a housewyf, strong and coarse of hande,
Who loved the sink the least in all the lands.
A coverchief hadde she upon hir head
Fetis it were and eek of scarlet reed,
Lank hange hir lockes, straight and blonde of hewe,
For she used peroxide, and this is trewe.
And lo! Somethyne to shock the toun,
Hanged from hir fulle red lippes doun
A cygarette, of brande Woodbyne,
Filtre-tipped, and of tobacco fyne.
Whenne she hadde prepared her husbande's tea.
Chippes fyne, and fisher fingers three,
Hastily she sped she hither to the toun,
For Byngo loved she more than anythynge.
For all thes faults, wel coude she sarp and synge.

Meg Wanless

Adding to your collection

Have some fun by creating new characters and describing them in similar imitation Chaucerian English.

Point of view poems

Do you remember the *Old Testament* story of Abraham taking his son Isaac to be sacrificed? Wilfred Owen rearranges the ending of the story in his protest poem about the First World War, 'The Parable of the Old Man and the Young'.

The Parable of the Old Man and the Young

So Abram rose and clave the wood, and went,
And took the fire with him, and a knife.
And as they sojourned both of them together,
Isaac the first born spake and said, My Father,
Behold the preparations, fire and iron,
But where the lamb for this burnt-offering?
Then Abram bound the youth with belts and straps,
And builded parapets and trenches there,
And stretched forth the knife to slay his son.
When lo! An Angel called him out of heaven,
Saying, Lay not thy hand upon the lad,
Neither do anything to him. Behold,
A ram caught in a thicket by its horns;
Offer the Ram of Pride instead of him.
But the old man would not so, but slew his son,
And half the seed of Europe, one by one.

Wilfred Owen

Imagine if this story was told from the perspective of Abraham's wife.

Always, Sarah Waits

Have you noticed that Sarah has no place
in the telling of the story?
Although she is the mother
the patient, ancient mother,
she is given no place.

She was the aged vessel to His child.
That was her only role.

65

And after that
it was all Men's Work.
It was God saying to Abraham
Take your son to a high place
Make an altar
Make a sacrifice of Him — to Me . . .

And did Abraham waver for an instant?
Did it cross his mind to say anything to Sarah?
To have a word to the little missus about it?
Not a word.
Not
one
single
word.
And why should he?

So off he went, Isaac in tow.
And Sarah waited.
And waiting,
what passed through her mind, I wonder?
And did she weep?
And did her old dry womb ache for Isaac, flesh of her flesh,
blood of her blood?

Did she curse Abraham?
Curse him for his obedience?
Curse him for his rectitude?
Curse him for his thoughtlessness?

And did she dare to mouth the words
or frame within her heart
the thought that Abraham, the Patriarch,
the Chosen One of God
had lost his marbles?

And did she in the end
dare the lament:

Oh more dangerous by far
than anger or fear or hope or love of all humanity
are those who believe
they hear the word of God?

Barry Carozzi

Writing from a different point of view

So many of the stories that we are familiar with have been written from a particular point of view. Try rewriting some of them from different viewpoints as Barry Carozzi and a lot of other writers have done. With most stories being traditionally male centred, one option is to write from the female point of view.

Helen of Troy

Oh come now,
you don't believe all that nonsense about
Helen being whisked away to Troy.
She wanted to go.
Menelaus was old.
Paris was young.
She had no choice.
She chose the better looking one, the one
she could control.
Besides Menelaus was a bore.
He spent all his time looking after the people
of his country and making money.
He didn't even go to Troy and fight for Helen.
Shows how much he really cared.
It was Agamemnon, Menelaus's brother
who fought for Helen for ten years.
Had he returned I wonder what he would have demanded
from his rich and powerful brother?
Helen only left Troy because she had to,
the whole place was destroyed,
and everyone in it killed.
And so Menelaus, that uncaring sod,
totally destroyed Helen's life. He didn't
even think about what she wanted.
Her happiness didn't matter to him at all.
All he wanted was what he thought was his.
Nothing less.

Nicole Raven

Helen's Lament

If Menelaus were to run off with Paris

He left me!
One day I got back from work
and he was gone.
He took the cat,
the TV, the VCR, CD player,
and even my CDs.
He took my son
and left a note
which read:
'I loved you once
but not anymore
I found my one real true love,
Paris, the man from down the road.
You must think I'm a toad.'

Ben Abbot

Perseus and Medusa

I'm scared, very dark, very cold, wet, I'm scared, going to die, won't make it, have to kill Medusa to save princess, can turn me into stone if I look at her, can't look, can't look, going to die, what was that, I heard something, oh no, I'm going to die, ahhhhh, ahhhhh, ahhhhhh, it's her, I'm dead, wait here, wait here, need mirror, need mirror, need head, need head, gotta kill her, gotta save princess, here it comes, knows where I am, gotta wait here, right next to me. Chop!!!!! Killed her, got the head, don't look, don't look, touch head but don't look. I won. Foul creature . . .

Chris Brown

Adding to your collection

Make a list of some more famous myths, legends and stories. Familiarise yourself with one in depth, then try writing a poem about it from a different point of view.

Relationship poems

A clear description of a character can be very effective in a poem, but when it is set alongside descriptions of characters related to the original character in some way, extra dimensions are added.

Each stanza in the poem 'Women Alone' deals with a different member of a family. By describing them individually and grouping them together, Pat Richardson makes a statement about the family and the society which isolates them.

Women Alone

A woman sits alone every night
watching TV,
in a house, high above Manly.
She is eighty-two,
widowed seventeen years.
Drives her yellow Mini
to lawn bowls twice a week,
reads the *Daily Telegraph*, and
murder mysteries, books with a red dot,
from Manly Library.
Once a week, on Sunday, the family
arrives for lunch,
for the baked leg of lamb, and
grandchildren fight on the floor.

Her daughter sits alone every night
watching TV,
in a unit, at Glebe Point.
She is fifty-six,
divorced eight years,
drives an old Holden,
attends poetry classes,
reads the *Sydney Morning Herald*,
is writing a book, loves bookshops,
listens to 2BL all day,
babysits grandson,
lived in the country,
drives to Morisset every Saturday,
across Sydney for lunch on Sunday.

Her daughter sits alone every night
watching TV,
in hospital, at Morisset.
She is thirty,
never married,
doesn't drive,
rarely reads, has schizophrenia,
each day is allowed one packet
of cigs, and one bottle of Coke.
The nurses are kind to her,
sometimes she writes poetry,
she is tired from dancing on
television every night,
her mother visits her every Saturday,
No-one else lives in her world.

They all watch TV every night,
alone in different suburbs, towns and houses,
they cannot live together,
they have not been raised to live together,
it is too late now to try.

Pat Richardson

⚡ Getting started

Think of your own characters that are connected in some way. They could be three
different generations of the one family. Or they could be a judge, a criminal and his
victim; actors and their audience; identical twin brothers. All you need to do is describe
each one individually. You may want to write a concluding stanza or you may want to let
the readers make their own connection. Either is appropriate.

A Woman Watches the Sun Rise

A woman watches the sun rise every morning
And dreams . . .
From her elegant balcony
She remembers things long forgotten.
She is fifty-two and growing older by the day.
During the day she enjoys her manicure
And taking her poodle for a walk.
Yet somehow she feels empty.

Her daughter watches the sun rise every morning
Awake before the kids begin to rise.
Enjoying the peaceful serenity of the rising sun
She remembers a distant woman.
During the day she feeds the children
And tidies her tiny black house.
Rushed with the hurriedness of the hours
She sometimes pauses to dream.

Her daughter watches her mother rise every morning.
Just turned ten with the innocence of a little girl
Yet she understands her mother's need for calmness.
She once got up to watch the sun rise,
But never again.
She needed her sleep.
During the day she tries to help her mother
As much as she can. She feels a
Sadness unknown . . .

Kelly Tisson

A Brother

A brother looks at his reflection in a pond
Thinking about someone.
It is his birthday.
He gets in his car and heads south.
His search begins.

A brother looks at his reflection in a window
Thinking about someone.
It is his birthday.
He boards a plane and heads north.
His search begins.

Brendan Bell

A Man Sits All By Himself

A man sits all by himself.
He is watching Mr Bean.
He is angry.
It's like watching a mirror.
He wears the same clothes
and has the same haircut.
Last week in the mall,
people were throwing money to him.
They thought he was a good impersonator.
His last name is Lentil and he hates it.
He wants to start again.
Change his name.
Change his clothes.
Change his life.
Change the channel!

Ashley DeBrenni

A Busker's Life

An old cold torn busker sat down alone to play,
every day in the same spot,
at exactly the same time. Nine.
He would release his instrument from its case
and set upon bringing life
to the dull and silent environment.
Gradually he became popular
and heard the familiar sound of coins
rustling in his instrument case. This
was enough to buy tonight's food
for him and his daughter.
He packed up his instrument
locked it back in its case and set off,
leaving the environment ringing.

Laura Duffield

Chill

A killer walks along the beach at night.
He sits on the beach as the tide rises.
The water wets him and chills him to the bone.
He doesn't care at all,
just sits and stares, and thinks about
what he has done.

A victim walks along the beach at night.
He sits on the beach as the tide rises.
The water wets him and chills him to the bone.
He doesn't care and is angry.
He cries and thinks of his wife who is dead.

A judge walks along the beach at night.
He sits on the beach as the tide rises.
The water wets him and chills him to the bone.
To get up he drives away in his Mercedes Benz
and leaves the murderer whom he set free
and the victim, alone on the beach
while the tide rises and wets them,
and chills me to the bone.

Cyprian Maynard

Adding to your collection

Write your own poem where you take two or three characters that are connected in some way. Describe each one individually, and allow the connections or lack of connections among them to make the point.

Poems as a source: pastiche

Poems can be made from other poems. Borrowing motifs from one or more well known poems is known as *pastiche*. Angelo Butera, Adam McCallum and Simon Priori have constructed their pieces by cutting up lines from a sample of five poems by Les Murray and Rory Harris. They made connections and wrote their own poems. The task was to construct new meanings on the themes, while at the same time staying true to the original poets' intentions. Angelo Butera develops repetition, changes pronouns and adds single words of his own to cement his poem together. Adam McCallum and Simon Priori add more of their own words, and both shift the focus of the sample poems. All write something completely different.

The Mystery of Love

In the midday light	1
his body leans	4
leans against a wall	4
In the midday light	1
her body leans	4
leans against a wall	4
She wants to leave herself	3
He wants to leave himself	3
together the distances between their faces close	2
She reads a poem	5
a poem about love	5
She reads the poem very well	5
a halo of force stood around him	1
and she blew a kiss	2
She climbed out of her body	3
He climbed out of his body	3
She climbed out of her head	3
He climbed out of his head	3
and turned into butterflies	3
and flew over landscapes	
that hold no discoveries except love	4/5

Angelo Butera

74

My Son

The son we surround,   1
the man   1
no-one approaches   1
weeps   1
in the midday light.   1
He falls in the middle of the road.
The traffic in George Street banks up   1
for half a mile   1
the crowd   1
stands back and ignores him
cars honk their horns
a drowning tone
In ragged clothes   4
his body leans
shuffles.
A boy rests   4
amongst the crowd
through the tall trees
to see what's going on.
The landscape is hard   4
tall buildings and a frozen crowd.
Why can't someone help
the stricken man
then
without hesitation
he walks to the middle of the road
'take my arm and I will help you.'
The crowd amazed, applauds.
The stricken man takes his son
and shuffles off along the footpath.
His sorrows disappear.
As they lean against a wall   4
the father looks at the tiny frame
of his son's body.
The man remembers
the words 'I love you.'   5
The boy then disappears
amongst the crowd.
The man smiles and stands tall.

            Adam McCallum

Simon Priori arrived home from school one day and received a phone call from his girlfriend saying that his good friend from work, Matthew Lee, had been hurt in a serious accident, so he wrote his pastiche poem for Matt.

for Matt

We all tried
As he burnt down main roads   1
And hurried through back streets   1
On the one thing he loves
All we could do was wait
For we all knew
What was to come
Some say they were shocked   1
As I too was shocked
But today it ended
We couldn't stop him
But knew today would come.

Simon Priori

1 An Absolutely Ordinary Rainbow

The word goes round Repins,
the murmur goes round Lorenzinis,
at Tattersalls, men look up from their sheets of numbers,
the Stock Exchange scribblers forget the chalk in their hands
and men with bread in their pockets leave the Greek Club:
There's a fellow crying in Martin Place. They can't stop him.

The traffic in George Street is banked up for half a mile
and drained of motion. The crowds are edgy with talk
and more crowds come hurrying. Many run in the back streets
which minutes ago were busy main streets, pointing:
There's a fellow weeping down there. No one can stop him.

The man we surround, the man no one approaches
simply weeps, and does not cover it, weeps
not like a child, not like the wind, like a man
and does not declaim it, nor beat his breast, or even
sob very loudly — yet the dignity of his weeping

holds us back from his space, the hollow he makes about him
in the midday light, in his pentagram of sorrow,
and uniforms back in the crowd who tried to seize him
stare out at him, and feel, with amazement, their minds
longing for tears as children for a rainbow.

Some will say, in years to come, a halo
or force stood around him. There is no such thing.
Some will say they were shocked and would have stopped him
but they will not have been there. The fiercest manhood,
the toughest reserve, the slickest wit amongst us

trembles with silence, and burns with unexpected
judgements of peace. Some in the concourse scream
who thought themselves happy. Only the smallest children
and such as look out of Paradise come near him
and sit at his feet, with dogs and dusty pigeons.

Ridiculous, says a man near me, and stops
his mouth with his hands, as if it uttered vomit —
and I see a woman, shining, stretch her hand
and shake as she receives the gift of weeping;
as many as follow her also receive it

and many more weep for sheer acceptance,
but the weeping man, like the earth, requires nothing,
the man who weeps ignores us, and cries out
of his writhen face and ordinary body

not words, but grief, not messages, but sorrow
hard as the earth, sheer, present as the sea —
and when he stops, he simply walks between us
mopping his face with the dignity of one
man who has wept, and now has finished weeping.

Evading believers, he hurries off down Pitt Street.

Les A. Murray

2 *junior primary*

Russell was sitting on my knee
one arm around my neck

the other around his story
he's reading, a voice

turning over
like a plough into earth

he's writing about
a bear being born

each lesson his story gets longer
but today it ended

with the cub
kissing the she bear

he was sitting on my knee
brought his face up to mine

& blew a kiss
to the distance between our faces
                              Rory Harris

3 *she wants to leave herself*

she wants to leave herself
climb out of her body
climb out of her head
& turn into a butterfly

which is not impossible
that she says this
pulling at the sleeve of her school tunic
& me listening
& she talking, is enough

enough for it to happen
to her, to me, to everyone

if we, if they
wanted it to

being able to do that
is like falling asleep during a movie
& waking up to the usherette's hand
on your arm
& all you can catch is the cleaner's shuffle
through the seats
which isn't part of the movie
or the last train home
if they're still running

& in the room
the idea exists

& she smiles & goes to a lesson
& I smile & go to a lesson

how many butterflies in a classroom

                        Rory Harris

4 *laying foundations*

his body leans
leans, against a wall

the mortar so soft it crumbles
like the milk teeth of a sick child

monuments fix history to earth
an English bronze can only point

the bricks, ragged as his trouser ends
uneven as a mountain range

here the landscape is hard
it holds no discoveries

a boy, rests
rests, against a wall

laying his own partitions in a school yard
they could come down around him

                        Rory Harris

5 this is going to be a poem / about love

this is going to be a poem
about love

today at school
a girl in grade 4

read to me a love
poem by a kid in year 11

from a school i'd worked in
years ago

she read the poem
very well

& at the end handed
me a piece of paper

with 'I love you'
written on it

her friend who had
been standing next to her

while all this was going on
said I ought to kiss her

& I should have

Rory Harris

🎵 *Using breath length poems*

In breath length poems, something similar occurs. The task is to create from, but still acknowledge, the borrowed source. Harris's 'breath' utilises the words, phrases and sentiments of the following quote

> The most disturbing and deplorable aspect of nineteenth century encounters with polar bears was a perverse manipulation of the bond between a female and her cubs, a common amusement of sailors aboard whaling and sealing ships. William Scoresby tells of the incident involving walrus hunters who had set fire to a pile of blubber to attract bears. A female and two cubs drew near. The female settled her cubs at a short distance and then started trying to hook pieces of blubber out of the fire. The men watched from the safety of the deck as she fought with the flames. They threw her small bits of blubber, which she took to the cubs. As she approached them with the last piece, the men shot the two cubs dead. For the next half hour she 'laid her paws first upon one, and then the other, and endeavoured to raise them up.' She walked off and called to them, 'she licked their wounds'. She went off again and 'stood for some time moaning' before returning to paw them 'with signs of inexpressible fondness.' Bored, or perhaps mortified, the men shot the female and left her on the ice with her cubs.
>
> (Barry Lopez, *Arctic Dreams*, Macmillan, London, 1986, pp. 111–12.)

breath

for Kerrie Armstrong

you held
her as

daughter
to both

of you
& wrapped

a world
around your

creation
& breathed

her animal newness

*

& after
the bear

cub had died
the mother

laid her paws
upon it

& endeavoured
to raise

it up
she walked

off & called
it, she

licked its
wounds

*

your own breath
cannot

keep her alive
your tears

fathered &
mothered

a legacy
of postcarded memory

collected & albumed
along the way

*

she went
off again

& stood
for some time

moaning
before returning

to paw it
with signs

of inexpressible
fondness

*

you have
buried your daughter

the toss
of a flower

into her grave
the short flight

echoes
heartbeat

on heartbeat
of family

Rory Harris

Using journal entries

A journal where you write day-to-day events can work in the same way. Here you can cut up, fine tune and develop your own writing. What was first written down in haste can be examined, redrafted a few more times and then made into poetry. These journal entries of 11–13 July 1994 were added to five more times before they became the poem 'somewhere on holiday'.

11–13 July 1994

the evenness
of hands
over granite
each child's step
high adventure
breathing deeply
holiday air
all coated
against the cloud's frown

the elbow of a bay
fish swim
in . . .
tide
from the
like . . .

and firefly light
along the ridges
a house full
of sleepers
the branches
graze the windows

the night
chins under covers

a wave
a scarf
around you

somewhere on holiday

the evenness of hands over granite
this holiday air
coated against the cloud's frown
crabbing under shadows
an elbow of bay draining the beach
night time electric fireflies along the ridges
branches graze windows
chins under blankets

Rory Harris

Adding to your collection

Think of a theme: the city, children, relationships, fashion, the beach, or something huge like love. Now go through this book gathering particular poems under your theme. Read them aloud many times and examine how the theme emerges. How do the poems work? Why did you select them? What do you like about them? Interrogate the poems. Are there ways of linking lines from one poem to another? Extract bits and begin creating your own. You may change pronouns and tense, but remember to stay true to the original intentions of the poets. Remember to acknowledge your sources. Also think about how to differentiate your lines from others in the final version.

'Tags' and 'To whom it may concern'

Everyone knows 'The House that Jack Built . . . '
This is the house that Jack built

This is the malt
that lay in the house that Jack built

This is the rat that ate the malt
That lay in the house that Jack built

This is the cat that ate the rat
that ate the malt
that lay in the house that Jack built . . .

It's simple, familiar, repetitive, cumulative and a model that Mike Ladd uses as the basis for his poem 'Tags' on the senseless killing of children during a civil war. Because it's a model associated with children, the killings and the final image of the children become even more poignant.

Tags

This is the gun so ready and new
placed in the hills where pine trees grow.

These are the men weary and mad
who aim the gun so ready and new
placed in the hills where pine trees grow.

This is the shell shrieking and clean
fired by the men weary and mad
who aim the gun so ready and new
placed in the hills where pine trees grow.

This is the roof with tiles of clay
hit by the shell shrieking and clean
fired by the men weary and mad
who aim the gun so ready and new
placed in the hills where pine trees grow.

This is the teacher holding a book
under the roof with tiles of clay
hit by the shell shrieking and clean
fired by the men weary and mad
who aim the gun so ready and new
placed in the hills where pine trees grow.

These are the children killed at their sums
next to the teacher holding a book
under the roof with tiles of clay
hit by the shell shrieking and clean
fired by the men weary and mad
who aim the gun so ready and new
placed in the hills where pine trees grow.

These are the tags tied on the feet
of children killed while at their sums
next to the teacher holding a book
under the roof with tiles of clay
hit by the shell shrieking and clean
fired by the men weary and mad
who aim the gun so ready and new
placed in the hills where pine trees grow.

Mike Ladd

 Let's begin

As a class focus on an object such as a clock and have your teacher write a tag poem of your own on the board.

This is the clock that holds the time
placed on the wall in Mr Fawcus's room.

These are the students at their desks
watching the clock that holds the time
placed on the wall of Mr Fawcus's room.

It won't take long before you get a feel for the rhythm and the pattern.

These are the chairs with legs of steel
that hold the students at their desks
who watch the clock that holds the time
placed on the wall of Mr Fawcus's room.

These are the turtles that swim to and fro
alongside the chairs with their legs of steel
peering at students who sit at their desks
who watch the clock that holds the time
placed on the wall of Mr Fawcus's room.

Peter McFarlane

 Looking at other poems

Leave the poem on the board as a reminder of the pattern and look at how these poems have been built up using a door, a letterbox and a fire as a focus.

The Door

This is the wall so white and so bare
built in the corridor where children pass.

This is the floor so dusty and worn
supporting the wall so white and so bare
built in the corridor where children pass.

These are the tyres full of air
resting on the floor so dusty and worn
supporting the wall so white and so bare
built in the corridor where children pass.

These are the pots of terracotta
above the tyres full of air
resting on the floor so dusty and worn
supporting the wall so white and so bare
built in the corridor where children pass.

This is the door out of the school
past the pots of terracotta
above the tyres full of air
resting on the floor so dusty and worn
supporting the wall so white and so bare
built in the corridor where children pass.

Patrick Phelan

Letterbox

This is the stamp, so sticky and perfect
in the bottom of the letterbox which the postman visits

This is the bill so hopeless and despairing
beneath the stamp so sticky and perfect
in the bottom of the letterbox which the postman visits.

This is the catalogue so vibrant and alive
next to the bill so hopeless and despairing
beneath the stamp so sticky and perfect
in the bottom of the letterbox which the postman visits.

This is the death threat so foreboding and bold
adjacent to the catalogue so vibrant and alive
next to the bill so hopeless and despairing
beneath the stamp so sticky and perfect
in the bottom of the letterbox which the postman visits.

This is the shampoo sample so small and pathetic
opposite the death threat so foreboding and bold
adjacent to the catalogue so vibrant and alive
next to the bill so hopeless and despairing
beneath the stamp so sticky and perfect
in the bottom of the letterbox which the postman visits.

This is the letter so yearning and pleading
across from the shampoo sample so small and pathetic
opposite the death threat so foreboding and bold
adjacent to the catalogue so vibrant and alive
next to the bill so hopeless and despairing
beneath the stamp so sticky and perfect
in the bottom of the letterbox which the postman visits.

This is the crushed egg so broken and sad
splattered over the letter so yearning and pleading
across from the shampoo sample so small and pathetic
opposite the death threat so foreboding and bold
adjacent to the catalogue so vibrant and alive
next to the bill so hopeless and despairing
beneath the stamp so sticky and perfect
in the bottom of the letterbox which the postman visits.

Joanne Hocking

The Fire

This is the cat, motheaten and old,
who basks by the fire, so warm and red.

This is the dog, all hairy and dribbly,
who pants by the cat, motheaten and old,
who basks by the fire, so warm and red.

This is the foot, resting on the footstool,
nearby the dog, all hairy and dribbly,
who pants by the cat, motheaten and old,
who basks by the fire, so warm and red.

This is the rising and falling body
attached to the foot, resting on the footstool,
nearby the dog, all hairy and dribbly,
who pants by the cat, motheaten and old,
who basks by the fire, so warm and red.

This is the grotesquely ugly head,
above the rising and falling body,
attached to the foot, resting on the footstool,
nearby the dog, all hairy and dribbly,
who pants by the cat, motheaten and old,
who basks by the fire, so warm and red.

This is the sound of the snore that emerges,
from the mouth of the grotesquely ugly head
above the rising and falling body,
attached to the foot, resting on the footstool,
nearby the dog, all hairy and dribbly,
who pants by the cat, motheaten and old,
who basks by the fire, so warm and red.

This is the thin piece of fluff in the air,
which vibrates to the sound of the snore that emerges
from the mouth of the grotesquely ugly head,
above the rising and falling body,
attached to the foot, resting on the footstool,
nearby the dog, all hairy and dribbly,
who pants by the cat, motheaten and old,
who basks by the fire, so warm and red.

This is the fire that burnt and ate up
floating, the thin piece of fluff in the air,
which vibrates to the sound of the snore that emerges
from the mouth of the grotesquely ugly head,
above the rising and falling body,
attached to the foot, resting on the footstool,
nearby the dog, all hairy and dribbly,
who pants by the cat, motheaten and old,
who basks by the fire, so warm and red.

Arwen Summers

✉ 'To whom it may concern' poems

Look at the poem 'To Whom it May Concern'. Adrian Mitchell creates a poem using repetition, violent images that accumulate and build on each other, and echoes of children's rhymes. The result is an amazing anti-war poem that builds to a crescendo and demands to be chanted or sung.

To Whom it May Concern

I was run over by the truth one day.
Ever since the accident I've walked this way
    So stick my legs in plaster
    Tell me lies about Vietnam.

Heard the alarm clock screaming with pain,
Couldn't find myself so I went back to sleep again
    So fill my ears with silver
    Stick my legs in plaster
    Tell me lies about Vietnam.

Every time I shut my eyes all I see is flames.
Made a marble phone book and I carved all the names
    So coat my eyes with butter
    Fill my ears with silver
    Stick my legs in plaster
    Tell me lies about Vietnam.

I smell something burning, hope its just my brains.
They're only dropping peppermints and daisy-chains
    So stuff my nose with garlic
    Coat my eyes with butter
    Fill my ears with silver
    Stick my legs in plaster
    Tell me lies about Vietnam.

Where were you at the time of the crime?
Down by the Cenotaph drinking slime
    So chain my tongue with whisky
    Stuff my nose with garlic
    Coat my eyes with butter
    Fill my ears with silver
    Stick my legs in plaster
    Tell me lies about Vietnam.

You put your bombers in, you put your conscience out,
You take the human being and you twist it all about
    So scrub my skin with women
    Chain my tongue with whisky
    Stuff my nose with garlic
    Coat my eyes with butter
    Fill my ears with silver
    Stick my legs in plaster
    Tell me lies about Vietnam.

Adrian Mitchell

Notice how the poem starts with a rhymed couplet, then builds a series of images line upon line.

To Whom it May Concern (Nudity)

I saw a shopful of manikins without their clothes
Dummies are all right naked I suppose
    So fill the cells with streakers
    Send nudity packing with a frown.

Turned on the cold tap and took a shower
Had to hide myself lower and lower
    So lop the breasts of statues
    Fill the cells with streakers
    Send nudity packing with a frown.

Or

To Whom it May Concern (Injustice)

Heard the idiot shouting down the street
Nothing but sandals on his feet
    So block my ears with beeswax
    Shut out the screams of a woman alone.

And so on.

Adding to your collection

Write a poem modelled on Mike Ladd's poem 'Tags' that is simple, repetitive and cumulative. Then using similar techniques to Mitchell write your own 'To whom it may concern' poem about an issue that you are passionate or disturbed or annoyed about. Your piece need not be an angry poem. You may find this form gives you the opportunity to write something humourous. Add your 'Tags' and your 'To whom it may concern' poems to your collection.

Dialogues of absence

'Dream of a Bird' is a model poem where students who speak English as a second language have constructed a dialogue with 'someone' somewhere else. The effect is an echo of rhetoric, convincing the writer and reader that the absence is more than geographic. The poem begins with the opening line: 'You ask me, what did I dream?' The line after the response follows the pattern: 'You ask me, why did I want to become a bird?' Each new question is based on the previous answer.

Dream of a Bird

You ask me, what did I dream?
I dreamt I became a bird.
You ask me, why did I want to become a bird?
I really wanted to have wings.
Why did I want wings?
These wings would help me fly back to my country.
Why did I want to go back there?
Because I wanted to find something I missed.
You ask me, what do I miss?
I miss the place where I lived as a child.
What was that place like?
That place was happy, my family was close together.
You ask me, what I remember best?
I still remember my father reading the newspaper.
You ask me, why I think of him?
I miss him and I'm sad.
You ask me, why I am sad?
I'm sad because all my friends have fathers.
Why does this matter?
Because my father is far away.
I want to fly to him like a bird.

Bach Nga Thi Tran

Dream of a Family

You ask me, what did I dream?
I dreamt I wanted to go back to Hong Kong.
You ask me, why did I want to go back to Hong Kong?
I really wanted to go back to Hong Kong to see my family.
Why did I want to go back to Hong Kong to see my family?
Because my family looked after me when I was young.
Why did I miss my family?
Because I wanted to see if my family had changed.
You ask me, how much do I miss my family?
I miss my family very much.
What was your family like?
My family was beautiful and happy.
You ask me, what I remember best?
I remember when I went out and ate with my family.
Why does that matter?
Because I went away from my family.

Wai Lun Lam

Girl

You ask me, what did I dream?
I dreamt that I became a time machine.
You ask me, why did I want to become a time machine?
I really wanted to go through time.
Why did I want to go through time?
This would help me go back to my youth.
Why did I want to go back to my youth?
Because I wanted to find someone I missed.
You ask me, who do I miss?
I miss the person from when I was sixteen.
What was she like?
She was beautiful.
You ask me, what I remember best?
I still remember the first time catching her hand.
You ask me, why I think of her?
I miss her and I am sad.
You ask me, why I am sad?
I'm sad because I love her so much.
Why does this matter?
Because she left me and went away.
I want to go back through time to her.

Tai Hoi Ming

Dream of a Business Man

You ask me, what did I dream?
I dreamt that I became a business man.
You ask me, why did I become a business man?
I really wanted to have my own business.
Why did I want my own business?
My own business would help me make money.
Why did I want to make money?
Because I want to help many, many poor people.
You ask me, why do I want to help poor people?
I want to help poor people because they have no food and no shelter.
What are poor people like?
I feel poor people are very sad.
You ask me, what I remember best?
I still remember poor people who are very sad.
You ask me, why no food and no shelter?
Why does this matter?
Because poor people are very sad.
So I want to help them.
I want to become a business man.
To help poor people.

Ng Hon Fung

Lam Siu Ki, my Mother

You ask me, what did I dream?
I dreamt I wanted to be an angel.
You ask me, why did I want to be an angel?
I really wanted to go to heaven.
Why do you really want to go to heaven?
Because I want to see someone.
Who do you want to see?
I want to see an important person.
You ask me, why do I want to see her?
Because she loved me when I was a child.
What does she look like?
She looks like a kind woman.

Ngai Man Ho

Adding to your collection

Keeping the same pattern, write your own dialogue of absence.

Possibility poems

Listen to this poem as it is read aloud and, without looking at it on the page, when the reader pauses, see if you can predict what the next line is going to say.

Possibilities for a Man Hunted by SBs

There's one of two possibilities
Either they find you or they don't
If they don't it's ok
But if they find you
There's one of two possibilities
Either they let you go or they ban you
If they let you go it's ok
But if they ban you
There's one of two possibilities
Either you break your ban or you don't
If you don't it's ok
But if you break your ban
There's one of two possibilities
Either they find out or they don't
If they don't it's ok
But if they find out
There's one of two possibilities
Either they find you guilty or not guilty
If they find you not guilty it's ok
But if they find you guilty
There's one of two possibilities
Either they suspend your sentence or they jail you
If they suspend your sentence it's ok
But if they jail you
There's one of two possibilities
Either they release you
Or you fall from the tenth floor.

Farouk Asvat

Farouk Asvat (who was banned by the South African government in the 1970s) is a medical doctor and poet who is particularly involved in social medicine and the problems of Black community health. 'Possibilities for a Man Hunted by SBs' explores the worst scenario using the two possibilities concept and takes on power as it gradually builds up to the final possibility.

There's One of Two Possibilities

There's one of two possibilities
Either you take it or you don't
If you don't that's OK, but if you do
There's one of two possibilities
Either you get caught or you don't
If you don't that's OK but if you do
There's one of two possibilities
Either the cops take you to the station
Or they don't
If they don't that's OK, but if they do
There's one of two possibilities
They will tell your parents or they won't
If they don't that's OK, but if they do —
You're dead meat!

Anon.

There's One of Two Possibilities

There's one of two possibilities
Either you go or you don't
If you go that's OK
But if you don't, there's one of two possibilities
Either you leave or you don't
If you don't that's OK
But if you do . . . You're fired!

Karrie McCann

There's One of Two Possibilities

There's one of two possibilities
Either you stop or you don't
If you do that's OK, but if you don't
There's one of two possibilities
Either you crash or you don't
If you don't that's OK, but if you do
There's one of two possibilities
Either you get hurt or you don't
If you don't that's OK, but if you do
There's one of two possibilities
Either you get squashed or you don't
If you don't that's OK, but if you do . . .

THAT'S BAD LUCK!!!

Wendy Harriss

Adding to your collection

Try writing possibility poems based on your own selection of options: either you kiss him or you don't; either they pass you or they don't; either you leave the house or you don't. The possibilities are endless.

Hate poems

Letting out our feelings can be cathartic. It can make us feel better. William Blake's 'A Poison Tree' advocates the importance of communicating and expressing our emotions so that negative feelings don't build up inside and cause us to be violent towards each other or 'explode' from within and hurt ourselves.

The Poison Tree

I was angry with my friend:
I told my wrath, my wrath did end.
I was angry with my foe:
I told it not, my wrath did grow.

And I watered it in fears,
Night & morning with my tears:
And I sunned it with smiles,
And with soft deceitful wiles.

And it grew both day and night,
Till it bore an apple bright.
And my foe beheld it shine,
And he knew that it was mine.

And into my garden stole,
When the night had veild the pole;
In the morning glad I see,
My foe outstretchd beneath the tree.

William Blake

Our own 'hate poems' can have a similar cathartic effect.

Hate

People hate
People like
Hate is a thing
People don't like

Megan White

I Hate Her

She's lookin' at me.
. . . I hate her!
and she knows it, too.
She sits there and perves on me boyfriend
while he's playin' footy.
Looks like her eyes
are permanently stuck on him.
I'm gonna hit her soon, you'll see!
Next Saturday at the footy, she'll perv,
I'll hit, she'll cry —
I can't wait. Stupid so-and-so!
I hate her!
She thinks she's an Impulse can —
Ya know, irresistible to men.
Well, she's not!
She's got a face like a twisted sandshoe.
. . . I hate her!
Why does she always look at me
and me boyfriend?
She knows we both hate her.
I wanna kill her —
then she couldn't look no more
and I could have me boyfriend
all to meself,
with no-one to interfere.
We're gonna get married one day, ya know.
We're gonna have kids too . . .
but always in the back of me mind
she will remain
and haunt me till the day I die.
. . . I hate her.

Robyn Blake

They Hate Me

Boy do they hate me.
They don't even know me,
But nothing will change their minds now.
Even if I'd just saved their life,
They'd still hate me.
They've got it set in their minds:
They hate me, and that's that.
I don't hate them.
How can I?
I don't know them.
I'm sure they're really nice people,
But they aren't going to let me find out
If they are or not.
Are they?

Tina Ferraro

I Hate Her

I hate her
That short cropped hair
Sallow lips innocent of lipstick
Bitter pin-piercing stones of eyes
Masculine, angular stature
Those grey trousers
Rigid
Untouchable
And they wonder why men
cannot weep
But how can I
When the male in me jumps out
Uncontrolled, accidental
Whenever she pounces?
Arrogance infects me
How can I weep
Before her splintered stare?

Sarah Le Page

Adding to your collection

Try writing some 'hate poems' for your collection. They don't have to be feelings of hatred towards a person or people, they could be directed at anything

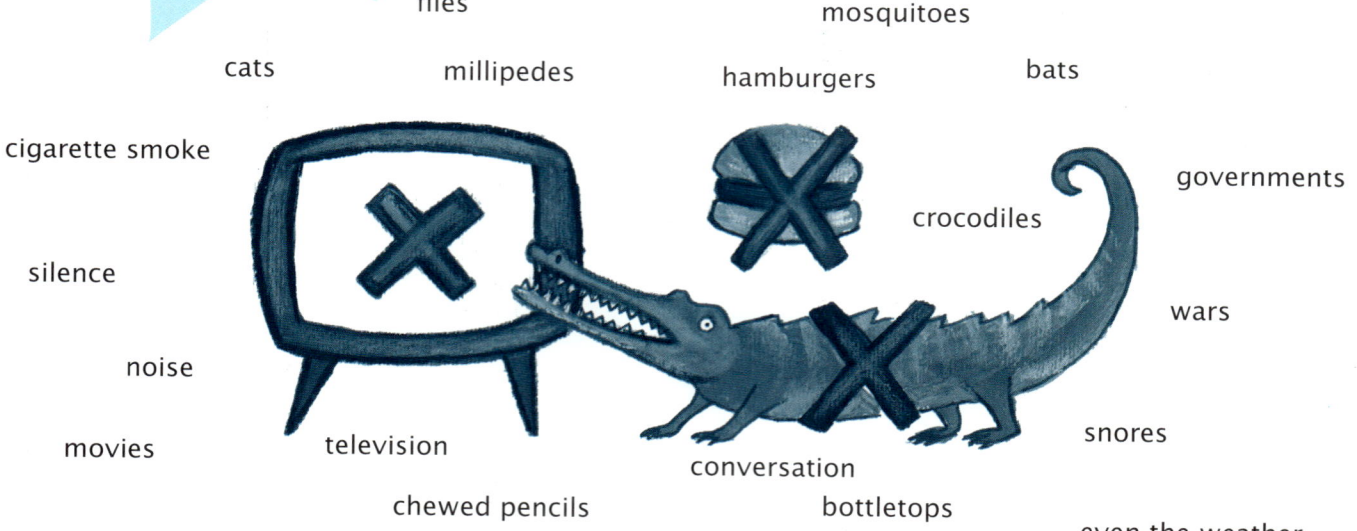

flies

mosquitoes

cats

millipedes

hamburgers

bats

cigarette smoke

governments

crocodiles

silence

wars

noise

movies

snores

television

conversation

chewed pencils

bottletops

even the weather.

Bad habit poems

We've all got bad habits. Even teachers have bad habits! Peeling sunburnt skin, clicking pens in class, nail biting, biscuit eating, snoring, putting people down, picking zits, not trusting, being hard to please, sniffing — the list of bad habits is endless, which makes them lovely topics for poems. The good thing is that you can have fun and make your habits even worse than they are, or if you're truly worried about them, you can cure yourself in an instant!

Picking Skin

I sit down
and slouch in the chair
roll up my sleeves
and start peeling.
Scratch scratch rip rip.
Ah, a nice big chunk of skin.
Oh oh, here comes mum.
Roll down my sleeve.
Quick, hurry up, go away.
Good, roll up my sleeve again.
Scratch scratch rip rip.
Another chunk of pale skin.
Search around for more pieces of skin:
under, over, left arm and right arm.
Oh no, none left.
Roll down my sleeve and sulk.

Renee Alberts

Bad Habits

As I sit back in my chair,
Sitting, watching, waiting,
For the teacher to turn around
(Good, he can't see me!)
I start clicking, clicking, clicking,
Sitting, watching, waiting, to make sure
That he doesn't see me.
'Come here you little rat.'
He yells across the room.
If I don't I will be kept in after school.
I get up and start towards the front.
Everybody starts to laugh at me.
How embarrassing!
I think I want to give up this habit.

Tanya Henderson

Watchin' TV

Watchin' TV
I feel like
somethin' to
eat so
I bite
and bite
nibble
nibble
one day
I won't
have
any
nails
left

Jason Cox

Sitting in the Classroom

Sitting in the classroom
bored as I could be
I roll up my sleeves
and look for a scab
At last I find one
I pick it and groan in agony
Then I see a beautiful big red puddle of blood.

Aaron Dunk

I Could But I Shouldn't

I could but I shouldn't
I might but I shouldn't
I'm seriously considering it
But I shouldn't
Damn it I will
SCRRRRRRRRRRRRRRRRRRRRCH
Fingers down the blackboard.

Kevan Watson

Adding to your collection

Think of your worst bad habit and write a poem about it. Don't be frightened to enjoy yourself!

Poems with rhythm

If a poem needs a particular rhythm, or if its rhythm is central to the point a poem is making, then the form of the poem should reflect it and contain the rhythm in some way.

The rhythm (or the beat) of a poem can be depicted by: the lopsided beat of a clock, the 'riddum' of John Agard's West Indian in 'Stereotype', the military beat of 'Ballad' as it helps tell us the story of a betrayed fugitive captured by soldiers, the computerised gobbledegook of automatic ticket machines as they swallow and spit out our tickets on public transport, or arcade games.

Listen to the variety of rhythms around you — dripping taps, traffic on the road, cats stalking birds, children playing games — and then look at the different examples of rhythm in the poems that follow.

The Roller Coaster

We have a jerky starting up the hill
When we're at the top
we start rolling at a comfortable speed
then we start to get faster

oh no

faster faster
and WHOOSH

down the hill, up the hill
round the corner, round the hoop
down the hill and out again
slowing down, jerking forward
slowly stopping
and

oh no

faster faster
and WHOOSH

down the hill, up the hill
round the corner, round the hoop
down the hill, almost over
ahhhhh to a halt
we survived

Belinda House

Tap

I know if I listen it's going to

        DRIP

in-ter-mit-tent-ly

     DRIP

  DRIP

    DRIP

      DRIP

  DRIP

     DRIP

    DRIP

    DRIP

     un-

      til

      I

       tight-

        en

        a

         wrench

          round

           its

           THROAT!

Peter McFarlane

And the Score

Ticka Tack Ticka Tack
Tack Tick Dinga Ding
Fingers play keys
In accord with the action
Ticka Tack Ticka Tack
Dinga Ding Ticka Tack
Ding
Fingers at work
On an icon
Ticka Tack Tack Tack
Tick Tack
Merry-go-round image
With each life intact
Significant
Tick Tack Ticka Tack
Ticka Tack Tack
Fingers play arpeggios
Slipping over stops and keys
Never a false move
Ticka Tack Ticka Tack
Tick Tick Tick
Ding
Nineteen thousand and sixty-five
Nineteen thousand and sixty-six

054800

Nineteen thousand and . . .
Twenty two thousand three hundred
Never missing
It's the winning that counts
Ticka Tack Tack
Aim the sights
Pull the trigger
Release the inestimable power
Create the false glow
On another screen
End of game —
And the score
One thousand million
Is inconsequential

Alan Laslett

Hyp - No - Tic

My clock's
got a limp
tick TOCK
tick TOCK
my clock's
got a limp
tick TOCK
tick TOCK
my clock's
got a limp
bing BONG

Peter McFarlane

Tennis at School

Ha, that's an ace!
Don't be stupid!
It's an ace!
Is!
Is!
Is!
OK

Nice shot

That one's out!
Out!
Replay?

Aah, fell over!
Would've!
Yes!
Yes!
Yes!
Replay?

Ha, an ace!
Was!
Was!
Was!
OK

Bull, it was out!
I'm not!
Bull!
Bull!
Bull!
Replay?

Thanks

Bull!
Bull!
OK

Wouldn't a' got it anyway!
Nooo!
No!
No!
No!
OK

Wasn't ready!
Wasn't!
Wasn't!
Replay?

Michael Hoffmann

Automatic Ticket Machine

IN***Naw nit*Naw nit*
*Naw nit****Naw nit**
Naw nit**Naw nit*****
Naw nit***TICKET*
Naw nit*OUT***Nit naw
Nit naw***Naw nit****
Do   dit********
***********STOP

Hilary Gold

Ballad

O what is that sound which so thrills the ear,
    Down in the valley drumming, drumming?
Only the scarlet soldiers, dear,
    The soldiers coming.

O what is that light I see flashing so clear,
    Over the distance brightly, brightly?
Only the sun on their weapons, dear,
    As they step lightly.

O what are they doing with all that gear,
    What are they doing this morning, this morning?
Only the usual manoeuvres, dear,
    Or perhaps a warning.

O why have they left the road down there?
    Why are they suddenly wheeling, wheeling?
Perhaps a change in the orders, dear,
    Why are you kneeling?

O haven't they stopped for the doctor's care,
    Haven't they reined their horses, their horses?
Why, they are none of them wounded, dear,
    None of these forces.

O is it the parson they want with white hair,
    Is it the parson, is it, is it?
No, they are passing his gateway, dear,
    Without a visit.

O it must be the farmer who lives so near,
    It must be the farmer so cunning, so cunning?
They have passed the farm already, dear,
    And now they are running.

O where are you going? Stay with me here!
    Were the vows you swore me deceiving, deceiving?
No, I promised to love you dear,
    But I must be leaving.

O it's broken the lock and splintered the door,
    O it's the gate where they're turning, turning,
Their feet are heavy on the floor,
    And their eyes are burning.

W. H. Auden

Stereotype

I'm a fullblooded
West Indian stereotype
See me straw hat?
Watch it good

I'm a fullblooded
West Indian stereotype
You ask
if I got riddum
in me blood
You going ask!
Man just beat de drum
and don't forget
to pour de rum

I'm a fullblooded
West Indian stereotype
You say
I suppose you can show
us the limbo, can't you?
How you know!
How you know!
You sure
you don't want me
sing you a calypso too
How about that

I'm a fullblooded
West Indian stereotype
You call me
happy-go-lucky
Yes that's me
dressing fancy
and chasing woman
if you think ah lie
bring yuh sister

I'm a fullblooded
West Indian stereotype
You wonder
where do you people
get such riddum
could it be the sunshine
My goodness
just listen to that steelband

Isn't there one thing
you forgot to ask
go on man ask
This native will answer anything
How about cricket?
I suppose you're good at it?
Hear this man
good at it!
Put de willow
in me hand
and watch me stripe
de boundary

Yes I'm a fullblooded
West Indian stereotype

that's why I
graduated from Oxford University
with a degree
in anthropology

John Agard

Poetry Jump-Up

Tell me if ah seeing right
Take a look down de street
Words dancin
words dancin
till dey sweat
words like fishes
jumpin out a net
words wild and free
joinin de poetry revelry
words back to back
words belly to belly

Come on everybody
come and join de poetry band
dis is poetry carnival
dis is poetry bacchanal
when inspiration call
take yu pen in yu hand
if yu dont have a pen
take you pencil in yu hand
if yu dont have a pencil
what the hell
so long de feeling start to swell
just shout de poem out

Words jumpin off de page
tell me if ah seeing right
words like birds
jumpin out a cage
take a look down de street
words shakin dey waist
words shakin dey bum
words wit black skin
words wit white skin
words wit brown skin
words huggin up words
an saying I want to be a poem today
rhyme or no rhyme
I is a poem today
I mean to have a good time

Words feelin hot hot hot
big words feelin hot hot hot
lil words feelin hot hot hot
even sad words can't help
tappin dey toe
to de riddum of de poetry band

John Agard

Adding to your collection

Keeping in mind these poems and all the sources of poetry around you, write your own poem with rhythm.

Dialect and Creole poems

A lot of poets around the world are choosing to write in Creole, that is, a pidgin which has become the primary language of a speech community, or a dialect — a special variety or branch of a language. Louise Bennett, Valerie Bloom, Grace Nichols and John Agard are four Caribbean writers specialising in a folk tradition using such speech traits and rhythms. Like two Australian Greek writers, Komninos and πO, who use similar techniques, they celebrate the language dialects that they write in.

Wha me Mudder do

Mek me tell you wha me mudder do
wha me mudder do
wha me mudder do

Me mudder pound plaintain mek fufu
Me mudder catch crab mek calaloo stew

Mek me tell you wha me mudder do
wha me mudder do
wha me mudder do

Me mudder beat hammer
Me mudder turn screw
she paint chair red
then she paint it blue

Mek me tell you wha me mudder do
wha me mudder do
wha me mudder do

Me mudder chase bad-cow
with one 'Shoo'
she paddle down river
in she own canoe
Ain't have nothing
dat me mudder can't do
Ain't have nothing
dat me mudder can't do

Mek me tell you

Grace Nichols

☞ *Writing your own dialect poem*

Copying the form of Grace Nichols, write your own 'Wha me Mudder do' poem. You may choose to do your own version of a West Indian dialect (it could be 'Wha me Fudder — or Brudder or Sistar — do'), or you may change it to a dialect of your own, one that you are familiar with and enjoy. Simply keep Grace Nichols's stanzas and change the words to fit.

Wha me Brudder do

Me brudder play basketball in back yard
me brudder is small so he play guard

me brudder play early
me brudder play late
me brudder break a window
da mudder go ape

me brudder take his basketball
run away

me brudder take his money
so de fudder have to pay

me brudder join de army
and he get tough
but he didn't go to war
cos it too rough

me brudder come back to live at home
but we gone north so he play alone
me brudder home alone

Yo mon

Geelong College

Try doing the same thing with another West Indian poem *'Tables'*, by Valerie Bloom.

Tables

Headmaster a come, mek has'e! Si-down.
Amy! min' yuh bruck Jane collar-bone,
Tom! Tek yuh foot off o'de desk,

Sandra Wallace, mi know yuh vex
But beg yuh get off o' Joseph head.
Tek de lizard off o' Sue neck, Ted!
Sue, mi dear, don bawl so loud,
Thomas, yuh can tell mi why yuh a put de toad
Eena Elvira sandwich bag?
An, Jim, whey yuh a do wid dah bull frog?
Tek i' off mi table! yuh mad?
Mi know yuh chair small, May, but it not dat bad
Dat yuh haffe siddung pon de floor!
Jim don' squeeze de fog unda de door,
Put i' through de window — no, no Les!
Mi know yuh hungry, but Mary yeas
Won' full yuh up, so spit it out.
Now go wash de blood outa yuh mout.
Hortense, tek Mary to de nurse.
Nick tek yuh han out o' Mary purse!
Ah wonda who tell all o' yuh
Sey dat dis class-room is a zoo?
Si-down, Head-master comin' through de door!
'Two ones are two, two twos are four.'

Valerie Bloom

Here is a similar piece in an ocker Australian accent.

Poe-Tree

G'day yous lot. Macca 'ere.
Gunna do some of this wicked poe-tree stuff today.
Gordo, you tryin' to make Tommo 'n Bennie kiss or sumpin?
Tommo, is that you or your monkey that's squeakin'?
Wellie, stop splashin' about there in that puddle you just made.
And KFC haven't you finished your mornin' burger yet?
Langie Loch Ness, stop eatin' Hardy Ha Ha's ears!
Jacko, I know you're a monkey, but stop swingin' around
And Gordo stop kickin' Langie Loch Ness.
KFC stop eatin' yourself. Why?
Didn't you eat your breakfast yet?
Vardy, why did you eat my recess?
And Ka Ka, I know you like doin' the can can
But 'ere's not the place.
Fatma . . . stop those smells!

Eater . . . stop eatin' Conquest House!
Scooter I know you like KFC
But please . . .
Jacko I've told ya before we're doin' poe-tree
Tommo, just what are you doin' with those monkeys?
'Ang on the 'ead's 'ere.

Mary had a little lamb, little lamb
Little lamb
Mary had a little lamb

Scotch College Junior School students

Dialect poems encourage you to enjoy the accents and variations in language that you
hear around you. Here's a piece of dialogue in a northern English country accent.

Ya Divvy

All right how's ya goin lad?
Pretty good laddy, how's ya?
Pretty good actually did ya see the football?
Yeh good eh, Manunited won
Ye want go out to eat?
No, what da ya think ya doin?
Naugh
Ya look like a divvy
Ya the one that looks like a divvy
Eh so ya wanna play tennis?
Yea ya wanna have duck for dinna?
Thought ya weren't hungry
Am now
Let's go then
All right I'll grab me flip flops

You'll need trainers for tennis
Ya right lad I will
Let's go ya divvy
I'm not a divvy
Ya are
Not
Are
Not
Are
Not
Are
Not
Ah get off, ya are
Not!

Anon.

Lachlan Walter uses a roll-call in a fantasy class to show the diversity of language, accent and dialect.

Class Room

John?	Here
Pete?	Yeah
Elvis?	A huh huh
Antonio?	Si
Joey, Elvis, Jimi?	Yo
Scott?	He's dead sir
Pardon?	He's dead
Pity	
Maxwell?	Uh, yes, I'm h-
	h-here sir
Rodriguez?	Si
Luigi?	I'm a here sir
Simon?	Yes
Roger?	Yes
Peter Franklin III?	Yes I am here
Tim?	Present
Tom? Tom?	
Take those headphones out of your ears!	Sorry sir.

Lachlan Walter

Adding to your collection

Celebrate the language you are familiar with, or a dialect you have heard or are a part of, by writing your own dialect poem and add it to your poetry collection.

Poems from sayings

A mark of the richness of a language is the number of different words and sayings it has for a certain thing or action. For example, how many words does the English language have for 'poor'? Write them down:

broke, penniless, unable to rub two cents together, being on the bean end . . .

How many did everyone get?

This was a task the writer Isaac Bashevis Singer gave the Stockholm Jewish community he was speaking to the night after his Nobel speech in 1978. He said that in English they would find only half a dozen words and sayings for 'poor'. Yiddish, the language he wrote in, was far richer.

> In Yiddish we've got pauper, beggar, destitute, wretched, shlepper, good for nothing, owner of a cabbage head, shirtless, miserable pauper, deep in grief. You can say that a man swallows his saliva, that he forgot the shape of a coin, that he drops dead from hunger three times a day, that things go as bad for him as a wicked person in the next world or a saint in this world, that he carries the soul on the end of his nose. You can say that he stumbles like a fool, that he barely has enough for water and grits, that all year long is Passover for him since he doesn't see a slice of bread. You can even call him Rothschild, with a slight wink, and everyone will understand he's dying of hunger. Only a crazy person would trade such a rich language for English.

Test Singer's theory on other English words. What sayings does the English language have for these, for example?

head

loaf of bread, bean, nut, scone . . .

dying

karking it, shuffling off our mortal coil, dropping off the twig, passing on, kaput, being no more, falling off the perch . . .

For a great humourous example of this, find the long list of words for 'dead' that the Monty Python team came up with in their famous 'dead parrot' sketch.

Barry Carozzi who has 'a good head on his shoulders' and 'plenty of grey matter', decided to have fun with sayings by extending this idea and putting together as many sayings for 'stupid person' as his 'fertile mind' could dream up.

He's

He's popped his cogs. He's dead between the ears.
He's nutty as a fruitcake; flipped his lid.
The lights are on, but nobody's at home.
He's bonkers, crackers — not quite the full quid.

He's off his chump, completely round the twist
Non compos mentis. Dippy. Off his tree.
He's barmy, potty, crazy. He's a Lulu.
Not in possession of his faculties.

The kangaroos are loose in his top paddock.
He's a tinny — maybe two — short of a slab.
He's round the bend. A few cents short of a dollar.
He's loony. Loopy. He's stark raving mad.

If he had another brain, it'd be lonely.
He's got a bloomin' screw loose. And what's more
If all his brains were dynamite, I tell you
They wouldn't blow his socks off, that's for sure.

He's mad as a March Hare. A silly-billy.
As silly as a two bob watch, that's him.
You call him a wit, and you'd be half right.
He's a drop kick. Not too bright. His wits are dim.

He's a drongo. Unintelligent. He's stupid.
Hasn't got a single brain up in his head.
He's thicker than two planks. A real nitwit.
From his neck upwards — everything is dead.

He's madder than a wet wheel. He's a dufus.
He's dorky. Dense. A simpleton. A tool.
He's madder than a meat axe. He's a dillpot.
He's a nincompoop, a ning nong, and a fool.

He's never had a thought in his whole lifetime.
He's a coupla sausages short of a barbecue.
He's a basketcase. He's off his brain. Demented.
When they gave out brains, he was way back in the queue.

He's got air between the ears. A real no-hoper.
He's lacking in intelligence. Insane.
You tell him something — it's straight through to the keeper.
He's a Wally. He's a wombat. Off his brain.

If he had a brain wave, it'd barely make a splash.

Barry Carozzi

 # Looking at other poems

People other than Barry Carozzi have created similar poems by selecting topics and piling up sayings and words that are used to describe them.

A place we're all familiar with

The Toilet

The bog house
The long drop
The reliever
The throne
The kingdom
THUNDERBOX
The retreat
Morning residence
The place that's never close enough
Toddler's hell.

Laura Bruce

A lover of motors

Petrol Head

Petrol head
Carburetor for a brain
Your mother's a 4 wheel drive
How do you get into first
in the morning?

Alasdair Rogers

A favourite landscape

It's

It's a spot to take your breath away
Unbelievable, awesome, truly unreal
It's . . .

Peter McFarlane

A football match

They're

They're burrowing in, applying the pressure
They're after the hard ball with guts and with skill
They're hunting in packs at the heart of the action
They're captains courageous who never say die
They're not chasing guernseys, they're not shirking danger
None of them are passengers or missing from sight
They're all chasing leather, they're all in there fighting
They're pulling down big ones, marks of the year
They're sending in passes and feeding their forwards
They're splitting the uprights, bisecting the sticks
They're kicking clear majors, they're not kicking minors
Their tails are up, they're in front, in the clear
They're bleeding, they're hurting, they're . . .

Peter McFarlane

Adding to your collection

Copy this idea and add your own 'poems from sayings' to your collection. Select a topic of your own and build a poem by piling up all the words and sayings you have heard to describe it. Try using repetition and variation. Avoid rhyme so that your focus is on a natural use of the sayings. If possible try to finish with a punch line, maybe a pun the way Barry Carozzi does.

Opening line poems

The opening line is the point from where the poem takes off. Use the following opening lines to begin your own poem.

'Here is a secret
I'm giving it away . . .'

'What do you know when yer just a kid . . .'

'Roll up! Roll up!'

'It's time to report . . .'

Where did you go? Where did the poets whose lines you borrowed take themselves and their readers?

How I Got to be the Grand Champion of Stirling East Primary School

Here is a secret
I'm giving it away
Because I'm getting on
And I'm probably past it,
Blast it!
It's a genuine, pure gold tip.
Once you've got it you can let yourself rip
And they'll all run.
It's fun.

It was when I was seven and new to fighting
Bar a bit of scratching and occasional biting,
I met this new boy at the top of our hill.
And he bailed me up to fight as strange kids will.
And he said with a horrible scowl,
I will smash you

And bash you
And stew you
And mash you.
Then he POUNCED
And I leapt with a terrified howl
And ran right down that lousy hill before you could say
'Knife',

Bolting for my life.
TO HELL WITH THAT FOR A LARK.
So I started my own career
And I wore the scariest sneer.
I was the first, hardest and most
With the nastiest face and the wildest boast,
And in no time at all there I stood
Chief Hood

Mind you
I couldn't hit
or throw
or punch
or gouge
or kick worth an old toffee,
But it didn't matter,
No-one stayed around long enough
To find out.

Kate O'Neill

What Do You Know?

What do you know when yer just a kid
And the old man's fighting a war
And yer muvver works in a factory
You don't know the score.

What do you know when yer going to school
Where nothing is taught that's useful
And it's took nearly twelve years through fighting and tears
And yer lucky if yer can read, or write.

What do you know when yer go out to work
And start with a job that's a bore
Drink booze with yer mates on the weekends
And with luck yer might make a score.

What do you know when yer twenty
And got some bird in the club
Get married, have kids and get into debt
Then get torn apart with frustration and sweat.
By thirty you've split, gone yer own ways
And yer dream of the times to come.

What do you know when you reach forty-five
And you've married again with more kids
But it's all gone sour just like the last.
You've made money to keep it together
But yer battling uphill and in misery still
Yer think what's the point, so yer go.

What do you know when yer fifty
out of work and live on the dole
You can't get a job, no-one wants yer no more
So you wander around, talk with yer mates:
Most have been through the mill, run the same race.

Why don't they teach you when yer a kid
What could be in store for this life
If you follow the rest in endless procession
With wives, work, debts, and useless possessions.

Then, maybe, you know if you're lucky
That you don't have to be like the rest
And to do the things with good judgement
Is better than having regrets.

John E. Ryan

Barefaced Barkers

Roll up! Roll up!
Buy your health in a bottle!
Canned cures here.
Weight loss in a wafer!

Make your way
past crutches hung by door flaps of our hallowed tent
through anterooms of cankerous growths,
formalin preserved by resurrected hosts,
to meet the saved consumers.

Such elixirs of life,
gorge on food of the gods
in the Network Marketers Travelling Fair.
Spruikers smile in three piece suits
while under lights in white lab coats
the product masters juggle facts and fantasy.
Circus glitter coalesces into packaging.

Ah, sir! At the back. Are you balding?
No matter.
The magic goes wherever your body calls.
Hair follicles will open their alleluia mouths
and sing out hair for you.
Pay now.
And while you wait in hope
listening
for the song,
we'll fold our tent and drive away
in ever faster cars.

Judith I. Pippen

The Greatest Circus

Roll up, roll up,
come and see,
The Greatest Circus,
and it's all run by me.

Horses with red spots,
mice drinking tea,
elephants tap dancing,
and it's all run by me.

Purple koalas,
cows in the sea,
cats and dogs raining,
and it's all run by me.

Seals in a sailboat,
a taunting turkey,
sheep holding shotguns,
and it's all run by me.

This may sound quite crazy,
all im-ag-in-air-ee,
but I tell you it's a circus,
and it's all run by me.

Victoria Entwistle

Unknown Soldier

It's time to report
I'm a missing person

It first happened
centuries ago

when men cut off
arms and legs

and even the heads
couldn't be fitted exactly

Meat tags and records
don't help

Neither do prayers
microscopes
nor helicopters.

So I'll live
with the bones
of the unknown soldier

and leave the rest
for cannibals and cat food

or Flanders poppies
depending where it happened

to make the quality humus
for growing primulas
where the wrens are singing

Jack de Vidas

Adding to your collection

Without reading the poems they come from, select opening lines from other poems in this anthology and let them be the starting point for a poem of your own. When you have finished your poem, compare your 'journey' with that of the poet who wrote the original poem.

Throwaway poems

Throwaway poems are just that — they work on the joke and the unexpected. They are delivered between the lines and find meaning when taken out of their natural context. They have a life of their own. Generally they have their point in the personal and fickleness of our lives and their impact is immediate.

Don't set out to write these poems. Just receive them. Let them come to you naturally, but make sure you jot them down when they arrive.

Fired With Enthusiasm

This morning
the boss
came into work
bursting
with enthusiasm

and fired everybody.

Roger McGough

Pedigree

Pet pedigreed halfwits
 long live the ignored
  long live those without
   any major obituaries
long live those who lived!

Ivan Rehorek

untitled

have you
ever felt
so lonely
that you
had to
hug
a
tree?

Shelton Lea

My Memory

What will happen tomorrow?
Will there be a tomorrow?
I just don't know anymore.
Yesterday — is just a memory.

Catrina Campbell

autumn comes
and leaves
(
fall
)

David G. Harris

Sometimes I get so depressed
it almost feels good.

Thomas Bohn

Sign on the Door

Examination in progress
Please pass quietly

Wayne Cooper

my car's got a toothache
& won't work on mondays

Rory Harris

Purgatory
is my life
Heaven is my dream

Rachel Purchase

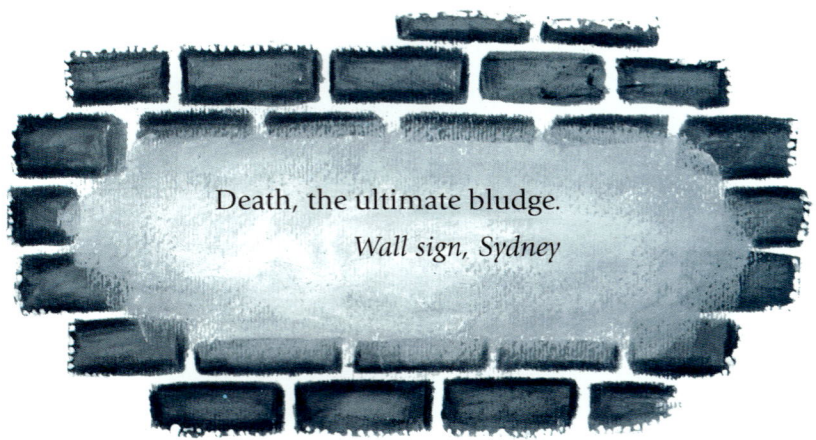

Death, the ultimate bludge.

Wall sign, Sydney

Adding to your collection

Make a point of having a 'throwaway poem' in your collection. Simply reread these examples and jot down the ideas and phrases they prompt. Eventually a throwaway poem will 'arrive'.

Theme and variations are familiar concepts in music. Composers take an existing tune and rework it in as many ways as they can. Poets have done the same thing with words.

Opening the Cage

14 variations on 14 words
I have nothing to say and I am saying it and that is poetry
John Cage

I have to say poetry and is that nothing and I am saying it
I am and I have poetry to say and is that nothing saying it
I am nothing and I have poetry to say and that is saying it
I that am saying poetry have nothing and it is I and to say
And say that I am to have poetry and saying it is nothing
I am poetry and nothing and saying it is to say that I have
To have nothing is poetry and I am saying that and I say it
Poetry is saying I have nothing and I am to say that and it
Saying nothing I am poetry and I have to say that and it is
It is and I am and I have poetry saying say that to nothing
It is saying poetry to nothing and I say I have and am that
Poetry is saying I have it and I am nothing and to say that
And that nothing is poetry I am saying and I have to say it
Saying poetry is nothing and to that I say I am and have it

Edwin Morgan

129

Someone is Always Leaving Something

Someone is always leaving something
Someone is something always leaving
Someone is leaving something always
Something is always leaving someone
Something is leaving someone always
Something is someone always leaving
Always someone is leaving something
Always something is leaving someone
Leaving something is always someone
Leaving someone is always something

Michele Morgan

✺ Devising your own variation

Try the following phrase taken from the poem 'The Crafty Butcher' by Susan Hampton and see how many variations you can devise that make sense.

the lack of pain after death
the pain of lack after death
pain after the death of lack
pain after the lack of death
of death the pain after lack
the lack pain of death after
lack of death the after pain

Peter McFarlane

Notice how each rearrangement throws new light on the meanings of the words. Try rearranging this collection of words from the newspaper.

judges slam drug laws
judges drug slam laws
slam judges drug laws
slam laws drug judges
drug laws slam judges

Peter McFarlane

Or these

Doing your best isn't enough
Doing enough isn't your best
Your best isn't doing enough
Your doing best isn't enough
Best isn't your doing enough
Enough isn't your doing best
Isn't enough doing your best?

Geordie Brookman

Adding to your collection

Now write a 'variation poem' for your collection by searching for a line that you think you can play with and writing as many variations of it as you can. If the variations are working, each new line will add wit, humour or significance to the words.

The edited poem

Most established poets have someone they trust acting as an editor on their work. Certainly there is a great deal of editorial input into any book before it is published. What good editors look for is poetry that moves them in some way, poetry that is fresh and original with clear ideas and images and precise language.

Usually we write too many words. The Australian poet Les Murray's advice to young writers is to chop off the last two lines of everything they write. But throwing out words is a very hard thing to do for a writer. Usually we need someone else to suggest an amendment before we take on the courage to do it.

Look at these three poems written by a Year 9 student, Denise Solomon. If you were her editor, what cuts and changes would you recommend (if any)?

The Shadow of Hiroshima

The shadow that faithfully follows us,
A lesson that must be learnt.

In the shadow,
Lie blistered faces
Death: with melting skin.

Unleashed
Apollo's sun chariot rampages.
Drowning heat,
That engulfs lungs.
An uncontrollable flood.

A child,
Staring back from the shadow.
her parents
Lost,
Amongst the shattered buildings.

The silhouette of an old man,
Crumpled like paper.
Someone lit that piece of paper;
Watch
His skin is burning.

Disturb the Universe

Look past my reflection,
Discover my true identity.

Listen to my silence,
It holds much more than emptiness.

Watch me disturb the universe,
With the wild, unpredictable beating of my
wings.

Discard the constitutions,
Of your neatly structured mind.
A human filing cabinet.
With suitable thoughts,
In rigid alphabetical order.

Release your soul from your property's
tenacious grip
Let it dance,
With the floating blue feathers of the sky.

The Love of a Spider

Broken pieces
Shards of yesterday's life;
A china plate,
Scattered with blue forget-me-nots.
The forget-me-nots,
Now withered-cracked.

Huddled
In the cyclone's eye.
The wind rampages around me.
I wait for your anger,
Waiting till the calm eye moves on;
(All around me, shattered plates and broken glass).

. . . Little Miss (Muffet)
Sat on a tuffet.
Along came a spider,
(A big, black enraged creature)
Who stood tall above her,
And frightened Miss Muffet
Away . . .

Crimson red,
Sharp and stinging anger;
Turning purple on my arm.
Submitting,
To bruises of devotion,
Ownership and your eternal love.

Denise was very happy with her poems, but she also wanted honest editorial comment so that she could learn from them and make her next lot of poems better. What kinds of things did the editor do to her originals? What do you think of the new versions?

The Shadow of Hiroshima

In the shadow
Lie blistered faces
Death: with melting skin.

A drowning heat
That engulfs lungs.
An uncontrollable flood.

A lost child
Staring back from the shadow.
The silhouette of an old man
Crumpled like paper,

His skin burning.

Disturb the Universe

Listen to my silence,
It holds much more than emptiness.

Watch the wild unpredictable beating of my wings.

Discard the constitutions,
Of your neatly structured mind,
A human filing cabinet
With suitable thoughts
In rigid alphabetical order.

Let your soul dance
With the floating blue feathers of the sky.

The Love of a Spider

Little Miss (Muffet)
Sat on a tuffet
Along came a spider
(A big black enraged creature)
Who stood tall above her
And frightened Miss Muffet
Away

Crimson red
Turns purple on her arm
Bruises of devotion
Ownership
And eternal love.

Adding to your collection

Select three unsolicited (or as we call them 'underground') poems of your own for your anthology, but ask your teacher and other members of your class for editorial comment before you include them. You may very well want to make a few changes. After the poem has been fine-tuned, read it aloud to discover any rough edges.

The editor should look for
- words that are repetitive or unnecessary
- words that might mean something to the writer, but are meaningless or incomprehensible to the reader
- vague general words like 'truth' or 'reality'
- the over-use of rhetorical questions
- self-conscious writing — poems that 'sound like poems'
- over-writing — the writer trying too hard, putting on a verbal display that congests the poem and destroys its impact
- fresh and original lines and phrases and highlight them.

Poems of the underground

It is natural to write poetry. Most of us do it. Usually we are a bit shy about showing it to anyone and we keep it hidden — part of the great poetry 'underground'.

For your poetry collection to be truly representative of your own poetry writing, you need to include your own 'underground' poems — poems that you write simply because *you* want to write them.

Often the topics you choose will be upsetting. It's strange, but when we are at our happiest, we are often too busy to write about it. However, you should try to. Like the writers of these poems, you should try to find words for the things of significance you find around you. These can be the things that amuse us and make us happy, as well as excited, disappointed, angry or sad.

Most importantly, you should include your poems in your collection. Like the writers of the following poems, you need to feel good about showing your work to a wider audience and if possible, having it published.

Why Lauren, What a Pretty Girl You've Become Since I Saw You Last

Oh, I know Auntie Lawrence it's . . .

Traumatic to be so good looking,
the hardships I have to bear,
my life is one constant battle
trying to keep boys out of my hair.

When I glance in the mirror, elegance sets in.
Immaculate figure, blonde hair and blue eyes.
Perfect teeth and brilliant long lashes,
I'm a fatally pretty young lass.

My face has not yet seen a pimple,
no blemishes are to be seen,
for cleansers, toners and moisturisers,
are what keep my skin clean.

The telephone never stops ringing,
guys asking me out on a date.
There's at least a two-month waiting list,
so I can be sure they will never be late.

Men use things like hammers,
saws, spanners and spades;
but mascara, lip gloss and eye shadow
are the tricks of my trade.

My slender-shaped legs are my highlight,
along with my fabulous thighs.
I guess my slim waist is a factor,
but my beautiful face is what girls idealise.

Guys crowd my front porch and driveway,
clamouring for love and affection;
but I'm too busy glued to my mirror,
gazing at my glamorous reflection.

Michelle Clark

Yuppies

They look but they don't see
Anything but your clothes
They hear, but they don't listen
To anything but how you speak
They may be nice, but you wonder
What they say behind your back
Their clothes are a façade
Where their personality hides.

Sarah Pearson

The Jetty

Out on the jetty
All the hoons are jumping
Off goes Mark, huge jetty wetter;
Off goes Matt, another huge splash;
Next it's Adam, Leigh and Dave.
'Come on Rich, have a jump.'
I've got no choice, either jump
or get thrown off.
I climb the rail,
Look down at the water;
Off I go, heading down.
Almost there, tuck up,
Bang, I'm under.
I rise thinking to myself, was it good?
I look up at my mates.
Everything's cool,
I got the thumbs up.

Richard Veltman

Questions

Why want something
If it always goes to someone else,
If you get your hopes up for it
And are left feeling down?
Why try hard to achieve
If you are always failing something,

Spending time and effort
And feeling left with time wasted?
Why be happy with what you've got
If it always slips away,
A fortune spent on what goes out of fashion anyway?
Why get close
If you always shut off those you like,
And clam up?
Why reach out
If you're always pushed away,
Asking for assistance with help
And someone else always a higher priority?
Why put yourself on the line
If everyone you ask out,
Always likes someone else?
Why have a beginning
If there's always an end,
If we all wind up dead anyway?
Why fall in love
If you always fall to the ground,
Believing you've found the one
But get crushed each time it's over?
Why let people in
If they always leave?
Why explain yourself
If you're always misunderstood?
Why talk for hours
If they only hear what they want to?
Why look happy
If you always feel sad?
Why smile and say you're fine
If there's always someone who seems to know you better?
Why go to sleep
If you always wake up with your problems,
Sitting at the foot of your bed waiting?
Why be optimistic
When death is totally pessimistic?

April Green

A Goldfish

A goldfish has a funny life, swimming
around & around
A brain span of two seconds
would mean
that everything is a new experience
you never do anything twice
except blink maybe
but goldfish don't
'cause they have no eyelids
they have to keep their eyes open
all the time
A funny life really
swimming & looking
but not remembering

Anna Ervin

Balloons

I cannot comprehend why
balloons choose to float high above —
wouldn't they prefer to pass
each day beside me, on Earth?

They could romp for hours
in our gladwrapped rivers —
instead they elect
to cruise the crisp air.

They could bicker all night
with our separated parents —
instead they elect
to live wild, like mountain hermits.

They could be raped or stabbed,
out late on our streets —
instead they elect
to roam our elegant sky.

They could doze, and dream
of never earning their pay —
instead they elect
to work rough with the wind.

It is truly remarkable.
I cannot comprehend why
balloons choose to float high above
when they could wither here, with me.

Jessica Webster

A Dream To Come

Soon it will be my turn
to open all the gifts
to fly around on unicorns
and run through all the mist.

Soon it will be my turn
to talk and laugh all day
to climb to the top of a beanstalk
and sing and dance my way.

Soon it will be my turn
to gallop in long grass
to do whatever I want
and fear not of what I'm asked.

Soon it will be my turn
to raise my head up high
to lead the world in victory
and wave the war goodbye.

Soon it will be my turn
to take a long earned rest
to close the future to an end
and do what is the best.

Lucy McFarlane

Finishing your collection

Each of us is a poet of the underground — writing whenever we can, getting ideas on what and how to write from other poets, other poems, our friends as well as the world around us, getting ideas from things that disturb us as well as things we know about and love.

Each of us is a poet.

Finish by adding your own 'underground poems' to your collection.

Drafting ★

How do we know when a poem is finished? I always know when I'm writing a poem when it's finished. I may have only made two lines but I know when it's finished. I know when it's there. It's interesting to find out why that happens, why a poem is just right or not.

Roger McGough, *Opinion*, April 1989

A poem is finished when it works in that time and place with the meaning you have made. Tomorrow it may not work. I tend to send poems off to magazines quickly so I can be rid of further editing. If it does come back rejected, I have another look at it and read the editor's comments. This way I distance myself from the poem and can look at it with renewed interest. By standing back I am more detached and more technically observant.

As the poem 'for Hazel' took shape, I read it and reread it, listening for the rhythm and 'bits' that weren't needed. This way, how the poem looks on the page can show the reader one way to read it.

Rory Harris

for Hazel

i cannot
imagine

a life
without

you, each
uncounted

embrace
each virtue

of ourselves
held up

& remembered
drawn, in

moments
of absolute

ordinariness
as when

i fold
our daughter's

clothes
fresh washed

& sorted
on the kitchen

table, where
in a few

hours we'll
sit as family

this which
means so

much to
me, that

i just
wanted

to tell you

Rory Harris

143

It is rare for me to finish a poem in one hit. My poems usually go through a lot of drafts where, if possible, I get editorial comments from my friends and associates. The record length for me to complete a poem is thirteen years ('Honeyeater'), while 'Slow Bike Race' only took five minutes. 'Hey Look Mum, I'm On Telly!' went through two drafts, and was finished once I compressed its concept by using my original last line as the title.

Peter McFarlane

Draft  *1*

Streaker at the Grand Final

What impulse of excitement
thrust
propelled you into the centre
of everybody's attention
of
amongst such spartan manhood
of bared thighs and tight shorts
muscles raised to fever pitch
libidos on the slack?
What invisible shield protected you
from players and policemen
who turned away or smirked
or snarled at women
            love
who aren't ashamed of their bodies
slippery as a dog to catch
already into slow motion reruns
fingers on the pause button?
You rode a ripple of irony
your white prancing nakedness
your happy skipping run from obscurity
upstaged lions and gladiators
undressed everybody who waved as you waved
'Hey look mum, hey look dad
I'm on telly! I'm on telly!'

Peter McFarlane

Draft No 2 (final)

Hey Look Mum, I'm on Telly!

for Helen D'Amico, streaker at the football grand final

What impulse of excitement
thrust you into the centre
amongst such spartan manhood
of bared thighs and tight shorts
muscles raised to fever pitch
libidos on the slack?
What invisible shield protected you
from players and policemen
who turned away or smirked
or snarled at women who love their bodies
slippery as a dog to catch
already into slow motion reruns
fingers on the pause button?
You rode a ripple of irony
a white prancing nakedness
your happy skipping run from obscurity
upstaged lions and gladiators
undressed everybody

Peter McFarlane

Acknowledgements

The authors and publisher are grateful to the following for permission to reproduce copyright material:

Ben Abbott for poem 'Helen's Lament'; Derek Bajer for poem 'A Gladstone Bag'; Nicholas Barnes for poem 'There Was a Punk'; Brendan Bell for poem 'A Brother'; Cassie Bentley for poems 'Window Seat', 'Cat and Mouse'; Nadia Berezansky for poem 'Chaos'; Thomas Bohn for poem 'Sometimes'; Chris Brown for poem 'Perseus and Medusa'; Laura Bruce for poem 'The Toilet'; Angelo Butera for poem 'The Mystery of Love'; Carcanet for poem 'The Red Wheelbarrow' by William Carlos Williams from his Collected Poems; Therese Crisp for poem 'Pete'; Mario De lonno for poem 'Rome'; Jack de Vidas for poem 'Unknown Soldier'; Helen Dowling for poem 'I Used to Have a Real Handbag'; Victoria Entwhistle for poem 'The Greatest Circus'; Anna Ervin for poem 'A Goldfish'; Faber and Faber for poem 'Ballad' by W. H. Auden; Angela Felton for poem 'The Traveller'; Tina Ferraro for poem 'They Hate Me'; Ron Frim for poem 'he cycles up the bike track'; Geelong College for poem 'Wha me Brudder do'; Alyssa George for poem 'My Dog Gizmo'; Hilary Gold for poems 'Automatic Ticket Machine', 'Quack!'; Katherine Gray for poems 'I Love', 'I Love Walking Slowly Along a Deserted Beach'; April Green for poem 'Questions'; Donna Gross for poem 'Dear Friends' from *The Personal Collections of Donna Gross*; Olivia Groufsky for poem 'Dogtags'; Vanessa Harmon for poem 'Face is One of a Friend'; Rory Harris for poems 'airstrip', 'somewhere on holiday', 'the lecturer's mark book', 'for both of you', 'breath' and 'for Hazel' from *Number 13 Friendly Street Reader*, Friendly Street Poets, 1989, 'conversation as a monologue', 'junior primary', 'she wants to leave herself', 'this is going to be a poem/about love', 'laying foundations', 'she collects firewood' from *From the Residence*, The Teacher's Publishing Company, 1984, 'she came in from the terminal' from *over the outrow*, Friendly Street Poets, 1982, 'my car' from *925*, 'picnic' from *The Weekend Australian*; Sophie Harrison for poem 'I Like to Run on the Banks of the Creek'; Wendy Harriss for poems 'There's One of Two Possibilities', 'Clock'; Ngai Man Ho for poem 'Lam Sui Ki, my Mother'; Joanne Hocking for poem 'Letterbox'; Matthew Jacka for poem 'It Was my Life'; Miles Jordan for poem 'If my Face Was a Giraffe'; Michael Julius for poem 'Waves'; James Kumar for poem 'he waits at a bus stop'; Mike Ladd for poems 'Tags', 'Beach Theory'; Wai Lun Lam for poem 'Dream of a Family'; Sarah Le Page for poem 'I Hate Her'; Shelton Lea for poem 'untitled'; Tanya Lintzens for poem 'I Can Feel my Lip Throbbing'; Katrina Lynch for poems 'I Love Watching the Cold Icy Waves', 'cold'; Naomi Martin for poem 'Eyes'; Cyprian Maynard for poem 'Chill'; Karrie McCann for poem 'There's One of Two Possibilities'; Lucy McFarlane for poem 'A Dream to Come'; Peter McFarlane for poems 'They're', 'Tap', 'Hyp-No-Tic', 'To Whom it May Concern (Nudity)', 'To Whom it May Concern (Injustice)', 'Grenades', 'judge slam drug laws', 'The Lack of Pain After Death', 'This is the Clock that Holds the Time', 'Hey Look Mum, I'm on Telly!!', 'Streaker at the Grand Final'; Luke McIntyre for poem 'A Big White Duck'; Thomas McNeil for poem 'Alone'; Osman Mewett for poem 'Suddenly I Noticed Quite a Fuss'; Bianca Millard for poem 'Why?'; Tai Hoi Ming for poem 'Girl'; Will Mooney for poems 'I Love Walking Though the Wilderness in the Morning', 'Shadows'; Tanya Morgan for poem 'As he Waters his Garden'; David O'Donohue for poem 'I Love Drinking Ice Cold Coke'; Kate O'Neill for poem 'How I Got to be the Grand Champion of Stirling East Primary School'; Overlin College Press for poem 'A Hand' by Miroslav Holub, first appeared in translation by

Stuart Friebert and Dana Habova in SAGITTAL SECTION, by Miroslav Holub, FIELD Translation Series, Oberlin College Press, 1980; Pan Macmillan Australia for poem 'The Questions' from *In Her Strapless Dresses* by Lily Brett; Aaron Paul for poem 'Moving to Australia'; Peter Fraser & Dunlop for poem ' To Whom It May Concern' by Adrian Mitchell from *Adrian Mitchell's Greatest Hits (The Top Forty),* published by Bloodaxe Books; Patrick Phelan for poem 'The Door'; Judith Pippen for poem 'Barefaced Barkers'; Simon Priori for poem 'for Matt'; Rachel Purchase for poem 'Purgatory'; Jess Radford for poem 'Friends'; Carolyn Ramsey for poem 'Finding Shirley's Smile'; Nicole Raven for poem 'Helen of Troy'; Julian Reichl for poem 'I Like Surfing at the Beach'; Tim Retrot for poems 'I Love my Dog' I Love my Dog Even Though', 'my dog'; Pat Richardson for poem 'Women Alone'; Nicola Riley for poem 'The Old Chair'; Nigel Roberts for poem 'The Red Wheelbarrow Extrapolations' from *Steps for Fred Astaire* by Nigel Roberts; Alasdair Rogers for poem 'Petrol Head'; Nichola Ross for poem 'A Champion Horse Racing'; Melanie Rottier for poems 'I Love to Discover People's Inside Beauty', You Can't'; Ingrid Ryan for poems 'He Tiptoes into my Room', 'Aeroplane'; John E. Ryan for poem 'What Do You Know?'; Jason Scarabotti for poem 'That Green Fishing Line'; Scotch College Junior School for poem 'Poe-tree'; Kate Sheehan for poem 'eyes'; Sharon Slade for poem ' I like Doing Bombers off the Jetty!'; Denise Solomon for poems 'Disturb the Universe' (and variation), 'The Love of a Spider' (and variation), 'The Shadow of Hiroshima' (and variation); Amy Spiers for poem 'I Love my Room'; Claire Spiers for poems 'I Love Entire Emptiness', 'Entire Emptiness', 'I Love the Winds and Waters'; Arwen Summers for poem 'The Fire'; Ryan Thomas for poem 'Girl at a Boys' School'; Ernie Tucker for haiku 'At the Edge of the Bush', 'By the Fibro Shack', 'Detached in the Pavilion', 'Dribbling Down the Creek', 'Fuming', 'In the Highest Leaves', 'The Last Drop', 'Through the Motel Window', 'Wire Coat Hangers', 'Two Currawongs Chortle'; Lucy Tucker for poem 'Black'; Morgan Vaudrey for poems 'I Love the Hot Sun Playing on my Face', 'hot sun', 'I Love the Wooden Chair'; Lachlan Walter for poem 'Classroom'; Ania Walwicz for poem 'Big Time'; Jessica Webster for poem 'Balloons'; Kellie Wheatcroft for poem 'Placed and Forgotten'; Megan White for poem 'Hate'; Elizabeth Young for poem 'They're Looking at me'; Joel Zika for poem 'Gaping Holes Spoken From Words'.

Many poems in this book were written by students participating in workshops. The authors would like to thank the following teachers and schools:

Brighton High School, South Australia; Suzanne Lennie and Jennifer Haynes, Camberwell Anglican Girls Grammar, Victoria; Petra Masters, Cleve Area School, South Australia; Rob Brown, Department of Education, Adelaide University, South Australia; Helen Fitzpatrick, Rod Cummins and Amanda Swaney, Geelong College, Victoria; Ian Parr, Geelong Grammar, Victoria; Helen Gillen, Gleeson College, South Australia; Rex Rehn, Golden Grove High School, South Australia; Kingscote Area School, South Australia; Jill McLaughlin, Marryatville High School, South Australia; Chris McCabe, Joe De Tullio and Tony O'Doherty, Mercedes College, South Australia; Dawn Webster, Morphett Vale High School, South Australia; Norwood Morialta High School, South Australia; Pat Hansen, Pembroke Junior School, South Australia; Jane Nelson, Prince Alfred College, South Australia; Kerry Coggins, Scotch College Junior School, South Australia; Andrew McKinnon, Andy Beauchamp and Ken Webb, Scotch College Middle School, South Australia; St Paul's College, South Australia; Steven Collins and Janet Johnson, Taroona High School, Tasmania; Sally Van Bavel and Jenny Storer, Walford Anglican Girls School, South Australia; Anne Miller-Arnold, Westminster School, South Australia; Wendy Dowd, Woodlands, South Australia.

Both Peter McFarlane and Rory Harris acknowledge support from Arts SA.

index of poets

index of poems